Pedagon

Studies in the
Postmodern Theory of Education

Joe L. Kincheloe and Shirley R. Steinberg
General Editors

Vol. 15

PETER LANG
New York • Washington, D.C./Baltimore • Boston
Bern • Frankfurt am Main • Berlin • Vienna • Paris

David Geoffrey Smith

Pedagon

Interdisciplinary Essays in the Human Sciences, Pedagogy, and Culture

PETER LANG
New York • Washington, D.C./Baltimore • Boston
Bern • Frankfurt am Main • Berlin • Vienna • Paris

Library of Congress Cataloging-in-Publication Data

Smith, David Geoffrey.
Pedagon: interdisciplinary essays in the human sciences,
pedagogy, and culture / David Geoffrey Smith.
p. cm. — (Counterpoints; vol. 15)
Papers published in various journals, 1988–1996.
Includes bibliographical references (p.   ).
1. Educational anthropology. 2. Humanities.
3. Postmodernism and education. 4. Education—Philosophy. I. Title.
II. Series: Counterpoints (New York, N.Y.); vol. 15.
LB45.S593   306.43—dc21   98-25589
ISBN 0-8204-2760-8
ISSN 1058-1634

Die Deutsche Bibliothek-CIP-Einheitsaufnahme

Smith, David Geoffrey:
Pedagon: interdisciplinary essays in the human sciences, pedagogy, and culture /
David Geoffrey Smith. –New York; Washington, D.C./Baltimore; Boston; Bern;
Frankfurt am Main; Berlin; Vienna; Paris: Lang.
(Counterpoints; Vol. 15)
ISBN 0-8204-2760-8

Cover art: *The Death of Shakyamuni*: Late eighteenth century ink on paper by
Japanese artist Ito Jakuchu. Courtesy of Kyoto National Museum. A parody of
lamentational representations, Shakyamuni is shown in recline as a daikon
radish, surrounded by mourners, all represented as fruits and vegetables. As a
parody, the work points to the way in which genuine wisdom of necessity is a
labour of dying.

Cover design by Nona Reuter.

The paper in this book meets the guidelines for permanence and durability
of the Committee on Production Guidelines for Book Longevity
of the Council of Library Resources.

© 1999 Peter Lang Publishing, Inc., New York

Printed in the United States of America.

For
Geoffrey Gordon—holy man, mentor
Jara Estelle—wild woman, smart

Acknowledgements

"Journeying: A Meditation on Leaving Home and Coming Home" was originally presented as an invited address to the Unitarian Fellowship, Lethbridge, Alberta, November 28, 1992. It was first published in *SALT: A Journal of Religious and Moral Education*, Spring 1994.

"Teacher Education and Global Culture" was originally prepared for the Lethbridge *Herald* as part of its University Information series, 1993. Subsequently, the paper was published by the *ATA Magazine* of the Alberta Teachers' Association, May/June 1993.

"Identity, Self and Other in the Conduct of Pedagogical Action: An East/West Inquiry" was originally published in *The Journal of Curriculum Theorizing*, Fall 1996, then in *Action Research as Living Practice*. T. Carson and D. Sumara, editors. New York: Peter Lang Publishers 1997.

"The Hermeneutic Imagination and the Pedagogic Text" was originally prepared for Edmund Short, editor, *Forms of Curriculum Inquiry*, New York: SUNY Press, 1991.

"Experimental Hermeneutics: Interpreting Educational Reality" was originally published in *Hermeneutics and Educational Discourse*, H. Danner, editor. Johannesburg SA: Heinemann 1997.

"Modernism, Hyperliteracy and the Colonization of the Word" was originally presented at the *Language in Education* Symposium, sponsored by the Canadian Association for Curriculum Studies, and held at the University of Lethbridge, June 18–20, 1990. The paper first appeared in *The B.C. English Teacher*, Summer, 1991, then in *Alternatives: Social Theory for Humane Governance*, Summer 1992.

"On Discursivity and Neurosis: Conditions of Possibility for (West) Discourse with Others" was originally presented at the International Conference on *Fragmentation and the Desire for Order/Unity,* held at Augustana University College, Camrose, Alberta, Spring 1994. The paper was first published in *Dianoia: An Interdisciplinary Journal of the Liberal Arts*, Summer 1994.

"Teacher Education as a Form of Discourse: On the Relation of the Public to the Private in Conversations about Teaching" was originally presented at WESTCAST: The Western Canadian Conference on Student Teaching, held at the University of Regina, Saskatchewan, February 16—18, 1991. The paper first appeared in *Analytic Teaching*, 12 (1) November 1991.

"The Problem for the South Is the North (but the Problem for the North Is the North)" was originally presented at the International Institute for Peace Education, held at Manila, Philippines, December 14—16, 1987. The paper first appeared in *Forum: The Journal of the World Council for Curriculum and Instruction*, II (2) December 1988.

"On Being Critical about Language: The Critical Theory Tradition and Its Implication for Language Arts" was originally presented at a joint symposium between University of Calgary and University of Lethbridge on the theme, "Forms of Inquiry in Education," Spring 1986. The paper first appeared in *Reading/Canada/Lecture*, 6 (4), Winter 1988.

"Modernism, Postmodernism and the Future of Pedagogy" was originally prepared under the auspices of the Institute for East and West Studies, Yonsei University, Seoul, Korea, Spring 1989. The paper first appeared as *Occasional Paper #9*, Institute for East and West Studies, Yonsei University, 1990.

"Brighter than a Thousand Suns: Facing Pedagogy in the Nuclear Shadow" was originally presented at the World Council for Curriculum and Instruction, Hiroshima Japan, August 2—5, 1986. The paper was first published in the conference proceedings, *Toward a Renaissance of Humanity: Rethinking and Reorienting Curriculum and Instruction*, Terrance Carson, editor. Edmonton AB: The University of Alberta Press, 1988.

"Children and the Gods of War" was originally prepared for *Elements: A Journal of Elementary Education*, Spring 1987. The paper has also appeared in *The Journal of Educational Thought*, 2 (2A) October 1988, and in *Phenomenology and Pedagogy*, 6 (1) 1988. Permission to reprint the cartoon is acknowledged from The Cartoon Bank Inc. and The New Yorker Collection.

"What Is Given in Giftedness?" was originally presented at "Girls, Women and Giftedness: An International Symposium," held at the University of Lethbridge, Alberta, May 25—28, 1987. The paper first appeared in *The Journal of Learning about Learning*, 1 (2), Winter 1989, then in *Girls, Women and Giftedness*, edited by Julie L. Ellis and John M. Willinsky. New York: Trillium Press, 1990.

Table of Contents

Preface

Pedagon is a neologism eliding two words, pedagogy and agony. Pedagogy, from the Greek *paidagogia,* originally referred to the work of leading children to school, but in more recent time it has taken on a much wider signification, referencing not only the formal practices and professions of teaching, but also that dense network of activities that surround general care for the young. I like to think of pedagogical sensibility as involving a thoughtful concern for all the multifarious ways children are under the influence of adult conduct, and this must include, therefore, not just the formal plans and intentions of parents, teachers, childcare workers and so forth, but also all of those indirect, subliminal, hidden and unconscious moments when children, on the basis of their experience, make interpretive decisions about the reality they share with adults around them. The great psychoanalyst Carl Jung once remarked that "children react much less to what adults actually say than to the imponderables in the surrounding atmosphere."[1]

"Agony" is from another Greek word, *agon,* that originally meant "a gathering or assembly," especially for public games. Later it developed the connotation of "contest" or "struggle"; indeed, "agony," the heart of which is precisely struggle or contestation over something of great importance, such as the condition of one's soul.

Pedagon, therefore, attempts to articulate the cultural space in which issues surrounding pedagogy are contested, enacted and inhabited. Invoking "culture" here gives notice of my conviction that the typical parameters of conversation regarding educational issues, particularly in the North American context, are far too narrow, largely because of the increasing specialization of professional languages consequent to the spread of industrialism. There is a need to broaden the scope of what is taken into consideration whenever we get together to talk about what should be done with respect to our progeny, whenever we get together to consider the character of responsible parenting, teaching and care. As adults, we inevitably suffer the cultural diseases of our time, but then we reproduce them in our children to the degree we have not healed ourselves.

I suspect my interest in approaching questions of pedagogy as questions of culture arises inevitably from the long after-effects of the culture shock I experienced as a young person coming to Canada in the early sixties. Being born in China during the Maoist revolution, then raised in Central Africa (Northern Rhodesia/Zambia) during the peak, then twilight, of British colonial rule, no doubt ensured that I would feel strange in my new North American home. Feeling strange or alien is the first prerequisite to a life of interpretation, as Wilhelm Dilthey once suggested,[2] so after many years of suffering through the typical immigrant agonistics of trying to fit into the patterns and codes of dominant culture, years of self-abnegnation and reclusiveness, eventually I began to realize that a life of difference, or a different life, is what makes possible a refraction of normalcy into strangeness, and that such work may be precisely what is necessary to the enormous contemporary task of mediating differences across cultures, that is to the hermeneutic task of making the world less fearful, more ecumenical.

The essays that are presented here, then, may at times seem to be only obliquely connected to matters of Education as we normally might understand that term. As meditations on culture however, they are intrinsically pedagogical in the sense of issuing from a concern for how our common life is, or has been, constructed. Such concern has a definite interest, too: the interest of bringing understanding, with the assumption that such understanding, or at least being involved in the work of it, is itself oriented toward making life better, and that a better life is one that is richer, deeper and truer in its interconnections between persons and the traditions which inevitably meet whenever people get together and face each other.

My own biography of journeying in the international sphere has led me to a distinct lack of interest in any form of theorizing or writing that does not begin from an addressing of the cosmopolitan context of everything we do today. Even if we live in small remote places, we are still inevitably tied to the grand narratives that have constituted the present arrangements of geopolitical influence and power. These narratives have to do with the history of Western imperialism and colonialism; the rise of Science and its influence in the shaping of political, social and economic ideologies as forms of Truth; and perhaps most especially, although also least explored in the public realm, the issue of the desacralization of the world which Science inaugurated, and the consequent loss of any credible languages of the holy. This last issue is one I believe to be of exceeding importance, not only because it has to do with how we might conceive of the world as a whole place, a holy place, sacred unto itself, but also because without such a vision it is virtually impossible to grasp our fundamental human commonality. Especially in the North American context perhaps, the seemingly absolute addiction to languages and constructs that actively cage individuals within their private, subjective fantasies serves most certainly to undercut any possibilities for a sense of shared community, even though the very language of individuality itself belies the fact that we have to talk *together* to talk about ourselves, showing that what we hold in common inevitably takes precedence over what divides us.

The three themes, then, of imperialism/colonialism, science, and secularism/desacralization, are ones that imbue most of the papers that follow, and they reflect the legacy of my own work over the last ten years in demythologizing, especially for myself, but taken up with a sense of collective pedagogical responsibility, what might be called the karmic infrastructure of Western culture. The most notable turn in the work might be easily seen as a turn to the East, which of course was the original etymological organizer for the term *orientation*, the task of getting one's Western bearings from an Eastern binary. In my own case though, the turn to Asian Wisdom. Traditions, came about as a consequence of seeing their extraordinary parallels with the formulations of postmodernism and deconstructionism, especially in the work of Derrida, but with one significant exception: Asian Way traditions open a way for genuinely creative engagement with the central problematic of contemporary Western experience, namely that of Identity. *Identity* constellates all of the focal agonistics of our time, those issues which enspace: the Self/Ego, Essence, Correctness, Nationalism, Cultural Identity/Multiculturalism, even Child-as-Social-Category. The problematics of Identity find their inspiration precisely within a mythic structure of dualism, the cultural architecture of which lies at the heart of the Western tradition, sustained by its Hebrew, Christian and, more recently, Islamic character. It is precisely this structure of dualism that Asian Way traditions, especially Buddhism, but also Taoism, have addressed most creatively, and which hold out the possiblity of helping solve the problem of me/us versus you/them. As David Loy has put the challenge: "the legacy of the eighteenth-century Enlightenment project—in social and scientific terms, that which liberates us from absolutism, dogmatism, and superstition—must dovetail into the enlightenment that frees me from *me*."[3]

Most of the papers here began as presentations at conferences, seminars, and such, then were worked into written form for publication. A list of sites for original presentation, as well as acknowledgements and publishers' permissions, is given at the front of the book.

The labor of my professional site in a faculty of education means that most of my time is spent in teaching and in working with students who wish to become teachers. A number of the papers offered here, therefore, resonate with a certain didacticism. This is because, as a teacher one is often presenting ideas to people who are hearing them for the first time. The required art calls for qualities of simplicity and clarity. Other papers have been written more centrally from the heart of my own visions. In both cases, the patience of readers is requested.

The final production of this book owes some special debts. My friend and colleague David Jardine has been unwavering in his belief in the value of putting these papers together, and without his inspiration, I probably would not have undertaken the project. The world doesn't need another book, I kept saying. Indeed, as I argue in one of the papers, the publishing industry itself may be partly responsible for the devaluation of the written word through the inflation of the same, and for the way in which, as Harold Bloom has put it, "Deep reading is a vanished phenomenon."[4] In my own case too, coming from several generations of Protestant preachers, and once completing a degree in theology, my natural inclination is oral: I'm a very reluctant writer.

Without the firm dedication and expertise of my former secretary, Helen Taylor, the whole project would have foundered on a pile of editorial details. I am also grateful for the assistance of Gisele Woods who, in the later stages, rescued me from the frustrations of being enmeshed in various incompatible word processing programs. Francis Noronha expertly copy-edited the penultimate draft. All remaining errors and misinterpretations, though, remain my responsibility.

Centre for the Study of Pedagogy and Culture
University of Alberta
Alberta Canada
1998

Foreword:
"It's All One Meditation"
by
David Jardine

I

> It is as if young people ask for, above all else, not only a genuine responsiveness from their elders but also a certain direct authenticity, a sense of that deep human resonance so easily suppressed under the smooth human-relations jargon teachers typically learn in college. Young people want to know if, under the cool and calm of efficient teaching and excellent time-on-task ratios, life itself has a chance, or whether the surface is all there is. And the best way to find out may be to provoke the teacher into showing himself or herself.

I utilized this passage from David Smith's essay "Children and the Gods of War", from this volume, in a recent course on the ethics of teaching. The attempt was to break through crusted notions of ethics-as-rules-and-regulations, and to invoke something of the notion of *ethos* as the characteristic spirit of a people, a place or a community. What ensued was painful for us all—an odd shock of recognition, that very little of our school experience (university and otherwise) involved any joy or any deep recognition of the ways of things. Children had devolved into either preciousness or monstrousness, and the disciplines of the world had devolved into "fun activities for the kids".

This passage became for these students, as it became and has remained for me since I read it first in 1988, a clarion of memory in our class, something each of us took to heart and remembered, recited and recalled as the class wore on and often down under questions like "Why didn't anyone tell us?" "Why does it have to be like this?" and, perhaps most painfully, "What in hell can we do now?" Most certain was the fact that none of us could henceforth pretend that we had not read these words and that we had not somehow recognized images and histories and traditions and discourses in which our lives were deeply and irremediably implicated. But even in the midst of the wonderful suffering that this passage caused, it was also quite evident that we, here, in this class, belonged together under the mark of these words and could take some comfort here, some common fortitude and strength. We all had to not only live individually with having read and understood these words. We had to live with the fact that these others, too, were here with us; all the relations, our teachers, our childhood's, our children, our elders, all called to account. A Great Council of Beings gathered, huddled around like-fires lit over ages, listening to the tales that hold us here. We, here, had a brief glimpse of what it might mean to say that pedagogy has to do with wisdom, "communities of relations" and small, meticulous obligations.

And we also recognized that passages such as this one will hold us because they proceed from a generousness and spaciousness that invites as it teaches. We all knew this passage was about us all and that it was (dare one say it these days?) *good work.*

Of course, we are all living under the newly fashionable education jargon of "community" that has already ruined these words before they even had a chance. The lamentation continues: jargon is rooted in an old Welsh term *iargoun*, which means "the warbling of birds". At least the warbling of birds is done with some tilting pleasure at the sun and the airblue arch that holds David's and my life together, this broad Chinook sky and the prairie abyss and the wind, and oh, the cold that cracks your bones, Alberta.

This is the sort of incident I've come to expect from David Smith's work—painful fits of often bloody-minded healing, unavoidable because their bearing is always slightly unanticipated. It is never quite clear from where the "calling" might call and just what might be at stake in such calling.

It will become evident as you read these texts that there is a critical edge to this work, similar, on the surface, to critical theory. Unlike critical theory, however, these essays do not begin with the self-satisfied certainty of what the problem is and who has it. The critical edge here is the crisis of a spirit dancing on the edge of the world coupled with a certain deadly playfulness, deadly because that is precisely what is at stake here: whether life itself has a chance. Many of us understand this crisis and the ways in which our children's lives, my child's life, my own life and the demons in the trees and Coyote howls in the wind are becoming co-opted by a consumptive panic endemic to our so-called postmodern era. As the fragments crack, the genuineness and spirit and address of David Smith's work are only understandable as hopeless naivete. Let us all be naive. Let us all give up hope. There, in that place of hopelessness, when the eschatological hallucinations of a "better world" are given up, there genuine love and compassion are possible. There, life itself has a chance out from under the vicious, well-meant glare of "improving our schools".

These essays slow the pace of attention and reveal, in odd ways, how the author has had to bear the agony of that slowing and the effort required to "live in the belly of a paradox" as he once put it—live, in fact, in the belly and the breath, and retain some courage to continue, not in spite of the agonies, but in love. David has taught me, in part through his work, in part through his example, that we must somehow love those students who make the request "Tell me exactly what it is you want in this assignment" (from the essay "On Being Critical About Language"), for they are bearing on our behalf the agonies of the world, showing us our own pains and foibles and fears, providing us all with openings and events that, if we read them generously and well, might lead us all to health, to sanity, beyond the breathless rush of schooling.

II

If we speed up the work in the garden, you'll just have to spend that much more time sitting in the zendo, and your legs will hurt more. It's all one meditation. I would like to take this all the way back down to what it means to get inside your belly and cross your legs and sit—to sit down on the ground of your mind, of your original nature, your place, your people's history. Right Action, then, means sweeping the garden.[1]

My debts to David Smith's work remain and they are the sort that don't demand repayment. It is his encouragement that has made the lilt of these words possible. Quite a feat, to hand a former asthmatic back his breath. If you read these pages slowly, space will clear, restlessness will become irrelevant and words will erupt out of your throat without warning: *makyo* nightmarish visions of the original nature that houses us all.

David Jardine
University of Calgary
Alberta, Canada

1

Journeying: A Meditation on Leaving Home and Coming Home

The word "journey" originally meant daily work (>L. *diurnus*, daily), so in a sense everybody is always on a journey. In the religious life, journeying is a particularly frequent theme. The biblical writer of *Genesis*, for example, tells us that the journeying of Adam and Eve is linked to a curse for their presumption to know the difference between good and evil. Later, the word Israel is given to mean "one who strives with God."[1]

For Hinduism, the guiding vision is of the soul or self (Atman) journeying to Ultimate Reality (Brahman). In Buddhism, the founder Gautama leaves his position as a prince of the warrior clan, the Kashatryas, to begin a search for the origin of human suffering and the true nature of reality. Mohammed's journeys on the trade caravans of the Middle East allowed him to see how Arabs were weakened in the international sphere because of a lack of unifying religion. From that came the distinctive call of Islam, the Shahadah: "There is no God but God, and Mohammed is his prophet."[2]

During his "lost years" between twelve and thirty, Jesus may have made sojourns to either Northern India or to Alexandria in Egypt. At least such is the speculation from some scholars examining the many strong parallels between Buddhism and the primitive gospel.[3]

If setting out on a journey is a central aspect of human experience, what are the motivations? Classical examples indicate the following: 1) To answer a basic concern about existence, such as the meaning of suffering; 2) To respond to an inner call; 3) To escape oppression, be it political, social, personal or intellectual; and 4) To discover a divine purpose, as in the vision quest of Native peoples.

It is important to remember, though, that going on a journey for such reasons is not exotic, or romantic. It is not a form of tourism. It issues from something much more basic, even ordinary, but also very deep. The ancient Greek philosopher Plotinus put it this way: "Question: Why do you go out? Answer: In order to come in." Why would one leave home? Well, in order to come home, but in a new way, a better way. In Buddhism, a Bodhisattva or

Enlightened Being is one who, after attaining insight into the nature of reality, goes back to his people to help them with their struggles. The most basic purpose of going on a journey, then, is the very ordinary one of learning to be at home in a more creative way, in a good way, a healthy way, a way tuned to the deepest truth of things.

Actually, undertaking a journey can be a collective enterprise as much as an individual one. In either case, though, what is involved is learning how to understand one's own tradition with greater insight and creativity, one's cultural heritage linguistically and ritually mediated. Indeed, given the general confusion of the times, for people in the Western tradition this may be a particularly appropriate historical moment from which to take the dynamic of journeying—leaving home, healing, coming back home wiser, more sane and generally compassionate—and applying it to the generalized condition of our lives. It's a matter of journeying into the story of our cultural construction to better understand our cultural pathologies.

To take but one aspect of our cultural story, it could be said that many of our contemporary difficulties find their formal beginning in ideas first celebrated in the sixteenth century through the Renaissance and Reformation. This is true whether we are talking about concepts of individual freedom, nationalism, the nature of authority, or of science. And as is usually the case when good news is taken up dogmatically, or celebrated unreflectively, there's always a downside. Through the new discipline of science, for example, the natural order was temporarily demystified, and over the course of four hundred years, enormous breakthroughs in medicine, healing, technology and so on occurred. It may be, however, that the downside has been the application of the same principles of science to the conduct of human affairs. Social engineering, whether in the name of behavioural psychology, Marxist rational state planning or free market economics taken as science—by and large these have brought heavy burdens to many people when applied as literal, definitive solutions to human problems.

As far as science is concerned, at the heart of the issue lie two more. One comes out of the new crisis of predictability within science, whereby the earlier Newtonian presumption of order in nature is less clearly defensible, so that predicting long-range outcomes from immediate actions is now seen as extremely difficult. The second issue concerns the modern problem of secularism which the former confidence in science inspired. Today in the West there is a dilemma, which can be framed as a question of whether one can live without the securities of the old science at the same time as live without the spiritual resources that the old science itself supplanted. Call this the social condition of a double vacuum.

The biggest challenge today may be to find a way of articulating a form of spirituality that honours the useful work of empirical scientific investigation in, for example, debunking literal interpretations of ancient sacred texts, while at the same time finding a way to live a life of vital faith, a faith that does not banish the unpredictable in the name of new false confidences. Those false confidences come in many guises, and not just the swaddling clothes of conservative religion, or the hypocritical seductions of consumer culture. More subtle forms include the evangelicalism of the Cult of Information, and the regressive pretentiousness of the new pedagogic fundamentalism which presumes to be able to transform the whole panorama of public education with a few grand gestures.

The need in the West for a new kind of spirituality is quite urgent. Ashis Nandy, a Third World social scientist, has said that "secularism is ethnocidal",[4] i.e., secularism kills people by killing their spirit, undermining their specific character and emptying their souls for nothing but a dust bowl of new conformities. So much of the rage that Muslim fundamentalism, for example, directs against the West comes from a profound indignation that the West seems to hold so little sacred, so little holy; that even traditional sources of inspiration like church and synagogue are too often too closely tied to the interests of big business and global militarism. There is a need for a kind of spirituality that is simpler, truer, and having its own integrity.

In my own work as a teacher educator, I often ask myself how young people today can ever develop the wherewithal to resist the culture of lying, duplicity and misrepresentation that now seems omnipresent, though very glossy and dramatic in a media driven environment. Without some kind of inner strength and autonomous interior resources, I do not believe such resistance is possible.

In the universal language of journeying, perhaps there is an invitation to consider a way through our difficulties. As a first step, it may be necessary to gain some objective distance from our received traditions, journeying to a genuinely free space. In Buddhism such distancing is actually achieved by a form of ritual stopping, a stopping of ongoing engagement with the usual round of active cultural illusions, and a gaining of what Tenzin Gyatso calls "equipoise".[5] In Judaism, the psalmist enjoins us to "be still" in order to know God.[6] In Taoism, the aim is to find the "stillpoint" where the finite and the infinite cohere.[7] In Islam, the term *waqt* describes the mystical experience of an "eternal now" in which time and eternity are understood as one. Christian theologians speak of "realized eschatology", whereby "end" time is in fact "now" time.[8]

The journey into stillness implied here in no way suggests a rebuke or rejection of any received tradition *per se*, but rather a making of oneself available, individually or collectively, for deeper insight into what the present moment holds. Call this a new kind of contemplative or meditative consciousness that works to gain the true measure of one's situation. Indeed the very word "meditation" comes from an old Indo-European root, *med-*, meaning "measure". At the heart of this is a form of silence which makes possible a kind of communion with oneself and with others which is not dependent on, say, literal notions of words and concepts, the usual currency of argumentation and dispute. Instead one works toward a space where one is genuinely free to engage the world openly and without pre-judgement. The great Trappist monk, Thomas Merton, used to speak of this as "wordless prayer," which creates a space "open to others," and "rooted in a sense of common illusion and in criticism of it".[9] The Tibetan Buddhist teacher, Chogyam Trungpa, describes meditative consciousness as "the art of making friends".[10]

The Wisdom traditions of the world understand very clearly that serious dangers lurk close at hand whenever the spiritual autonomy that meditative or contemplative consciousness produces is not well understood. Particularly severe is the problem of narcissism or self-enclosure, which arises whenever the pleasures of spiritual practice are taken to be the ultimately intended purpose. Spirituality, even belief in God, easily becomes a form of Valium substitute. In the ancient Pali language, this danger has been termed *Jhana*, meaning "absorption in inner activity". The true aim of contemplative practice is called *Upacara*, referring to the fact that once inner peace has been found, one must embark on the difficult new journey of investigating one's "outer activity", piercing its illusions and repudiating its claims when necessary.

Piercing through the illusions of modern life is extremely difficult, given a culture where advertising and other media forms are organized so persistently to produce mass public deception. The common manipulation of the public will to serve narrow vested interests is one of the most outrageous scandals on the human record. That people should be led to believe that their dignity and self-respect are inseparable from an alignment with certain consumer products; or that particular interpretations of political events can be so orchestrated as to obliterate the line between fact and fiction—well, such conditions point to a depth of social pathology from which only the most enlightened and determined of souls will be able to heal themselves.

The German philosopher, Max Scheler, once remarked that for Western civilization, the entire evolutionary journey has been "a one-sided and overactive process of expansion outward".[11] Certainly since the Renaissance one can trace this trajectory, with science, technology and commerce, often with the blessing of official, state-sanctioned religion, leading the way outward from Europe to bring the rest of the world into its sphere of influence. Apart from the more obvious tragedies of rape and plunder wrought by conquest, the most serious consequence may have been the gradual evacuation of the inner life of people, and the production of a form of humanity concerned only with surfaces. Maybe this is the time to embark collectively on a new long journey inward, not for the purpose simply of celebrating our personal or collective subjectivities, but for the more noble one of laying down the outward things that presently enslave us. Then a new engagement with the world may be possible, one that is more friendly, honest and true.

2

Teacher Education and Global Culture

The preparation of teachers never takes place in a vacuum. In shaping both the curriculum and manner of teacher education, larger developments in society have always played an important role. Early in this century, for example, John Dewey's famous "experimental method" of teaching was influenced by his positive interest in industrialism. Dewey thought that by encouraging children to experiment with practical materials they would not just engage in meaningful creative activity for self-development: he also believed that, at the same time, they would learn the skills necessary for the expansion of American industry.

Our long-standing preoccupations in education with measurement and evaluation are largely an inheritance from Dewey's contemporary, Edward L. Thorndike of Columbia University, who was part of a broad movement looking for ways to make the study of human life more "scientific". He applied statistical principles to the observation of teaching acts in an attempt to make educational judgements that were as "objective" and "impersonal" as possible.

It is to the famous theorist of evolution, Charles Darwin, that we owe most of our ideas about "development", "adjustment" and "adaptation". Today, one of the buzzwords is "globalization". What should we take this to mean, and how might it affect the way we prepare teachers? Actually, as for most words, the meaning of globalization is slippery, implying different things to different people, a condition that holds both dangers as well as opportunities. For some, globalization simply refers to the world becoming a kind of global village through the new technologies of communication, international travel and so on. Teachers, it is argued, need to be aware of the latest developments in, say, information technology so they can prepare students who are at the breaking edge of everything new. Success in business probably depends on such a position, although for teachers to be seduced by this latest cult of information is to forget the words of the ancient Chinese sage Lao Tzu: "Whoever wishes to rule the country by knowledge alone will harm the country".[1]

For others, globalization refers to themes surrounding Third World Development, and in school curriculum circles is usually associated with Development Education. Students are introduced to such issues as the politics of world hunger, the international debt crisis, peace and disarmament questions and so on. This is important work, because without doubt our collective future depends on how well we can deal with such matters.

In a way, though, globalization may also operate as a kind of glamour word that hides subtle but profound difficulties in our culture. For one thing, as a concept "globalization" is an abstraction, so that while on the surface it seems to speak for the condition of the whole world, in reality this is a false promise, because who—what person, what group—can claim to know the world in its entirety? People who make such claims are usually dictators or tyrants. Even astronauts, while they are the only human beings who can claim to have seen the earthly planet whole, suspended in space, at the same time cannot claim to know the whole world intimately in all of its variation and depth. And so, as the writer Wendell Berry has said, there is a certain "futility" in global thinking[2] because while on the one hand it would be comforting to be able to say what the whole world is like (it might make the human world easier to control, for example), realistically we know how impossible this is. In fact, because human knowledge is always partial and incomplete, it is good to be wary of those who try to make the term globalization serve their own narrow, limited interests, whether it be in the name of commerce, politics or even education, because chances are we will end up being nothing but items on their corporate, political or educational agendas. That is how abstractions work: individuals and their situations are diminished in the name of big ideas and rationalizations.

Indeed it is this quality of rationalization, of trying to organize life according to abstract versions of universal laws of reason, that is both the crown and curse of modern life. It is the legacy in Western culture of the rise of science, and eighteenth-century principles of Enlightenment. This journey began in the Renaissance and peaked, arguably, with the development of nuclear weapons. Communism was the most daring experiment in applying principles of objective reason to the business of human living, and as the president of the Czech. Republic Vaclav Havel, once stated, the fall of Communism contains a vital message to the human race. The end of Communism marks the end of the modern age as a whole, the end of a particular way of thinking about human affairs, the end of "the belief that the world is a wholly knowable system governed by a finite number of universal laws that we can grasp and rationally direct for our own benefit".[3]

In teaching and teacher education, our most profound challenges lie in dealing creatively with the relation between our rationalized conceptual systems and the emerging uniqueness of life as it presents itself in the lives of our students. Teachers who think teaching involves nothing but the correct application of professional knowledge they learned in college or university soon burn out, because it is young people themselves who hold at least part of the answer to the question of how to teach. Good teaching requires getting to know one's students personally, uniquely, individually, so that a genuine conversation can exist between you, and knowledge is mediated in a way that has a human soul.

As a teacher educator I am often distressed by the way new concepts like "collaboration", "restructuring", "journalling", even "whole language" get taken up as forms of absolute truth, with attempts to apply them literally across the board in schools and classrooms. What is violated in such attempts is the kind of intuitive wisdom seasoned teachers have gained from years of experience, involving an understanding of how each child brings to the classroom a different life story with its own particular ways of proceeding to meet the world. Good teaching depends precisely on an ability to tune into and embrace that way in order to lead it to a fuller maturity.

Modern educational systems, like modern systems of business and industry, are products of the Enlightenment optimism over rational planning. As a consequence, they often operate as if children and teachers are just sociological categories to be manipulated according to the whims of social engineers or political visionaries. If a concept like "globalization" is taken in education as a simple, vulgar rallying call to match the Japanese or Germans in international business competitiveness through the reform of our schools, then that is a shortsighted sellout to a way of thinking about life that is already in its death throes. If, on the other hand, we can understand the world itself as emerging, in a slow, painful way, into a new kind of global culture liberated from heavy-handed political, social, economic and even educational dogma to a life more tolerant of cultural and ethnic differences, more at ease with things not immediately understood, more patient in dealing with life's essential difficulties and more hungry for a simple love of the world itself as our earthly home—if we can gain a glimpse of this, maybe we have a chance for taking one small creative step into the future.

3

Identity, Self and Other in the Conduct of Pedagogical Action: An East/West Inquiry

I

Identity is a problematic at the heart of almost all debates in the contemporary Western tradition. In this paper I wish to examine the notion of identity as both a Western preoccupation and, differently, as a central theme in Eastern wisdom traditions. In the process, I will also relate the discussion to questions about the conduct of pedagogical action. By pedagogical, I mean an interest in how both the implicit and explicit values of a people get mediated through relations with the young. It is in this sense that an interest in identity is also an interest in action, namely that any form of action, pedagogical or otherwise implies a theory of identity. As a teacher, the question of "what is to be done" with respect to Others (a particular child, or group), depends on who I think the Other is, and who I think I am in relation to them.

I also write as a person formed by both Eastern and Western traditions, born in China during the Maoist revolution, but formally educated in the British liberal tradition, so in a way I write from middle space, neither east nor west, looking for a way through the kinds of intellectual and cultural binaries that seem to so hopelessly ensnare creative thinking in the contemporary context. My argument will be that the West is currently at a kind of intellectual and cultural impasse, even a state of exhaustion, precisely because of being stuck in a particular kind of desire with respect to identity. Only through an abandonment of that desire, along the lines, say, of ancient Ch'an Master Huang-po's "great relinquishment" may it be possible to enter the broader ocean of wisdom that can enlighten our lived burdens as parents, teachers, colleagues, friends and especially enemies. Matisse once said of his paintings: "I never finish them, I just abandon them." Such abandonment may be the only means through which what is genuinely new can find its life, but it requires very careful understanding. Certainly abandonment cannot mean a giving up of our deepest human responsibilities.

II

As a field of discourse in the Western tradition today, *identity* is talked about in many different ways. "Identity politics", for example, is allied to the "politics of representation" and the question of how my identity, especially as a racial, sexual being gets constructed and defined within the overall configurations of culture. The topics of Self and subjectivity, with their complementary labour of (auto)biography, story and narration are driven by a belief that one's identity is somehow knowable in itself if only one could find the right way to it.

In pedagogical terms, identity is stubbornly entrenched as the theoretical axis around which virtually all the defining concerns revolve. This is true whether one is speaking of child development (presuming progression from one identity [child] to another [adult]—the myth of adultomorphism, as David Kennedy describes it[1]); the psychology of individuation, aimed at cultivating a strong sense of "self-esteem"; curricular judgements about the degree to which school texts accurately reflect a presumed state of actual affairs; or teacher education models driven by standards of achievement and excellence determined to be normative.

These examples all reflect fairly recent history, however, and are in a sense symptomatic of the end-point of a long chain of cultural experience and reflection.[2] The belief that there is an essential, irreducible *I* that is knowable, stable and discussable may be largely an inheritance from Aristotle, particularly his theory of Substance, which covered three different aspects, namely: substance; being possessing attributes (the subject); and that of which one predicates qualities. Aristotle's theory was borrowed by the early Christian church for its description of the nature of God as being of one substance but three personal expressions—the doctrine of the Trinity.

Current interests in autobiography have a serious precedent in Saint Augustine of the fourth century. His *Confessions* were an experiment in the art of introspection, with introspection being the means by which to unravel and describe all of the ways the human soul could be devious in the search for its true, divinely inspired identity.

The contemporary split in Western academies between philosophy and psychology first arose in the eighteenth century through the work of Immanuel Kant, who proposed that every person's Self was actually composed of two aspects, a transcendental subject or ego which is the ground of all knowledge and perception, and an empirical ego which is what we observe when we introspect, or the thing we impute to other people with qualities, attributes, and so on. The former became the domain of the philosophers, the latter of psychologists. Actually Kant's formulation of the split subject was very reminiscent of the ancient Etruscan understanding of "person", which comes from the Latin word "mask" (L. *persona)*. Certainly I am the person you see, but there is another person too behind the mask of the public self.

If the theme of identity seems to dominate so many fields in the West today, this may be largely due to two factors, the first identified by German sociologist Max Weber at the turn of the century,[3] and the second by writers in the area of postmodern and postcolonial theory.[4] Weber argued that industrial, technical cultures are publically dominated by excessive rationalization, intellectualization and especially by a certain "disenchantment of the world". This drives people inward to try to reclaim personal values deemed to be under threat by the increasing specialization and compartmentalization of knowledge, and the widespread impersonal controls over how the average citizen lives. Capitalism is the quintessence of such rationalization, whereby the ends (making money and profit) completely dominate the means of personal expression and creative outlet. The Self thus becomes the last haven for any sense of individual possibility.

By far the most important influence in current debates about identity is that developed through the literature on postmodernism and postcolonialism. In brief, the suggestion is made that the identity "West" can no longer be accepted as a pure thing, because it depends on a refusal to recognize and honour its own dependencies. Since the Renaissance, Western ascendance in the geopolitical sphere, in terms of economic and political power, depended upon the subjugation, enslavement and even obliteration of Others, others now claiming their place within the new configurations of world order. The West is now having to "face" itself in the faces of those it once oppressed, and the challenge is very unsettling, particularly for those who have a lot to lose in any new equation of, say, redistributed wealth. In this sense, the new crisis of identity in the West is not so much an intellectual issue as a concrete practical one of how to re-think a world in which the West and all of its prized assumptions about nature, man, and truth, are literally "relativized".

Today, then, the Western Subject has been "de-centered," to use the term of Michel Foucault. In the field of education, and especially curriculum studies, the de-centering of the West has meant widespread re-evaluation of the central canons and *oeuvres* that have defined school and university programs to this point, with a bringing forward of what has been systematically excluded in the "standard" works of the tradition as taught. Where are the voices of women, blacks, aboriginals and the colonized in the triumphalist male, white, European imperial tales? This has been a guiding question in curricular discussions for the last ten years or so.

It is the condition of feeling of de-centred which is, according to literary critic Terry Eagleton,[5] "the true aporia, impasse or undecideability of a transitional epoch," the epoch in which, as Western people, we now find ourselves. At the heart of this undecideability is, as Eagleton describes it, "an increasingly clapped-out discreditable, historically superannuated idealogy (sic) of Autonomous Man". Eagleton's argument is that the fiction of autonomy is the anchor myth of liberal capitalism, whereby each person is educated to believe that they can discover themselves through their various accumulations and achievements. In fact, however, the success of consumer culture depends precisely on the Self *not* being a reducible concept, with a consequent sustaining of people's generalized anxiety about such a condition. As David Hume said in the eighteenth century, "The Self is a justifiable but unprovable concept".[6] Consumerism is sustained precisely by the feelings of lack that people have about themselves, and the (false) promise of satisfying that lack with an endless array of material goods, circulating ideas about psychological fulfillment, and so on. Capitalist pedagogy exhausts itself with endless busy(i)ness predicated on an assumption that student or teacher agitations are the consequence of allowing feelings of lack to rear their ugly heads, with the remedy being to labour even more intensively to fill any empty spaces with variations-on-a-theme activities.

The collapse of Autonomous Man has produced a fierce competition to redefine the character of the human project. It is, however, a curious but perhaps inevitable feature of the new identity politics that while the configuration of identities has been changing, to be more inclusive, more pluralistic, the consequences still seem full of pathos, because somehow the social grammar has remained the same. Step one may involve the overthrow of old stereotypes, alliances, identities; step two, the formation of new ones. But has anything really changed? No longer a Yugoslavian, now I am a Croat, and as such now I fight Serbs instead of the Stasi police. No longer a dysfunctional heterosexual, now I am positively gay or lesbian, yet still I find myself entangled in the same jealousies and bitternesses of hetero intimacy; no longer a slave without a vote, now I am an African-American determined to participate in democratic process, but still I have to confront myself within the limits of democracy, manipulated as it is by big business and conservative government; no longer exclusionary high school English literature texts, now texts that attempt to include stories about everyone, everything, as if such could be possible. What is a fully representational textbook anyway?

The point is that within this new identity politics, identity is still linked to a profound *desire* for identity, and there is something neurotic, something of the nature of tail-chasing at work in the whole enterprise. It all still depends on an assumption of the possibility of identity, that somehow if only I could change my circumstances, the real me would have a chance to flourish, to find itself. But perhaps it is this assumption that must bear scrutiny, with the fiction of identity being precisely what sets up the possibility of persons being set against each other, or in collaboration to serve a common purpose at someone else's expense.

So what is left? A neo-Nietzschean inversion into cynical nihilism? A swirling postmodern dance of surfaces that leaves everyone burned out and suicidal? A collapse into market-sponsored media inventions of personhood, with an endless fashion file of consuming souls drained of all ethical substance and psychic interiority?

III

There have been several recent attempts by notable Western scholars to rethink the notion of identity away from the usual, basically Aristotelian, typifications of a stable unified subject. Joanna Macy, for example, working from a systems-theory model influenced heavily by Indian Buddhism, proposes that we should understand persons to be much more fluid and impermanent in their respective manifestations. Persons must be seen in terms of "their relations rather than substance" so that "personal identity appears as emergent and contingent, defining and defined by interactions with the surrounding medium."[7] A person does not so much *have* experiences, in the manner of Descartes's ego, as exist inseparably from those experiences.

Such a formulation however, while solving the problem of the irreducibility of the Self by pointing to its necessary relations, still is in a sense atomistic. The Self is sustained through its relations, but the relations in turn are sustained by the participation of the same Self. There is no one without the other, yet still they exist together as a self-sustaining entity.

In pedagogical terms, collaborative learning and classrooms organized around principles of ecology reflect this kind of systems theory view, and for that very reason can be very depressing, heavy places for children to be. "Whew! Now I am actually *tied* to you, whether I like it or not. We *have* to collaborate, because independent thinking is now somehow shown philosophically to be false thinking". I may be tied to my field of relations and influence, but whether this is burdensome or emancipatory requires further consideration.

In *Self as Other*, Paul Ricouer[8] similarly suggests that any attempt to define the Self exclusively as a question of who or what "I am" should be abandoned in favour of realizing that identifying our own selves depends on the presence of and our interaction with "others" as necessary context. The narrative self is a kind of story-telling ego who identifies him or herself as the centre around which is constelled series of Others who provide the necessary conditions out of which the drama of the Self can be revealed. There is an inextricability of Self and Other, with the Other maintained as a kind of Other-for-the-Self.

Pedagogically it can be seen how this view sponsors a certain requirement of friendliness with others, a new kind of ethical foundation for social relations. If I harm you, somehow my own self requirements are diminished, or at least the context of my life is harmed. One can see, though, how the kind of self-conscious interdependency at the heart of this orientation might easily produce a certain hypocrisy in human relations, insofar as ultimate self-interest inevitably overshadows any genuine interest-free concern for another's welfare, or love of another purely for their own sake. Others simply provide the backdrop for that autobiography in which inevitably I am the hero.

In what follows, I wish to work through the issue of Identity from a kind of "third space",[9] a move which relegates the whole identity question to a different kind of frame, and invites certain reconsiderations of our Western prejudices over the matter.

IV

"You should know that buddha-dharma is to be studied by giving up the view of self and other".[10] This statement by thirteenth-century Japanese Zen master Dogen is easily de-exoticized for Western readers by pointing out that *buddha,* in the original Sanskrit simply means "one who is awake," and *dharma*, again in Sanskrit, means literally, "carrying" or "holding." Studying the buddha-dharma, then, refers to the action of being awake to, or attending to what carries, upholds or sustains us as human beings.

Typical responses in the Western tradition to the question of what sustains us include, for example, positing the god(s) concept, whereby everything that is unexplainable by my received rationality is dumped into a cosmic cargo container for "explanation later", producing a phenomenology of postponement in the now, a kind of intellectual and moral torpor with respect to current problems. Teaching requires a kind of amnesiating Subject who deflects students' hard questions with responses like: "Don't worry, when you grow up you will understand". A teacher formed by the god concept inevitably plays the god role in the classroom.

Another response D. T. Suzuki has called "the homocentric fallacy"[11], the idea that the whole of creation is focussed intentionally around the human species, and that survival or fall depends exclusively on what human beings do or neglect to do. This theory has iterations in Marx, for example, who established the theory of subjectivity on the basis of the historically materially productive activities of human kind. The social-construction-of-reality myth that dominates contemporary social science in the West arises from this. The pedagogical analogue might be found in blind encouragements of students to "be whatever you want to be", as if to be human means being free at all times to shape and mould oneself according to will.

Then there is the response of what can be called one-turn negation, an adolescent protest against meaning and the refusal to take any creative responsibility for human difficulty, except perhaps for one's own. The refusal to see the question of what sustains us as a matter of public concern, with a lapse instead into private visions, undergirds most of our secular systems of education. Teaching becomes a kind of "informatics", a condition that celebrates decontextualized "bites" of information. Here, so-called facts, in isolation, are privileged over their interrelated meaning, and the hard task of interpretation is left to specialized others—philosophers, priests, witches. The closest a teacher gets to being "philosophical" is to declare everything a matter of point-of-view, the curse of perspectivism that haunts most of today's classrooms.

Why should it be important to consider the question of what sustains us, as Dogen urges? In grand terms, the answer might be in order to discover the world more clearly as our true home; or to find ourselves in the world in terms of the world itself, rather than fighting against it, or demanding that it be hammered into the template of our concepts of it. More clearly, it is a matter of having all our work and action ever more finely tuned to the realities of the world, according to the world's own nature. In speaking this way, we are not just talking of the world as the planet earth, with New York, Teheran, Soweto, and so on, all vying for attention on the present world's stage. Instead, the appeal is to the world as in the Old English *w(e)orold*, meaning "age", from the Greek *Aeon*. In this sense of world, time and space intersect, or are inseparable, even identical. It is the sense one gains by staring into the sky on a clear night, and seeing the stars and planets, asteroids, comets, gas clouds and so on, all in continuous motion, all in a state of the most intimate intermingling, interfusion and co-origination, all so big and far away, yet so near. One's meditation inspires the feeling of being part of an ongoing drama, one without beginning or end; one is unequivocally in it, even though as a human being one feels so small, so insignificant in the Face of it. One thinks of the forces that are at work, constantly, as the universe undergoes its endless transformations, out of which the earth has momentarily appeared, and into which eventually it will disappear, to be re-worked into new forms in new ages. This "I", this Self, which meditates on these things is sustained, shaped, moulded, carried and upheld both by and in the midst of these transformations, but only in a certain sense, and it is one that offends our common sense because it is a condition not of lively, self-conscious affirmation, in the spirit of the Happy Face of good liberal capitalism. Instead it is the primordial condition of both creation and destruction, to be awake to which means that whether I live or die really seems quite beside the point. To truly live, then, in the way this world shows its way to be, I must embrace without equivocation the truth of my mortality as part of my vitality. As the contemporary Vietnamese Zen Master Thich Naht Hanh has put it, "Birth and death are fictions, and not very deep", [12] by which he means that even when I die, I continue living, in the plants and insects that consume me for their nourishment and life, and in the memories of those with whom I have lived for a brief span, and who themselves go on living. Similarly, as I live by the grace of the animals, plants and insects that give me life, so too am I dying, eventually to be taken in again for other purposes. Every identifiable "thing" is itself in a condition of constant mutation, completely infused with everything else, never 'this' for more than a moment; soon to be "that", or '"his-and-that". In spite of everything, the whole remains whole; teeming with fluid ambiguity, but never without integrity.

If we are to get closer to the sense of what sustains or upholds us, these last examples, of how dying and living are themselves concepts that require deep meditation, may point to how that very meditation can lead us to a healthy abandonment of the concepts of Self and Other. It is not that there is no Self and Other, as in the one-turn negation, but rather that the formulation puts the emphasis in the wrong place. There is a place where Self and Other cannot be identified separately because the moment one is identified so too in that very instant is the other named or brought forward. The game of trying to separate them is one, not just of futility, but worse, of utter violence, because they are always everywhere co-emergent, with a denial of one being a denial of the other.

In the third century, Indian philosopher Nagarjuna declared that in the life of true liberty, "there is neither yes nor no, nor not-yes or not-no". [13] He was trying to point to the futility of dualistic thinking, drawing attention instead to the pre-existent unity by which all dualisms are already held together. Here we might say, "Not Self and Other, and not *not* Self and Other". In other words, Self and Other should not be held as independent entities, yet too, neither should we deny that Self and Other exist. After all, common sense tells us that I am me and You are you, and these separations are required for simple functioning, for example, within the space limitations of our homes, schools and other institutions. What Nagarjuna is saying, though, is that we should not rest in our common sense perceptions, complacency with which provides all the ammunition one needs to set oneself against the other should the "I" be threatened. As Peter Hershock has put it, "...the gathering with which we identify ourselves is actually a learned process of simply divorcing that over which "I" cannot exercise direct control". [14]

Living in the pre-existent unity of the world, or rather living in such a way as to put the awareness of that unity in front of the desire for the usual discriminations that inevitably emerge from language, tribe and nation, is a form of life-practice that is "to be realized and not sought", as Chih Tung, disciple of Hui Neng, founder of the Ch'an (Zen) school in the seventh century, has put it. [15] One cannot seek it, because that would put it "over there" somewhere, while it is already "here", inherent in every present moment. Also, to posit it over there means it would have to be apprehended by some pre-existent Ego that somehow lies outside of the whole process. So the truth of living awake to the way that sustains us requires a different manner of proceeding, a manner not dependent on language, rationality or culture; it requires a simple openness to that which meets us at every turn, in every thing, every thought, feeling, idea, person. Everything is a reminder of who and what we are, a kind of calling back to our more essential truth. Becoming awake to what sustains us is a form of realization of what it is we already are. Indeed, as David Loy has put it, "What you seek, you already are". [16] Sometimes this is spoken of as the process of finding one's "Original Face". [17]

Being in the presence of someone who is truly awake can be very unnerving, especially for those who have not "faced" themselves. The person seems like a mirror in which one sees oneself for the first time and is aghast. There is an uncanny stillness present, reminding us of our constant agitation, our frenetic searching for that which we cannot name but feel we should be able to if only one more turn be taken with this or that. The stillness of one who is awake does not arise out of passivity, quietism or simple resignation but rather from deep attunement to the coherence and integrity of everything that is already and everywhere at work in the world as it is. The face of one who has found their Original Face seems to contain everything and nothing all at once. It is as if the face could burst forth with joy at any moment, or register the most profound anger. It is the Face of complete potentiality because indeed it has seen everything. It has seen human misery in its darkest expressions, joy in its most robust celebrations. In the presence of one who has faced himself, one feels understood, found, unconditionally accepted, but this acceptance does not necessarily induce pleasure. It does not mean an endorsement or condoning of bad things, things that hurt others, for example. Rather, in facing one who has faced herself, one has the feeling of being seen, deeply, and in that very instant one begins to see the foolishness of one's own ways, perhaps for the first time, ways that arise precisely out of the desire to arbitrate the boundaries of Self and Other, to secure or justify the Self against the Other. And in seeing one's actions as, in a sense, arising out of ignorance, one is filled with desire to live differently, with greater awareness.

What would be the face of teaching for a teacher who is awake to what sustains us?

In Sanskrit, there is a word, *upaya*, used precisely to describe the teaching style of an Awakened One.[18] Literally, it refers to "skill in means, or method". It also has the connotation of "appropriateness", of knowing exactly what is required in any specific instance. Students under the tutelage of one who is awake often find the teacher to be a bundle of contradictions, because what is said to one may be completely reversed in instructions to another. This is because the teacher understands the unique needs and capabilities of each, honouring their differences, and knowing what is best for each.

In terms of contemporary pedagogy, we can see the way *upaya* refutes any systematic approach to instructional conduct, making possible an opening of a much fuller range of expression on the part of both the teacher and the student. The interest of the teacher is not to teach, in the usual sense of imparting well-formulated epistemologies, but to protect the conditions under which each student in his own way can find his way. One of the key conditions for this effort is to be vigilant of students' motives. Is the learning simply for personal aggrandisement, careerism, a way by which to assert the Self over the Other? Or is it oriented to an ever-deepening humility (literally, "groundedness" > L. *humus*) which arises from seeing the interconnectedness of everything and the essential humour of our co-origination. In such circumstances, one student may need severe discipline, another strong encouragement; always the concern is for each one to discover a sense of what upholds them, and the original face that bears their hope for a new originality in the present.

There is a likeness here to the practice in many aboriginal cultures in North America of appointing elders gifted with discernment to the post of "child watcher". Their job is to keep watch over the children, at play, in community activities, and so on, to see what the particular gift of each child might be, as it arises naturally in the context of everyday life, and then to guide each child into efforts that can bring the gift to its fullest expression. Such a practice holds up for criticism all those pressures in modern capitalist culture which encourage students to fit themselves to the requirements of the corporate agenda, taking a narrow, time-bound characterization of success to be of universal application.

As far as classroom management is concerned, pedagogy which faces itself may elaborate the suggestion of Thich Nhaht Hanh: "We need to look at a conflict the way a mother would who is watching her two children fighting. She seeks only their reconciliation".[19] From the point of view of full compassion, war arises precisely out of Self and Other, with attempts to name the virtue of one at the other's expense. Wisdom, however, desires the loss of neither, seeing their essential mutual necessity within the integrity of what sustains us.

If facing oneself as a teacher is a task to be realized and not sought, that is, attended to as an already inherent potentiality rather than something to be obtained and validated by external certification, what are the safeguards to ensure that one's teaching practices are not simply the manifestation of a new blind narcissism or a celebration of a newly realized subjectivity? Again, those who have gone before, have understood the problem. In the ancient Pali language, there are two terms that identify stages along the way of finding one's way as a teacher who is awake. In the first stage, *jhana*, the aim is to achieve a kind of stillness of heart and mind through ritual stopping of intellectual and cognitive habits.[20] It is the process of emptying the mind of thoughts, worries, fantasies, and so forth, by accepting their unresolvability. They cannot be resolved in any final sense because they are themselves simply products of the mind, that jumping monkey which tries so hard to not let us rest.

In the condition of stillness, it becomes possible to hear new sounds, or old sounds in a new way; appreciate tastes once numbed out by old habits of taste; see a child, spouse, partner, parent, in a way that honours them more fully, instead of constrained by the usual fears, desires and projections. One begins to understand how pedagogical confidences learned in one's teacher training may have only limited application in the face of any classroom's true complexity; and that dealing with that complexity requires not yet another recipe for control, but precisely the opposite, namely a radical openness to what is actually happening therein, in the lives and experiences of both students and oneself, and an ability to deal with all of it somehow on its own unique terms. Again, such an ability requires first and foremost a true facing of oneself and others as sharing in a reality that at its deepest level is something held in common, something that upholds one and all together in a kind of symphony.

At the age of fifty-one, Confucius had not yet faced himself, and was therefore not yet a teacher. One day he went to his Master, Lao Tan (Lao Tzu), who asked him how he had been spending his time. Confucius replied that he had been studying mathematics for five years, light and darkness for twelve years and memorizing perfectly the Six Great Books, called The Odes, History, Poetry, Music, The Changes, and The Seasons Spring and Autumn. Lao Tan then began to talk to Confucius about the way which upholds us, sustains us and carries us. Confucius retired to his hut for three months, and then returned to his teacher, saying, "I have understood now. The crows and magpies incubate their eggs, and fish plan their spawning; the locust engenders itself by metamorphosis; the birth of the younger brother makes the older cry. For a long time now I haven't participated in these transformations. *The person who does not participate in transformation, how could such a person transform others?*"[21]

Confucius' last remark signifies the second major turning point on the way to waking up as a person, on the way to becoming a teacher, and that is taking up the hard challenge of self-transformation. The meaning is carried in the Pali word *upacara.*. The task is chiefly one of beginning to pierce through all of the social, political and cultural illusions by which one's identity has sustained itself to the present point. Without doubt, therefore, it involves culture criticism, criticism of bad economic practices that destroy the common realm for the greed of the few; criticism of social structures and attitudes that demean others of different race, class or gender in order to affirm only one type as the "real" thing. More than anything else, however, it forces a recognition of how one is oneself always and everywhere complicit in such ignorance, and that the hardest work, the work that provides the only true authority for teaching others about social tranformation, is by addressing the condition of one's own ignorance. Rwanda does not just exist in Africa, Rwanda also exists in my own heart-mind, to deny which is to deny, and hence not face, the vicious fantasies I am quite happy to entertain, even maintain, about the family across the back lane, for example, whose barking dog keeps me awake at night and who refuse to discipline the same, in spite of my mock-friendly overtures. I have to face the fact that I myself am really not so distantly removed from committing a vile atrocity; that though I have a naturally smiling face, often it hides feelings of hatred. I know that I am capable of the most calumnious and vituperative delusions. These Other sides of my face I must face too, if I want to be a teacher, or more accurately if pedagogic authority is to flow out of me in the manner of the world's upholding, in a way that reveals the deepest truth about the world rather than acting against it. I may have a teaching certificate, a civil license to teach, but whether I am a teacher, really, depends on something else. It depends on the ability to "be still, and to know God",[22] as the Hebrew psalmist has expressed it, which means the ability to dwell openly in that which cannot be named but within which we live and move and have our being. Without attention to this which contains both this and that, self and other, you and me, life becomes nothing but a half-life, a kind of fake optimism about the Now which is fundamentally conservative because it refuses to love the Other as Itself, to see them as one, instead banishing the Other as enemy, or potential enemy of the "I".

"Your enemy is your teacher", says Song-chol, head of the Chogye Order in Korea.[23] "Adversity is the only teacher", said Aeschylus, the early Greek dramaturgist.[24] "When you have eaten the bread of suffering, and drunk the water of distress, then you will see your Teacher face to face" said the Hebrew prophet Isaiah.[25] All of these examples imply the truth well understood by Freud that what we keep at bay, what we hate, what we demonize, is most typically what we fear. What we fear, we repress, and what we repress comes back over and over to haunt us, in our dreams, in our compensatory actions, until the day comes when we can no longer run away from it, and have to make friends with it, and embrace it as part of what sustains us. Isaiah understood this seeming contradiction well: suffering and distress are like bread and water, forms of nourishment. To accept this, however, requires a discerning of how they act together within a deeper truth of things, a truth that is deeper than any pain I might feel when I have lost my beloved, my job, my country. In fact it is precisely such experiences of loss that can divest us of the illusion of trying to secure ourselves, yet in that very divestment we can see more clearly the security already manifest in the world, the world which is already carried, upheld and sustained in spite of our most advanced management systems, comprehensive insurance policies and hyper-developed health care products—those monuments to human cowardice that reveal our reluctance to be taught the things of greatest importance.

To be a teacher, then, requires that I face my Teacher, which is the world as it comes to meet me in all of its variegation, complexity and simplicity. When I do this, I face myself, and see myself reflected in the faces of my brothers and sisters everywhere. If I look to see myself only in the faces of those portrayed in glamour magazines, or in *Fortune 500*'s "Top Ten CEOs", I suffer a fundamental double impoverishment. Not only will I be disappointed in myself, but also I will miss the point that such people represent only a small dot on the mirror of reality, and to try to copy them is to force myself to become equally small. By facing too those whose faces have been burned by the fires of life, seeing myself in them, I become more fully human, more open and generous, more representative of the real thing we call Life.

In conclusion: Western critics of Eastern philosophy often suggest that the latter sponsors only quiescence and pacifism, and does not take full enough responsibility for dealing with the hard, concrete problems of existence on this side of the river. Such a remark, of course, only points to the priority the West gives to action and activism, and does not face at all those negative consequences that Western activism has inflicted on the world. Even in the field of medicine, for example, the rush to interventional practices too often gets in the way of natural healing, and a true pedagogy of suffering. Ashis Nandy has eloquently drawn attention to the phenomenon of "iatrogenesis",[26] whereby acts of treatment themselves often cause different kinds of disease. In Western medicine, the patient is no longer allowed to be patient, the clinical vultures always hovering overhead waiting to dive in with the latest "procedure".

Certainly the most profound disease in Western pedagogy is activism, or action for its own sake. Children in today's classrooms have virtually no time to simply dream, wait, think, ponder or learn to be still. There is so little opportunity to find one's original face, because every space is seen to require some sort of instructional intervention. Indeed, using the language of this paper, Western pedagogy is too often precisely an act of de-facement, for both teachers and students, as they struggle mercilessly to fit themselves in to codes and agendas that maim and scar the soul. Ironically, such maiming arises precisely out of good intention and great earnestness. But that very earnestness itself gets in the way of self-understanding, because the Self cannot understand itself until it loses itself in the work of great relinquishment, of being born again in the ocean of wisdom wherein Self and Other have no time to negotiate their differences. In the ocean of wisdom, the moment Self and Other have been identified they have disappeared, or been transformed or mutated into yet another unfolding of the drama in which all things, all people regardless of race, gender or class, participate. Whether that participation is creative or destructive depends on whether one clings to or reliquishes old identities that have already passed anyway. To find one's original face as a teacher means to stand before one's students as the embodiment of true liberty, known everywhere by its mark of deep humour, which arises from the awareness that at the heart of life is a contradiction. To find myself I have to lose myself, otherwise death comes in the most vainglorious guise, death by a thousand Self achievements that leave me isolated in the cage of my own subjectivity, bereft of the companionship of the world.

We might note in closing the profound engagement between one who is awake and children, or, as it might be described, the universal attractiveness of Wisdom to children. Ryokan-osho, an eighth century enlightened hermit, was described in the following terms:

> Hair unkempt, ears sticking out,
> His tattered robes
> Swirling like smoke,
> He walks home
> With hordes of children
> Swarming all around.[27]

The image has a mirror in the Christian story of the children "coming to Jesus".[28] As teachers and teacher educators we might ask what is it that makes genuine enlightenment attractive to children. I think it has something to do with the way the teacher who is awake has recovered themselves from the snares and entrapments of Self and Other thinking, now accepting all others in the way a very young child does, trusting the world as being the only world there is, engaging it without fear. Fear comes later.

4

The Hermeneutic Imagination and the Pedagogic Text

At the end of a recent graduate course entitled "Interpretive Inquiry in Educational Research," a course in which phenomenology, critical theory, semiotics and poststructuralism were all made topical along with hermeneutics, one student remarked, "But it's all hermeneutics, isn't it?" Whenever we are engaged in the activity of interpreting our lives and the world around us, we are engaging in what the Greeks called "practical philosophy," an activity linkable to the character of Hermes in the Greek pantheon.[1] Hermes, as well as being the deliverer of messages between the gods, and from the gods to mortals on earth, was known for a number of other qualities such as eternal youthfulness, friendliness, prophetic power and fertility. In a sense, all of these features are at work in the hermeneutic endeavor to this day, as the practice of interpretation attempts to show what is at work in different disciplines and, in the service of human generativity and good faith, is engaged in the mediation of meaning. There is one further aspect of Hermes that may be worth noting, namely his impudence. He once played a trick on the most venerated Greek deity, Apollo, inciting him to great rage. Modern students of hermeneutics should be mindful that their interpretations could lead them into trouble with "authorities."

One might ask why hermeneutics is such an ubiquitous feature of the contemporary intellectual landscape. One finds the term not just in the older traditions of philosophy and theology, or more recently in literary criticism. In recent years also, for example, there have appeared texts on the hermeneutics of psychology[2] and economics.[3] Canada may be distinguished in forming the first society specifically oriented to the exploration of the relation between hermeneutics and postmodern thought.[4]

The answer to the question of hermeneutics' attractiveness to the times resides, perhaps, in the general state of exhaustion of what Karl-Otto Apel has called the "dogmatic-normative"[5] traditions of epistemology and metaphysics as they functioned foundationally in the establishment and continuation of contemporary discourse domains from the eighteenth-century Enlightenment to the present day. The critique of "foundationalism"[6] inherent in the current poststructuralist movements signals what many people already understand intuitively, which is that, for Western cultures at least, there is a crisis of value at work that cannot be resolved simply by appealing to traditional forms of logic and authority. It may be precisely the inability of traditional (Western) forms of discourse to deal single-handedly with the lived problems of the present day that makes interpretation or re-interpretation of contemporary paradigms and their institutional embodiments necessary. Indeed, H-G. Gadamer, likely the foremost philosopher of hermeneutics in this century, has so summarized the situation: "Only when our entire culture for the first time saw itself threatened by radical doubt and critique did hermeneutics become a matter of universal significance".[7] One might quibble with the right to speak of universals, but not with the link between social trouble and the need for interpretation.

In educational terms, the hermeneutic imagination throws open the challenge to inquire into what we mean when we use words like curriculum, research and pedagogy. We are challenged to ask what makes it possible for us to speak, think and act in the ways we do. From the perspective of postmodern hermeneutics,[8] the project is even more searching, namely, a concern for how we shall proceed pedagogically after we have given up the presumption of ever being able to define in unequivocal foundational terms all of the key referents in our professional lexicon. For example, how might we orient our lives with children when we can no longer take for granted what a child is in any discrete sense, when we make problematic all of the usual categories for understanding childhood in our culture (development, cognition, achievement, etc.), or when we take up the question of the meaning of children as one which is not answerable except self-reflexively, that is from the question of who I am in-relation-to my children?

The United Nations' *Convention on the Rights of the Child* underscores how it is that in spite of enormous public expenditure on formal educational programs for children and good rhetoric speaking on children's behalf, in actuality children are the most frequently abused and neglected of all the world's citizens, in countries like the United States and Canada as well as in the Third World.[9] It may be that the meaning and place of children in our lives is the most important consideration to be taken up in education today, not just because the voice of the young has been translated out of any meaningful involvement with the powers that be,[10] but also because the question of the young (their conception, care and nurturance) devolves precisely on so many of the defining issues of our time, such as the structuration of power, gender relations and the matter of how we might learn to live more responsibly within the earthly web of our planetary home. But not only that: Hermes was "a young god always",[11] which means, in a sense, that the hermeneutic imagination works from a commitment to generativity and rejuvenation and to the question of how we can go on together in the midst of constraints and difficulties that constantly threaten to foreclose on the future. The aim of interpretation, it could be said, is not just another interpretation but human freedom, which finds its light, identity and dignity in those few brief moments when one's lived burdens can be shown to have their source in too limited a view of things.

Hermeneutics from Aristotle to Gadamer

Hermeneutics has a long history. [12] Aristotle once used the word in the title of one of his works (*Peri Hermenia*), and there was a school of interpretation in ancient Alexandria. It was not until the Reformation in the sixteenth century, however, that the question of interpretation itself became problematic. The issue was one which still inheres in contemporary debates, which is whether the authority for the meaning of a given text resides within a traditional interpretive community such as the Church (or now the State), or whether a text has its own internal meaning and integrity which can be recovered by any well-intended individual possessed with the right skills. In 1567, Matthias Flacius Illyricus wrote the first "methods text" for hermeneutics, the *Arts Critica*, inspired by the need of Protestant theologians to validate their efforts through scriptural interpretations that were independent of Roman Catholic tradition.

In the eighteenth century the question of method assumed full prominence, and this was the case not just for the interpretation of sacred texts but also for the newly emergent understanding of science which characterized the Enlightenment. Johan Martin Chladenius wrote a treatise in 1742 outlining procedures for "The Correct Interpretation of Reasonable Discourses and Books". The timing is notable for its temporal location between those foundational texts which have underwritten virtually all economic, political and philosophical activity in the modern West, such as Descartes's *Discourse on Method,* Mill's *Logic* and Adam Smith's *Wealth of Nations*. The point is that eighteenth-century philosophers were full of optimism that life in general could be systematically brought under the control of correct logical procedure. It is that assumption, of truth being ultimately a methodological affair, that much of contemporary hermeneutics wishes to challenge.

The most under-appreciated of all hermeneutical thinkers is probably Friedrich Schleiermacher, who in the nineteenth century was part of the early

Romantic movement inspired by the aesthetics of J. G. Fichte and H. Schelling.[13] From Schleiermacher on, three themes in hermeneutic inquiry have always been present: namely, the inherent creativity of interpretation, the pivotal role of language in human understanding and the interplay of part and whole in the process of interpretation. That process later became articulated as "the hermeneutic circle" at work in all human understanding.

For Schleiermacher, interpretation and understanding are creative acts, not just technical functions. Texts, works of art, and so on, are expressions of a creative spirit which any interpreter must somehow engage if interpretations are to be made that are faithful to an author's original intention. This process of engagement Scheiermacher termed "divinitory", as distinct from "comparative". The divinitory character of interpretation is the "feminine force in the knowledge of human nature", a knowledge made possible by the deep commonality of all people. The comparative approach on the other hand is "masculine". Depending as it does on the employment of typologies, it is incapable of "yielding a unity". A unity occurs when the singular and the common "permeate each other" by means of "intuiting" or divining what is at work on the part of the original author. In this last formulation can be discerned perhaps the most abiding contribution from Schleiermacher, namely, a pointing to the way in which good interpretation involves a playing back and forth between the specific and the general, the micro and the macro.

When this interplay is applied to the understanding of persons, one is inevitably drawn into a consideration of how language both encourages and constrains a person's self-understanding. As Schleiermacher put it, "every discourse depends on earlier thought... (and) it follows that every person is on the one hand a locus in which a given language is formed after an individual fashion, and on the other, a speaker who is only able to be understood within the totality of the language".

There is foreshadowed here all subsequent attempts to show the articulation between language as general system and language as individual speech and utterance. Ferdinand de Saussure's distinction between *langue* and *parole*[14] and Wilhelm von Humboldt's characterization of *Sprache* and *Rede*[15] are perhaps the two most notable of such attempts. Schleiermacher's emphasis on the creative spirit in any work, that is, on the inner driving integrity which gives an interpreter access to its specific aspects, resonates in Julia Kristeva's later stress on understanding the "desire" in language[16] and Paulo Freire's challenge to "grasp the human aspiration" of a people's speech and action.[17]

If Schleiermacher's romanticist hermeneutics marked a watershed for the nineteenth century, Wilhelm Dilthey's work showed the way to twentieth-century interests in philosophical hermeneutics and the methodological concerns of the social and historical sciences.[18] Dilthey was profoundly influenced by the philosopher of history J. G. Droysen who refined from von Humboldt a distinction still residual today in the so-called quantitative/qualitative debate in educational research, the distinction between the historical sciences and the natural sciences. Droysen designated the term *Verstehen* to refer to "understanding" as the method appropriate for the historical sciences, while causal "explanation" (*Erklarung*) was the methodological foundation of the natural sciences. Dilthey later developed this distinction in his efforts to define the human sciences as their own speciality, the *Geisteswissenschaften*. Pushing away the mechanistic models of explanation which were the order of the day, Dilthey, under the influence of the new phenomenological investigations of Edmund Husserl, began to explore "understanding" as a methodological concept which has its origin in the process of human life itself. Human understanding is a "category of life" (*Lebensausserung*) in texts, artifacts, gestures, voices and so forth, and we understand them to the degree to which we can show how they emerge from "lived experience" (*Erlebnis*), that deep sediment and texture of our collective life. Good interpretation shows the connection between experience and expression. There is a strong affinity here with the ideas of the later Wittgenstein who argued that the meaning of words and statements is reflective of specific "forms of life" (*Lebensform*). We might note, too, that Dilthey was one of the first to suggest that written statements are the most elevated form of human expression, an idea which pre dated Paul Ricoeur's attempt to formulate textual interpretation as a foundation for a general hermeneutic,[19] and also Jacques Derrida's critique of phonocentrism, the Western predisposition to privilege speech over writing.[20]

Any serious consideration of the development of hermeneutics must inevitably point to Edmund Husserl as the most significant shaper of all of the interpretive streams of human science which have flourished since the turn of the century. Not only did Husserl introduce the notion of the "life-world" (*Lebenswelt*) to characterize our sense of the world as it is there for us before we say or do anything about it, but he also laid the ground for those later phenomenologies of human social behaviour such as Alfred Schutz's interpretive sociology[21] and Harold Garfinkle's ethnomethodological studies.[22] Most important of all, however, was Husserl's massive project of overturning the Enlightenment ideal of objective reason. Through his theory of intentionality, Husserl showed that we never think or interpret "in general" as a rhetorical activity that bears no necessary connection to the world at large. Rather, thinking and interpreting are always and everywhere precisely about the world. I cannot abstract thinking itself out from what it is that I am thinking about. A clear split between subjective thinking and objective thinking is not sustainable because my subjectivity gets its bearings from the very world that I take as my object. Furthermore, the world is always a world I share with others with whom I communicate, so my descriptions of the world are always subject to modification on the basis of what I share communicatively.

From Husserl on, words like "understanding", "interpretation" and "meaningfulness" are rooted, hermeneutically speaking, in a sense of the dialogical, intersubjective and conversational nature of human experience. Husserl forged the possibility of a new unity between Self and Other, and, I suspect, inaugurated a foundation for a more friendly relation between human beings and their earthly habitat. The political, social and economic implications of the Husserlian revolution have never been adequately worked out. One of the poverties of postmodern formulations may be shown, for example, in the evidence of what happens when a liberation from objective reason is not linked to a recovered sense of the Other. Interpretation easily lapses into a dalliance of interpretations rather than leading to a renewed embrace of the Other and the world in the service of a fuller appreciation of the human prospect.

Husserl's student Martin Heidegger gave a radically new meaning to the term hermeneutics by incorporating it into his unique rewriting of the Western philosophical tradition around the question of Being. After Heidegger, hermeneutics is no longer a particular domain of metaphysics or a special school of speculative philosophy; rather it is the foundational practice of Being itself. Interpretation is the means by which the nature of Being and human be-ing is disclosed. Interpretation is the primordial condition of human self-understanding so that a phenomenology of Being reveals its fundamental mode to be precisely hermeneutical. As Heidegger expressed it in *Being and Time*, "The phenomenology of Being (*Dasein*) is a hermeneutic in the primordial signification of this word, where it designates this business of interpreting."[23]

Heidegger's casting of interpretation as the primordial mode of human existence (he later allied the notion of interpretation to the Greek sense of "thinking"[24]) put Dilthey's project of a method for the human sciences into crisis because thereafter method could never attain a status independent of the project of thinking itself. Method could never achieve a kind of solitary stable state ready for universal application, because indeed it bore the same character and quality as that to which it sought access. This was the point taken up more fully by Heidegger's student Hans-Georg Gadamer, who in his landmark work *Truth and Method*[25] argued that the appropriate method for interpreting any phenomena could only be disclosed by the phenomena itself through a kind of Socratic-dialogical engagement between question and phenomenon.

There is not room here to explore other key themes in Heidegger's hermeneutics of existence except to highlight two aspects which Gadamer later developed in his own work, namely, the historico-temporal quality of human experience and the linguisticality of understanding. According to Heidegger, human experience of the world takes place within a horizon of past, present and future. Understanding that which confronts us as new is made possible in the "now" by virtue of the forestructure of understanding which is already in us through past experience. Gadamer pursued this idea in two important respects. The first was to reinstate in a positive way the manner in which pre-judgement is a necessary requirement of all understanding. This he emphasized as a counter to the objectivist thrust of the natural sciences and its claim that knowledge could be free from human interest. For Gadamer, prejudice (pre-judgement) is not a swear word, but rather a sign that we can only make sense of the world from within a particular "horizon" which provides the starting point for our thoughts and actions. Understanding between persons is possible only to the degree that people can initiate a conversation between themselves and bring about a "fusion" of their different horizons into a new understanding which they then hold in common.

Putting the matter in a slightly different way, it could be said that Gadamerian hermeneutics validated a new appreciation of tradition as the received life-stream out of which it is possible to say or do anything at all. For Gadamer, tradition is not sclerotic, nostalgic or antiquarian; rather it always opens out into the future to engage what comes to meet it as new. This understanding of our temporal nature Gadamer called "effective historical consciousness" (*wirkungs-geschichlisches bewusstsein*), and its character is revealed most pristinely in the structure and function of language. Inevitably I speak the language into which I was born, but my language already contains within itself in a sedimentary way the evidence of its own malleability and evolution, reflective of the political, economic and social changes in which my forebearers engaged through the course of their personal and collective lives. My language contains within it the evidence not just of the openness of my life, but, in a deep and subtle way, its anticipation of being transformed in the face of new lived realities. How I will be transformed depends upon my orientation and attitude toward what comes to meet me as new: whether I simply try to subsume or repress it within prevailing dispensations (a possible prelude to war or hostilities) or whether I engage it creatively in an effort to create a new common, shared reality.

In this so-called postmodern era, Gadamer may be described as the last writer of a hermeneutics of continuity, a hermeneutics which attempts to hold the structure of understanding together within a language of understanding. As such, his hermeneutics supports all of the recent work in the study of narrative and story,[26] which proceeds from an affirmation of the traceably constitutive nature of human understanding and its roots in recollection and memory. Indeed, it could also be argued that, since Gadamer, as a result of the ascendent poststructuralist interpretive movements and even the neo-Marxist critical traditions which work from a vision of radical rupture and separation rather than conversation, the question of continuity has assumed a status of vital importance. Of great pedagogical and curricular significance, it devolves on the question of whether understanding is, say, a necessarily cumulative, evolutionary work in progress, linear and sequential, or whether it is a more complex clustered affair with occasional bursts of illumination but not working on a plane of any sort nor in any particular direction. It may be fair to say that Gadamer stands as a link between the totalizing proclivities of hermeneutics up till the last quarter of the twentieth century, and the contemporary hermeneutics of "play" and "desire" signified in postmodern writers like Derrida and Kristeva.[27]

Indeed, in many important ways, Gadamer prefigures postmodern hermeneutics. His description of play as the basic modus of understanding, his articulation of the way in which within everything said there is something unsaid and his working through of a theory of the relationship between speech and writing—these matters are all central in the interpretive activity of the present time. Whether or not such activity is formally called "hermeneutics" seems almost beside the point now, except that no contemporary writer in the human sciences can proceed without eventually acknowledging a debt to those figures referred to in this section who all at one time or another were preoccupied with the question of the nature and character of our subject. Of course in these Derridean days, the very desire to know what something like hermeneutics "is" in its essential nature, a desire laden with imperial, masculine, "logocentric" baggage, is what is now thrown into question. But logocentrism or the metaphysics of presence can only be deconstructed because deconstruction itself is an interpretive hermeneutical activity.

The Nature of Hermeneutic Inquiry

Reviews and summaries like the foregoing are inevitably incomplete, and because of that, like all forms of writing they contain a certain violence. But it remains for us now to ask how the hermeneutic tradition can inform the interests of curriculum, research and pedagogy. We have seen that hermeneutics is not just one thing nameable and applicable in some vulgar instrumental sense. Rather it refers to a whole range of topics and questions which had their internal legitimacy within a context of German and European philosophy. That context might be seen as something which inevitably constrains or even devalues the potentiality of the interpretive project, located as it is within an undeniably Eurocentric origin and nexus. Quite notable, however, is the way in which the hermeneutic imagination has the capacity to reach across national and cultural boundaries to enable dialogue between people and traditions superficially at odds. Hermeneutics is able to shake loose dogmatic notions of tradition to show how all traditions open up onto a broader world which can be engaged from within the language of one's own space. Impressive interpretive work in this kind of cross-cultural mediation has been undertaken by such scholars as Zhang Longxi in the Chinese context,[28] Oh Mahn Seng in Korea,[29] and Cynthia Chambers with North American aboriginal peoples.[30] All three draw specifically on hermeneutic formulations to problematize the hegemony of dominant culture in order to engage it transformatively. These three examples also provide excellent models of a kind of interpretive research that curriculum developers of the future will require as they face the challenge of mediating meaning in the midst of cultural difference. Given that teachers throughout the Western world are now working in classrooms increasingly cosmopolitan in makeup, curriculum and pedagogy cast in frames and conceptions which do not address the new realities of global intercourse will be severely impoverished. The hermeneutic insistence on the articulation between whole and part in the development of understanding invites new considerations of what we mean by a "world", a challenge taken up, for example, in the work of the World Order Studies movement.[31] Later we will briefly discuss the implications of this for interpretive life-world research.

Is there such a thing as "the hermeneutic method" of inquiry that can be applied to concerns in curriculum, research and pedagogy? The answer to this question is perhaps best answered not directly but contextually. We saw briefly in the previous section how the matter of method has been dealt with within the hermeneutic tradition itself, showing our contemporary preoccupation with it to be a modern construct linked to the sciences of control. Here it may be most helpful to show the hermeneutic imagination in relation to the two other most currently dominant traditions of educational theorizing in the West, the critical tradition and, so we might call it, the tradition of consciousness. Then we can ask for the unique contribution of hermeneutics in a more practical sense.

By the tradition of consciousness is meant the long journey of Western culture to establish the mind as the locale and arbiter of knowledge and experience. Rooted in Aristotle's logic and systems of classification, Cartesian dualism, and Kantian idealism, the tradition of consciousness valorizes the work of perception as the means by which the human subject grasps reality then anchors it as reality through the legitimating codes of the times embedded in users' language. The tradition of consciousness shapes curriculum decision-making as fundamentally a form of arbitration over the correctness or appropriateness of ideas, that is as a judgment of the degree to which they "re-present" reality,[32] with the truth of things being defined according to standards of orthodoxy such as science or communal tradition. The modus of the tradition of consciousness is argumentation and dispute so that winners can be declared. Given that maturity is measured by the degree of an individual's subjective appropriation of the so-called objective world, personal autonomy is the most celebrated social quality, with loneliness and anomie the most common personal complaints. Fundamentally conservative in tone and gesture, the tradition of consciousness proceeds on an assumption that once things are arbitrated as true, they are true once and for all, storable or transmittable as needs arise at any given moment. Pedagogy is most basically an act of cultural reproduction and transmission. Research involves getting the facts of a particular case right and conveying them accurately.

The critical tradition shares with the tradition of consciousness a common lineage through Kantian idealism and the determination that the nature of reality can be decided in advance of a full experience of it.[33] When categories such as class, labor or surplus value, for example, are taken as ultimately fixable determinants of social reality, instead of being simply interpretive frameworks which themselves can be interpreted, then as categories they can be used as conceptual weapons by which to brow-beat others and the world into a preordained recognizable form. This accounts for how the implementation of critical pedagogy programs in the name of equality and justice sometimes seems to do violence to the very people the programs are designed to assist.[34] Dialogue in the critical sense becomes dialogue with a hidden agenda: I speak to you to inform you of your victimization and oppression rather than with you in order that together we might create a world which does justice to both of us. The interest of the critical tradition is not just persuasion but a predetermination to shape the social order in fixed directions; it requires material evidence of ideas translated into practice. The curricular agenda of the critical has the character of a blueprint operating in the name of justice. Pedagogy is concerned with mobilizing the social conscience of students into acts of naming and eradicating the evils of the times. The social end in view is utopian (Greek *u-topos*, no place), a community of ideal speech and life-order free of distortion, inequity and duplicity.

The frustration of the critical vision resides precisely in the very ambiguity and complexity of language which hermeneutics tries to uphold.[35] That is to say, all programs and practices have to be mediated linguistically (we have to talk together about what is to be done, write memos, policies and so on), and the only way this can be carried on without violating the participants concerned is to ensure that there is a genuine meeting of the different horizons of our understanding. The fact that rectitude is not always decidable in any clear sense presents a profound difficulty for the critical tradition, leaving the necessity of frequently suspending judgement on the actions of others if basic trust in human relations is not to be undermined.

It is not difficult to see how and why the tradition of consciousness and the critical tradition are constantly at war in educational circles, each finding its identity as the binary opposite of the other. The one seeks stability and the solidification of culture, the other repudiation and a new world. Not only do they compete as siblings within the same grand Western epistemic tradition, but as the poststructuralists (especially Derrida) have helped us to understand, that tradition itself is predicated on the desire to put interpretation to rest. Call that desire the predisposition to theologize, and call theology the war over the true name and nature of things. Both the tradition of consciousness and the critical tradition begin by wanting to get things right, which means there will always be a war over whose interpretations can be taken as being so. In the face of resistance, the pedagogical practice of the tradition of consciousness leads to tantrums over metaphysics; the critical tradition leads to physical exhaustion from the social activist efforts of self-reproduction.

But Hermes is neither concerned to make a word mean one thing and one thing only, nor is only one preconceived way of doing things the only way. The hermeneutic imagination constantly asks for what is at work in particular ways of speaking and acting in order to facilitate an ever-deepening appreciation of that wholeness and integrity of the world which must be present for thought and action to be possible at all. As a child, I am born into a world that "seems" complete. But I learn the language of my community only to find holes and difficulties which point to the limits of our collective understanding. Those borders and boundaries which serve to secure our life together and give us an identity are permeable. As Paulo Freire has put it, reality is always "hinged".[36] Reality is always reality-for-us but it always opens out into a broader world which serves or can serve to enrich our understanding of who we are. Again, for us as educators this requires a consideration of what we mean by "world" when we speak of the world of curriculum, research and pedagogy. This is a profound hermeneutic requirement, given the way in which the hermeneutic tradition has shown that all understanding takes place within an articulation of whole and part.

One of the most important contributions hermeneutics makes to all contemporary social theory and practice, then, not just to curriculum and pedagogy, is in showing the way in which the meaning of anything is always arrived at referentially and relationally rather than (for want of a better word) absolutely. The final authority of concepts, constructs or categories does not reside in the concepts themselves but within the dialogically arrived at agreement of people to consent to them. The hermeneutic deflection of absolutism in favour of relationism does not elevate the relational as the new absolute except in the sense of supporting the view that relationality (living together creatively on the planet) requires a new set of conditions for pedagogy and the procedures of inquiry. In the terms elaborated by Gadamer and Richard Rorty,[37] the hermeneutic modus has more the character of conversation than, say, of analysis and the trumpeting of truth claims. When one is engaged in a good conversation, there is a certain quality of self-forgetfulness as one gives oneself over to the conversation itself, so that the truth that is realized in the conversation is never the possession of any one of the speakers or camps, but rather is something that all concerned realize they share in together. This is a point well stated by Thomas Merton: "If I give you my truth but do not receive your truth in return, then there can be no truth between us".[38]

The conversational quality of hermeneutic truth points to the requirement that any study carried on in the name of hermeneutics should provide a report of the researcher's own transformations undergone in the process of the inquiry, a showing of the dialogical journey, we might call it. Underscored here is a profoundly ethical aspect to hermeneutic inquiry in a life-world sense, namely, a requirement that a researcher be prepared to deepen her or his own self-understanding in the course of the research. Other people are not simply to be treated as objects upon whom to try out one's methodological frameworks. We might note briefly, too, that another aspect of conversation is that it is never finished. As in good improvisational jazz, one thing leads to another, but success has one foundational, definitional requirement, which is that group members be committed to staying "with" each other, constantly listening to subtle nuances of tempo and melody, with one person never stealing the show for the entire session. Hermeneutic pedagogy, for example, requires a giving of oneself over to conversation with young people and building a common shared reality in a spirit of self-forgetfulness, a forgetfulness which is also a form of finding oneself in relation to others.

Requirements of the Hermeneutic Imagination

In his working through of a hermeneutical position for our contemporary situation, Gadamer has suggested that it is not possible, in genuine inquiry, to establish a correct method for inquiry independent of what it is one is inquiring into.[39] This is because *what* is being investigated itself holds part of the answer concerning *how* it should be investigated. Genuine inquiry always has much more the character of a kind of dialogical messing about, in tune with what the Greeks simply called "thinking." Schleiermacher called hermeneutics a "commonsense endeavour".[40] There are, however, a number of requirements that must be attended to by those who find hermeneutical formulations fruitful for new lines of research in the human sciences. The first is to develop a deep attentiveness to language itself, to notice how one uses it and how others use it. It is important to gain a sense of the etymological traces carried in words to see what they point to historically. Every hermeneutical scholar should have a good etymological dictionary at her or his side. The loss of philology as a core subject in modern universities is a great loss, a sign perhaps of the eclipse of a genuinely historical consciousness in favor of the more efficient proclivities of a technical age. But gaining a sense of how one's collective language works, what drives it, what its predispositions are in terms of metaphor, analogy and structure, and so on, is quite essential for the work of the interpretive imagination, because in a deep sense our language contains the story of who we are as a people.[41] It is reflective of our desires, our regrets and our dreams; in its silences it even tells us of what we would forget.

A second requirement for hermeneutical explorations of the human life-world is a deepening of one's sense of the basic interpretability of life itself. This is a matter of taking up the interpretive task for oneself rather than simply receiving the delivered goods as bearing the final word. This sounds trivial, perhaps, but we live in a world already heavily interpreted, with ideologies and fundamentalisms masquerading as forms of truth lying beyond the reach of interpretation itself. Indeed, in a time when the very act of thinking has become a target of intense commercial and political manipulation, the need is great for persons who can meaningfully deconstruct what is going on and propose alternative, more creative ways of thinking and acting.

In the graduate Interpretive Inquiry seminar at the University of Lethbridge, we have been experimenting for a number of years with different ways of shaking loose our own dogmatic (culturally predetermined) ways of interpreting the details of our daily experience, trying to deepen our sense of what is implicated in the specifics of our thought and actions. Of course, as the hermeneutic tradition always reminds us, how we interpret details is very much related to our macro-frames, so we struggle continuously and contingently to extend our sense of what is at work, relying not only on the more conventional perhaps-on-the-verge-of-exhaustion grand narratives of Marxism, psychoanalysis or critical analysis, but also, importantly, on the more suffocated narratives of our time, such as those concerning spirituality (eastern, western and aboriginal), feminism and the new discourses about north-south relations and global interdependence.[42] In orienting (interesting word) ourselves this way, we also affirm the hermeneutic insight that good interpretation is a creative act on the side of sharpening identity within the play of differences, and we thereby give voice to and show features of our lives ordinarily suppressed under the weight of the dominant economic, political and pedagogical fundamentalisms of the times. This is all in the service of that deeper etymological sense of what it means to be fundamental, namely, showing a connection to the earth (Latin, *fundus* land). Living as we do as inheritors of the Enlightenment principles of abstraction, we are discovering that so many of our modern pains issue from a cultural determination to refute or refuse the interconnectedness of everything.

The interpretational activities of the seminar are not just focused on texts *per se*, but on the deep texture of our lives. So we engage in Icon Studies, using semiotics theory to interpret the iconic character of the educational world revealed in signs, pictures and photographs as well as in simple everyday things that we explore as "artefacts."[43] In Sound Studies, we examine the relationship between sound structure and social structure, investigating the sonic environment of pedagogy. Here we draw particularly on the theoretical work of Canadian musicologist R. Murray Schafer in his studies concerned with the "tuning of the world" and the field studies of Steven Feld from the University of Texas at Austin.[44]

Conversation Windows is an activity involved with the deconstruction of conversation fragments taken from street corners, coffee shops, hallways and so on, undertaken in an attempt to hear what people are saying about their lives before a microphone is pushed into their faces or an interview schedule predetermines what should be of interest. We pay careful attention to the tone, mood and context of the speech as well as to its tropes, spaces and structure. Time Studies invite seminar students, many of whom are practicing teachers during the day, to reconstruct in as great detail as possible certain time frames of their professional day. This is done to try to recover a sense of how professional practices are constructed through the "minutiae" of day-to-day events, through responses made to certain students in their classroom, through staff interactions, through interruptions, and so forth. All of these activities help to give our lives a sense of text which we can then interpret, discovering what is at work in practices we once engaged in dogmatically, that is, as if there was nothing more to be said about them.

Citing these activities points to a third important aspect of hermeneutical research, which is that hermeneutics is not really concerned with hermeneutics *per se,* that is, with its character as another self-defining imploding discourse within a universe of other discourses. Far more important is its overall *interest* which is in the question of human meaning and how we might make sense of our lives in such a way that life can go on. As such, the hermeneutic imagination works to rescue the specificities of our lives from the burden of their everydayness to show how they reverberate within grander schemes of things. Hermeneutics is about finding ourselves, which also, curiously enough, is about losing ourselves, that is, giving up the precious "fundamentalist" logocentric impulse in the name of a greater freedom and dignity. Constantly engaged in the practice of interpretation, the hermeneutic imagination is not limited in its conceptual resources to the texts of the hermeneutic tradition itself but is liberated by them to bring to bear any conceptualities that can assist in deepening our understanding of what it is we are investigating. This means that the mark of good interpretative research is not in the degree to which it follows a specified methodological agenda, but in the degree to which it can show understanding of what it is that is being investigated. And "understanding" here is itself not a fixable category but rather it stands for a deep sense that something has been profoundly heard in our present circumstances. Similarly, "hearing something in the present" does not just mean simply being aware of vibrations on the eardrums, but a registering of them within the deep web of sounds and voices that make up the structure of one's consciousness as language, memory and hope. This means that hermeneutical consciousness is always and everywhere a historical consciousness, a way of thinking and acting that is acutely aware of the storied nature of human experience. We find ourselves, hermeneutically speaking, always in the middle of stories, and good hermeneutical research shows an ability to read those stories from inside out and outside in. Hermeneutical research is a multidimensional enterprise, not just a vertical (theological) one or horizontal (empirical) one. Weak research is concerned only with surfaces, whether in the name of statistics or psychologism. Pedagogically, the highest priority is in having children and young people gain precisely a sense of the human world as being a construction that *can* be entered and engaged creatively; to have a sense that received understanding can be interpreted or re-interpreted and that human responsibility is fulfilled in precisely a taking up of this task.

A fourth aspect of hermeneutical inquiry implicit in all of the others suggested so far has to do with its inherent creativity. Hermeneutics is about creating meaning, not simply reporting on it. This distinguishes the hermeneutic effort from, say, ethnographic and grounded theory formulations wherein the task is to try to give an account of people's thoughts and actions strictly from their own point of view.[45] Hermeneutically we understand how impossible such a task is, given that I always interpret others from within the frame of our common language and experience so that whatever I say about you is also a saying about myself. Within the hermeneutic agenda, however, the purpose is not to translate my subjectivity out of the picture but to take it up with a new sense of responsibility—to make proposals about the world we share with the aim of deepening our collective understanding of it. This involves what Gadamer has referred to as "the art of hermeneutic writing" which necessarily has the character of a certain exaggeration requiring for its completion the voice of another. Good hermeneutic writing is "strong," to use the word in the meaning of social philosopher Alan Blum;[46] its desire is to provoke new ways of seeing and thinking within a deep sense of tradition, bringing about new forms of engagement and dialogue about the world we face together.

It is precisely the hermeneutical suggestion that the full truth of things can never be the conscious property of any one person or group that incites the fulminating Apollonian rage on the part of those who would wish to have the foundations of knowledge secured before proceeding with an engagement with the world as such. And given that the "foundationalist" view is the one that has underwritten most pedagogic practices today and is responsible for the artificial distinction between thinking and doing (the theory/practice split) which haunts the modern destruction of the world in the name of science, what is the shape and texture of the world that the hermeneutic tradition itself must presume in order to make the claims that it does? Perhaps the most important point to affirm here is that there is an integrity to the world that somehow must be preserved even at the same time as we inquire into how best to alleviate our pains while living in it. Gadamer's question, "Does what already supports us require any grounding?"[47] at once makes relative all parochial logocentric attempts to have the last word about defining the unshakable foundations of things, at the same time as it invites us deep into the hermeneutic project of articulating a more full sense of the world which affirms local identities. Instead of the imperial, triumphal, subsuming and distinctly masculine languages which have characterized the self-descriptions of the Western tradition to this point,[48] the hermeneutic way points to how meaning is always "webbed", challenging us to speak about our life in a way that is both ecological and ecumenical, two terms derived from the Greek word for "household" *(oikos)*. The task is one of "understanding", the character of which the hermeneutic tradition has been at great pains to elucidate, not just because "understanding" is now one more thing co-optible by the human sciences, but because without an ongoing search for understanding we are reduced to terror, xenophobia or the kind of isolation that breeds complacency, hubris and self-contempt.

All writing is in a sense autobiographical, and as I have worked through the ideas of this paper, many times I have wondered about my own interest in the subject of hermeneutics. How is that Hermes and I found each other? I think the matter has partly to do with the fact that my pre-adult years were all spent in different parts of the world (particularly Africa and Asia). Wherever we went, not only was I always acutely aware of being different, but in every place too I witnessed how the question of difference seemed to inhere in virtually all of the historical, politico-economic, and pedagogical struggles at work in those locations. Everywhere there seemed to be a need for a language of "understanding" that could take up "difference" not as a problem to be solved but as an invitation to consider the boundaries and limits of one's own understanding. Hermes and I found each other, I suspect, because of a mutual recognition that identity means nothing without a set of relations, and that the real work of our time may be defined by an ability to mediate meaning across boundaries and differences, whether those boundaries and differences be concerned with gender, race or ideas. And somehow it seems to me that the hermeneutic imagination has an important contribution to make to that task, not to settle everything once and for all by assigning people and things to their (so it might be thought) "essential" places, but for the profound pedagogical purpose of affirming the way in which present arrangements always border on and open onto the space of an Other whose existence contains part of the story of our shared future. And whether there will be a future indeed depends on the full power of creative interpretation. Hermeneutics for everyone?

5

Experimental Hermeneutics: Interpreting Educational Reality

The project of education arises whenever certain people determine that the world would fare better if certain other people, especially but not exclusively young people, learned certain things. Such things might include the technical skills of basic survival, forms of traditional wisdom or the arts of politics or war. The heavily financed state public schools and academies of the industrialized Western world are but one example of education in action. Other no less significant examples include, say, the Quranic schools of the Muslim world, sometimes consisting only of a teacher, a copy of the Quran, and a few students sitting under a tree; or the revolutionary schools of political independence movements in Asia, Latin America or Africa, organized by those determined to break the cognitive habits of colonial rule.

In a sense, educational actions are always everywhere at work, not only as people attempt to influence each other directly, but also as we come under mutual influence in unspoken ways. Indeed, it is almost impossible not to be an educator of some sort. As a parent or teacher, one might wish on occasion that this were not true, as when children learn and repeat things from one's own behaviour best left unrepeated.

Hermeneutics is sometimes called "the philosophy of the middle way". This should not be confused with, say, an orientation to compromise, or a simple doctrine of the mean. Instead, it points to the way hermeneutics always takes up its work right in the middle of things. Unlike the orientation of conventional science, hermeneutics does not seek some pure ground, some place of objectivity from which to view and analyse people or situations. Instead the hermeneutic voice attempts to speak always from the centre of action. This is based on an assumption that it is impossible for an interpreter to be completely or absolutely separate from that which he or she is investigating—that the very languages and constructs I use to think about the world are themselves very much of the world itself. They are languages and constructs that I share with others, and without which human communication would not be possible. Even if I am aware that I speak a language different from others, to recognize this means to recognize first and foremost a relationship, in this case a relationship of difference. So as an investigator, I am always in what I am investigating, just as what I am investigating is somehow already in me even before I begin. This point is best understood not conceptually but phenomenologically, that is, through experience. One of the tasks of this paper will be to show the human interdependence of understanding in pedagogical situations. There is another aspect of this same point, well appreciated in hermeneutic work, which is that the universal and the particular play off each other symbiotically, so that in the details of life is the big picture, and vice versa. This insight is not unique to the hermeneutic tradition, of course, but perhaps hermeneutics brings it to a pedagogical focus, namely that seeing the big picture in the details means precisely to find oneself in the picture at the same time. The art of hermeneutic investigation is pedagogical in the sense of bringing about the reintegration of experience that was rent by the objectivistic proclivities of science. Hermeneutics is about articulating the integrity of the world lying beyond the violence inflicted upon it by ideology, politics and war. In this sense, hermeneutics could be called the art of pedagogical homecoming.

The Western legacy from Descartes has taught us to objectify the world from a position of pure subjectivity, a move which renders human experience of the world to a game between subjects and objects, and ensures the breakdown of genuine communication between persons and of relations between human and natural worlds. Hermeneutically, one speaks instead of the intersubjectivity of everything, of their mutual interpenetration and influence. To see this, however, requires a particular kind of imaginal discipline, especially an ability to see connections which may not be superficially apparent. That very ability itself requires an openness to experience which goes beyond dependence on conventional categories of explanation, or on tradition received as a final word. Putting it in the language of postmodernism, the hermeneutic imagination requires an openness to the Other of experience, an openness to that which knocks from beyond the boundaries of what is known. To open the door means to have one's experience transformed into a new reality shared with new Others.

The hermeneutic tradition has always well understood this point theoretically, metaphysically, but in the context of contemporary global realities it requires challenging and creative reinterpretation. The hermeneutic tradition originated and developed within the limits and constraints of European culture with its preoccupying interests in Reason, Truth, Essence and so on. However, the new cultural interfusions which mark the character of late twentieth-century life demand that most of the treasured social, economic and political institutions that embody those interests be re-examined. Such investigative work must include the examination of educational practices, the task which forms the central subject of the present paper.

In taking up this task I am reminded of Heidegger's claim that interpretation is the "primordial" work of human experience.[1] Not fundamentally a methodological affair, interpretation is most simply yet profoundly the work of thinking, of thinking through the implications of facing what comes to meet one as new. As such, the modus and temperament of hermeneutic work is predominantly poetic, imaginal and suggestive, rather than systematic and dutiful to pre-established registers.

Furthermore, hermeneutics is not really about hermeneutics *per se*, just another academic discourse about academic discourse. Instead the concern must always be with life as it is lived, with a desire to understand the same, interpreting it in a way that can show the possibilities for life's continuance. Human vitality depends on being able to show the conditions and constraints of the day-to-day as having boundaries that are permeable and open, not fixed and closed. Hermes, after all, is the border crosser.

For the hermeneutic process to begin self-consciously, we require a text for exploration, or more accurately, we must turn to life itself as a text, to see life as something readable and interpretable. For the purposes of this paper, I have chosen three educational texts: a film, a local school situation and an exploration of hermeneutic pedagogy in the context of teacher education. In this engagement I have been mindful of a recent comment by Ione Davies that "any study which ignores the analysis of education as culture is in danger of trivializing the entire subject".[2] Here, then, I have attempted to explore ways in which the "interpretation of educational reality" must inevitably involve an interpretation of the culture in which educational reality has its life. For me, this has largely involved making problematic the organizing figure "West", as in Western culture, and especially my home locale of North America. However, the interpretations are offered as an invitation to readers of all traditions to open up their own experience, so that in the new challenges confronting us all mutually in a newly configuring world, we may be able to face each other with deeper shared understanding.

Text One:
Interpreting the Film
Menace II Society

Allen and Albert Hughes's brilliant film *Menace II Society* depicts the daily life of black teenage gang culture in Los Angeles, California. The plot is organized around the lead figure Cain (perhaps from "cocaine", but also suggestive of the accursed one of the Bible), and his neighborhood relationships. Opening with a scene in which Cain's friend kills an immigrant Korean shopkeeper, a murder which Cain witnesses, the rest of the film traces the building of his ultimately failed attempt to try to leave the 'hood for a new life in Atlanta with his girlfriend.

The film has pertinence here not only because it is about young people, African-Americans in this case, but because for an educator one of the most telling moments in the film occurs when Cain, reminiscing about his formal education, openly declares: "I didn't learn f____n' sh_t in high school". The remark has particular poignancy because unlike many African American males, Cain actually received his high school diploma.

For the viewer, it is painfully clear how Cain could have made the remark he did. The web of experiences into which most young black men in the ghettos of Los Angeles (or any other major American city) are drawn have very little to do with the heavily abstracted world of texts and standard white English at most high schools. That non-school life is rich and dense with the primordial instincts of basic survival, here the abiding undertone of which is fear of death at the hands of rival gang members. The life of the school is presented as reasonable and ordered, while life on the streets is chaotic, anarchic and self-destructive.

The story and action of the film serve as a binary to the "Other" Los Angeles of the common mythic imagination—the City of Angels, blonde nubile women and beautiful beaches, Disneyland fantasy, and most especially Hollywood, the world capital of image making. This Other Los Angeles is never shown in the film, but its power resides latently in the viewer's imagination to establish the tragic character of Cain's world. Indeed, for a white viewer much of the power of the film comes from this, from having to face the knowedge that one's mythic understanding of the City of Angels has been guided by only a half-truth, by a denial of its underside, its shadow. Hermeneutically, it can be suggested that the pedagogic failure of Cain's school experience precisely results from a severance of the tension between the micro and macro worlds on the part of school authorities. Or, better put, the macro interpretations of the dominant culture have failed to acknowledge their "Other" side, in this case the presence of African-American culture as a living alternative to the surface fantasies of the white agenda.

Hermeneutically speaking, what themes would need to emerge in Cain's education for the world of African-American experience to register as a living voice within the school curriculum? Here one might draw upon H-G. Gadamer's description of "effective historical consciousness"[3] to point up both the possibilities as well as fundamental tensions in American culture. Taken positively, as pure theory, "effective historical consiousness" denotes the way that self-understanding (personal and collective) always takes place within a horizon of past, present and future, a horizon in which I understand myself "now" through recognizing myself as having a past, and being oriented towards a future which itself will somehow contain the "now". What is presupposed is an understanding of historical process as open and dynamic, always changing.

So it could be suggested that for Cain and his friends the most imporant thing would be the constant revivification of African-American cultural memory, to give the present a sense of continuity with a living tradition, and provide a basis for orienting towards an open future. Certainly, it was this vision that inspired the black civil rights movement of the 1960s and in the film several of the people posing as positive black role models, including one male teacher, take this line.

Perhaps only liminally, Cain seems to grasp its limitations. For one thing, his experience tells him that in a white-dominated society, his education is no guarantee for a job, especially a meaningful one. But more importantly, to enter the question of his historicity would be to open one of the most profane acts of hermeneutic violence in the history of Western culture, namely African slavery. The success of slavery in America depended precisely on the elimination of African memory. Africans were severed from their historical roots, and taken to the New World as abstracted anonymous labour. Males, being especially prized, suffered especially by being separated from their children and women folk so that normal affections could not develop and African culture could never consolidate to become a political force. So it is not surprising that Cain could once declare "the black man has no future in this country". The former slave class, though now emancipated in this "age of decolonization" as Cornell West[4] describes it, still harbours the legacies and traces of oppression, the lack of self-belief turned into litanies of self-destruction.

Actually Cain's rebuke of his education may be seen as a good first step on the road to affirmation, the first step in the process of decolonizing his mind—a firm naming of the artificiality and irrelevance that had been urged upon him. Pedagogically and hermeneutically, another turn could be taken too which is to draw attention to the chimerical qualities of dominant white culture itself. It can be pointed out that white dominance is itself a historical construction, not an immutable fact; that it has its own dependencies and vulnerabilities, not least of which are connected to Cain and his historical legacy. Without slave labour, the emergence of white power itself would not have been possible.

The point is, hermeneutically, not just that the macro and micro play off each other to create the tension of existence, but that the micro is *in* the macro, and vice versa—that the particulars are unseverable from the universal, and cannot be banished to some other place so that those claiming the dominant position can claim a pure space, free of "others". After all that very space is made through the lives of others. It is not enough for teachers to bemoan the lack of application of their black charges to set studies if those studies do not open a window through which students can gain access to an understanding of their current situation. Not only that however; the pedagogical agenda of dominant white culture itself requires a kind of hermeneutic deconstruction to show its own poverty, its own lack, its own inability to read the Other as somehow necessary to its own self-identity. It is precisely this state of denial on the part of dominant culture that produces black rage, rage against the monolithic amorphous, seemingly impenetrable self-identity of those who mask their fear of the Other with benign indifference.

Cain's principal teacher in the film is, iconically, as a pure image, Hermes. Her skin tones are ambiguous; she could pass for either black or white. In the age of decolonization, she stands as a border person, in position to mediate cultural differences, to translate between worlds, and bring about understanding. At this point though, she is hermeneutically immature. Her pedagogical practices mirror her institutional training in the languages, values and orders of dominant culture: analysis, textuality, writing, the prosaic. In many ways she is a tragic figure, caught between black and white, unable to bring the two into creative conversation, maybe unwilling to enter the true *agon* through which new worlds are brought into being. She reflects the tragedy of "professionalization" in teaching, one of the marks of the industrial age, the age of specialization. Her professional specialization gives her a mock security while at the same time rendering her impotent to genuinely address what is right in front of her pedagogically, making her instead a subject of mockery to her students. She is no longer a real person, full of the tensions of reality; instead now a smiling conduit for state policy, full perhaps of her own form of self-hatred, that condition which haunts the purely dutiful.

There are two other important aspects of the film that need to be addressed. First, there is the figure of the Korean shopkeeper whose murder precipitates the larger narrative of the story. The presence of a sizeable Korean community in Los Angeles can be taken as a semiotic trope for a much broader phenomenon within contemporary global culture, namely significant ethnic and minority demographic movements which in turn introduce a lacuna of profound self-doubt within any tradition that takes self-identity to mean homogeneity without difference. Linked largely to the history of global capitalism, these demographic shifts are part of the broader devolution of Western culture signified most clearly in what J-F. Lyotard calls the "postmodern condition",[5] the character and implications of which will be examined later.

The second theme emerging from the *Menace II Society* story has simply to do with the circumstances of my own access to it. It is the current preponderance of video culture that made it possible for me to see the film. As a former school teacher and now instructor in a university program for the preparation of teachers, I live in a small, fairly isolated country town in southern Alberta, Canada, far away from the ghetto of Compton, Los Angeles. Yet within a matter of minutes I can go to a video outlet, pick up a film like *Menace II Society*, return home and view it in the comfort of my living room. Obviously, the film has moved me deeply. As a teacher, I feel challenged to be more mindful of the cultures of difference that increasingly predominate our classrooms. The film underscores the way knowledge-forms are connected to forms of life, so I cannot in any way pretend that what I teach is somehow value-free or not connected to the structures and politics of power in my own society. In the local schools, native aboriginal students routinely do badly on tests and other performance registers that have cultural roots only in white European culture. Now as a teacher, I have to interpret my own educational tradition as somehow implicated in the longer story of the oppression and marginalization of Others, searching for the assumptions, modalities and beliefs that made it possible. Such work will take a long time, and will take long conversations with the officially silenced Others of my tradition, Others not listed in the dominant curricular interpretations, or at least referred to only in passive ways. Any pedagogical confidences I may have had have suffered an irruption not appeaseable only from within the languages and constructs of my own tradition. From now on, I have to be more open, more willing to listen. My self-understanding as a teacher has gone through a kind of identity crisis, and I realize that the crisis is not mine alone, not just a personal problem. It is a crisis I share with all people who trace the authority for their actions back to Plato, Aristotle, Jesus, the Church, Columbus, Thomas Hobbes, Isaac Newton and so on.

The advent of video culture is itself part of my received tradition, an extension of a four hundred year line of scientific and technical development. Video formats are said by many educational experts to mark the coming wave of educational reform, and increasingly television and computer screens are part of the educational landscape. Certainly it is an awesome thing to be able to watch a film and be transported in one's imagination not just to Los Angeles, but to virtually anywhere in the world—to the Galapagos Islands, to Thailand, to Bosnia, to Rwanda. Some scholars have wondered whether we have entered the age of "the end of the book".[6] Harold Bloom has suggested that "deep reading is a vanished phenomenon".[7] If such is the case, it is a cultural shift that carries profound pedagogical implications which require interpretive understanding.

Text Two:
Mrs. Jablonski's Grade Three:
Video culture and the postmodern classroom

Mrs. Jablonski has been an elementary school teacher for almost thirty years. Not long ago I was visiting a student teacher working in her classroom when Mrs. Jablonski commented: "You know, it almost seems impossible to teach any more. The children have such little ability to concentrate". Now Mrs. Jablonski has a long established reputation for being a good teacher. Several students in the class are there by special request of parents who themselves were once her students. The pedagogical difficulty she relates, therefore, must be seen as much more profound than a passing irritation. As we explore the subject together it becomes apparent that she is speaking of nothing less than a kind of transformation of consciousness in young people, a transformation that has left her as a teacher increasingly unable to connect with her students in the ways she would prefer.

As Mrs. Jablonski herself admits, her whole orientation to teaching, through her training as well as through her natural proclivity, is guided by a love of books—a care for the written word, and for the spoken word disciplined by the written word. Her students however increasingly cannot relate to books; even their own stories emerge not from what they have read but from what they have seen, on television or in the movies. As a teacher, Mrs. Jablonski feels herself to inhabit a "different world" from that of her students, and in the twilight of her career she is struggling with feelings of personal failure.

The cultural shift from books to video, from textuality to iconicity carries with it a shift in the work of imagination and cognition. A different kind of human embodiment is part of this shift, a transformation of the ways we receive and then act upon the world. According to a recent survey of the A. C. Nielsen Company, the average North American home has a television set switched on for nearly eight hours a day. Cultural interpreter J. Mander has suggested that American society is "the first in history of which it can be said that life has moved inside media",[8] by which is meant that increasingly people are living not from within the matrix of their own thought and action but vicariously, living through representations of life constructed by others. This condition has many aspects to it. For one thing, as Mander says, the human brain is increasingly operating in what is called the *alpha* mode, characterized by noncognition and a passive-receptive modality whereby images and information are received into the brain directly, without thinking or participation. Paradoxically however, there is a coincident acceleration of the nervous system and the production, especially in children, of hyperactivity and what can be called "jumping mind". The imaginal hyperstimulation gained through non-stop action images, linked to the diminishment of personal agency in the act of watching, produces a cycle of passivity and aggression in which what is passively seen requires for resolution an ultimate enactment by the viewer. When the television set is turned off, children who a moment earlier were sitting quietly entranced, may suddenly burst forth with frantic disorganized behaviour, only to be calmed when the set is turned on again.

The perceptual speed-up which prolonged television watching produces also produces a kind of boredom with the natural world, and cynicism about real or unrepresented life. While the power of television resides in its ability to represent the things of the world in a very real and vivid way, its duplicity lies in the fact that what is presented can be *nothing but* a re-presentation, a semblance or seeming to be true. The narrative and temporal rhythms of the normal nonrepresented life-world inevitably suffer a breakdown and transformation into artificial and highly constrained forms. A life that took eighty years to live can be reduced to an hour; a problem that took a year to solve can be shown as solved in a matter of minutes; a journey of months is related in seconds. Because young peoples' experience of the world has yet to register the natural requirements of day-to-day living, the representations of television, by virtue of their sheer vividness, place the ordinary world itself into the role of liar. Unrepresented life seems too slow, too pedestrian to be real. Real life is boring, something to be rejected. E. B. White, a journalist who was invited in 1936 to witness the first experiments in television production, wrote this as his first response: "Television will advertise the Elsewhere.... It will insist that we forget the primary and the near in favour of the secondary and the remote."[9]

The advent of video consciousness however should not simply inspire nostalgia for a lost era, especially in this instance with respect to education and teaching. Mrs. Jablonski's perplexity about teaching today is as much about one teacher being caught between worlds as it is about the specific difficulties of teaching in the contemporary context. What needs exploration is not how to restore a lost order so that teaching might proceed as before, but an investigation into what should be the unique character of teaching in a culture of images.

Whereas a textual education attempts to lead the student to the world through the instrumentality of books, a responsible education in an iconic world may need first to interrupt the flow of represented reality in order that reality may begin to appear more clearly in consciousness simply as it is. This of course has been the clarion call of the phenomenological-hemeneutical tradition since Husserl's *zu den Sachen Selbst*, "to the things themselves". A responsible hermeneutic pedagogy for today may first and foremost involve an invitation to the primary and the near, a kind of "pedagogy of presence",[10] involving the learning of new ways of paying attention to what is right in front of us.

Actually video consciousness, or "videoism" as it might be called, itself can be taken as a kind of analogue or tandem carrier for a much deeper and broader transformation of the collective imagination of Western culture, a transformation named most accurately by J-F. Lyotard as the "postmodern condition." This is not the place to rehearse all of the debates that currently surround postmodernism, debates that have permeated virtually all of the humanities and social sciences in the last ten to fifteen years, especially in North America. Indeed, whether or not there is such a thing as "postmodernism" can be argued about philosophically, intellectually, but there is little doubt that at the experiential level of many people there is a sense of deep transformations taking place in the public realm that have profound personal implications.

The postmodern condition has been described by many writers in different ways. Lyotard himself speaks of a generalized "incredulity to grand narratives",[11] meaning an unravelling of belief with respect to the possibility of any unifying grand theory. Frederic Jameson describes postmodernism as the defining condition of late capitalist culture, characterized by, among other things, a decline of historical sensibility and a living for the present alone, a coincident erosion of the depth dimension in experience, and a constituent relationship to technology, whereby people feel themselves to be constructed by technology just as much as they might use it for their own purposes.[12] Arthur Kroker identifies "hyperkinesis" or superspeed as the prevailing ambience in postmodern "panic culture".[13] All of these themes emerge as a consequence of the breakdown of the monolithic univocal character of Western self-consciousness that had endured from the Renaissance until the devolution of European empire in the age of decolonization.

The following description may show the postmodern condition in its lived character in a contemporary North American classroom. Several weeks ago one of my graduate students reported on a classroom activity she recently engaged in with a teaching colleague at school. As part of a new program in Global Education, the Grade Five class was commemorating "The World Day for Water" with a simulation game called "The Game of One Hundred", which attempts to teach students about the politics of diminishing drinking water resources in the so-called Third World. The details of the game are not important here, except to note it as a "simulation", a contrivance designed to make a disembodied epistemic point, or we should say a game which produces that "seeming to know" which is fundamentally characteristic of a culture of representation. Indeed the videotape of the class taken by the student shows the teacher in charge beginning the lesson with: "Today we are going to try to show you the *real* world. This game represents what the real world is like. Let's start with Africa...." Three minutes later: "Okay, now we come to Asia...." Towards the end of the video the teacher is interviewed, and she explains that as part of the overall Global Education course, "the students are creating a mural of animal life in Zimbabwe" in their Art class. The regional Social Studies consultant is shown saying: "We need to infuse the curriculum with global perspectives". After the Social Studies class, the students engaged in thirty minutes of Physical Education, followed by an hour of Science. Prior to the Social Studies lesson, students had had an hour of Mathematics, and an hour of Language Arts.

One witnesses in the speech of the teacher, as well as in the structure of the class timetable many of the characteristics of which we have spoken. The rapid flitting from one topic to another, one country after another, one activity followed by another activity, not only reflects the hyperkinetic quality of contemporary life in the technical, industrialized world, but also the lifeworld of the learning atmosphere oriented toward a profound superficiality, to say which is not oxymoronic. It speaks instead of the depth of depthlessness in the contemporary classroom, the settlement into a way of proceeding which is content to be forgetful of the deep questions of its own sustenance. Pedagogy is reduced to a pointing to the parade of facts and information available through the multiple technologies of the age, with little attention to the way the facts carry a story of culture. Not just is this an analogue for the kind of video consciousness spoken of earlier, so also does it inspire a kind of "panoptic",[14] touristic self-confidence that one actually knows about Africa and Asia in some grand sweeping sense, even though such knowledge is radically decontextualized, disembodied and completely beyond the interlocutory reach of those persons in Africa and Asia of whom it speaks.

The classroom of postmodernity has its origins in the European Enlightenment dream of all possible knowledge being unifiable within a universal principle of Reason; the belief that knowledge leads to understanding of the world precisely because its essential character is the same everywhere. Teaching and learning require no heavy justification because their value can be taken as self-evident. They are the portals to a new universal civilization. It is this dream that justifies the teaching of "everything" in the contemporary classroom, even at the same time as that teaching has introduced through the backdoor of its own project a certain cynicism and despair of purpose. The computer-driven Cult of Information[15] has produced a situation in which knowledge has exploded, the explosion being an epistemic dis-integration rooted in the incapacity of reasonableness to hold together in one frame the full load of what has been revealed, Internet notwithstanding.

The postmodern classroom, then, currently contains an immobilizing tension between the myth of coherence and the truth of disintegration. As guardians of the myth of coherence, teachers dutifully instruct as if, given a correct sense of personal discipline, or the application of the right method, everything should be at least "masterable". In the meantime, the whole configuration of the human world has changed since the days of easy optimism of the Enlightenment social engineers. Auschwitz, Hiroshima, Bhopal, Chernobyl, Gandhi, Sharpville, Vietnam, Watergate, Feminism, Black Power, Hamas, Jihad—all these have pointed to a profound crack in the Eurocentric egg, a crack now calling for creative interpretation. Either it can be read as a pathological condition requiring nothing but further apparatuses of control, or it can be read as an invitation to reformulate the modus and orientation of dominant institutions in the "light" of challenges coming from the margins. In the next section an exploration will be undertaken of the possible character of a form of Teacher Education which attempts to work hermeneutically from the centre of the new complexities.

Text Three:
Hermeneutic Pedagogy in the Context of Teacher Education

What would be the face of pedagogy oriented by a hermeneutic imagination? Here I wish to explore that question in the context of my own work as a teacher educator, as someone involved in the preparation of teachers. What does it mean to be prepared to teach? Every culture has its teachers, after all, yet the roles and functions vary for each. In traditional societies, teachers are usually persons in charge of "the teachings", the corpus of collective wisdom which bind the community together over generations. Often such a responsibility is associated with a priest class, with the clergy operating as the primary mediators and interpreters of the culture. In secular societies such as those of the industrial West, since the State took over reponsibility for education from the Church, it could be argued that teachers, as mediators of culture, represent a kind of secular priesthood. Certainly the weight of hope for social betterment projected onto the public schools seems to point to their soteriological legacy.

A hermeneutic pedagogy however must begin not from a sense of grand future hope nor from a nostalgic relationship with the past. Instead the concern must be with the present, in which the past and the future both reside, but only hermeneutically. That is, past and future can be invoked interpretively, but never literally. At the same time, the purpose of such invocations is to show that the present is always a living, present one vibrant in the NOW with memories, hopes and dreams. This situatedness in the now ensures that when persons of different traditions meet, they bring their respective horizons to a common meeting without brutality, aware that for any tradition to survive requires a creative engagement with whatever comes to meet it as new. If what is met as new immediately gets interpreted only through old filters, then the pedagogic significance of the new gets lost, banished to a mythological Outside. Similarly, whatever the future, it will contain what exists today to the degree that what is met can be read as genuinely participatory.

Hermeneutically one understands that nothing can ever be pushed to an exteriority of existence, that everything is always already everywhere present. Even though politics, geography and simple energy may determine that at any particular moment some things have salience while others only latency, still there is only one world within which everything coheres to form a unity. This is the foundation of the kind of ecological consciousness now seen by many to point a way through the dualistic wars of modernity.[16] And while such understanding has been well understood by the world's Wisdom traditions for millennia,[17] the insight is also well formulated in the hermeneutic tradition through the influence of Edmund Husserl in his massive project of overturning the Enlightenment project of Objective Reason.[18] It is not objectivity that is the basis of knowledge, said Husserl, but intersubjectivity, a relation between subjects. I gain my humanity through reciprocal relations with the world and with others. My identity is not something fixable in advance of those relations, but is found precisely through them.

What shall I say to my first year undergraduate seminar convened around the theme "Orientation to Teaching"? Coterminous with the seminar is a practicum experience in local schools, so the students bring lots of stories from "the trenches", as one teacher described classrooms. Actually, that could be a start right there. Why would a teacher invoke the language of war to describe his work, a language also carried in preoccupations with "target objectives", "drills" and "strategies"? Is the classroom a battleground, with children as the enemy? Certainly the teacher's linguistic turn reflects a culture of dualism in which Self and Other, adults and children, face each other as two solitudes, one in a position of power and authority, the other only in position to rebel, aquiesce or wait.

So I choose not to proceed dualistically. I have to take a risk and open up my own horizon with them as an invitation for them to do the same in order to create a shared space. I suggest to them, for example, that if they find my speech a bit odd or strange, as a colleague in linguistics once told me it was, it may be because I speak from a different history to theirs, in this case a history of exile. I was born in China during the Maoist revolution, then ejected with my family as "foreign". I grew up in Central Africa, then after the political independence movements of the late 1950s-early 1960s it was clear that my white face reflected a presence not appropriate to the new political reality. My parents were "missionaries", one of the great swear-words of secular materialism, and I have to acknowledge that in a tradition of proclamation, such as the Protestantism in which I was raised, listening may be the most underdeveloped skill of human communication. I share with them my hard-earned lesson that speaking actually implies listening; that autodiction without audition inevitably inspires violence against the speaker precisely because speaking alone violates a central truth of language itself, namely its derivative character. Words are not just things to be put at the service of the will; "words are people" as James Hillman has put it,[18] living organisms that carry the lived experience of others. Teaching cannot mean just telling. More than anything it must be an act of engagement in which the teacher shows the way by which it is possible for a young person to understand

and enter his or her own tradition as a living stream. Tradition is neither brute nor inert, but to be neither requires creative interpretation, the reponsibility for which falls on the shoulders of each new generation. My students are invited to enter the stream, to lay down at least temporarily all their preconceptions about teaching, especially teaching as the means through which to reproduce oneself and one's cultural tradition unreflectively.

In the Canadian context, most undergraduate students can trace their stories back one or two generations to accounts of immigration either from Europe, or more recently from the West Indies, India, Pakistan, China and so forth. It is always interesting to hear these stories because they bring into the present moment traces of all the major global developments of the last one hundred years or so. Tales of war, refugee camps, determined numbed silence, stories of privilege or hardship—all these may be part of the mix of a typical class. Students are often themselves amazed to find their personal family stories as participating in something much bigger than themselves. As an instructor, I am often startled at how frequently students relate how their parents or grandparents saw public education as the means through which personal stories should be subsumed, even lost within the greater story of the broader realm. Especially for non-English-speaking immigrants, education was seen as the means for gaining anonymity in order to progress through the ranks of dominant culture.

Such confessions by students open doors by which it is possible to consider how forms of cultural dominance are constructed and sustained through linguistic, racial and historical convention. These considerations in turn show the way for new opportunities for self-respect on the part of those occupying the underclasses. For example, they can begin to see their lack of representation in history books as a comment on the nature of History itself; History as itself a historical construction largely written by the self-described winners of historical developments. Actually even in terms of the teaching profession, the question of who is represented in it is a very important one; that although the racial and cultural mix is diversifying somewhat, teachers remain largely a white middle class group.[20]

Teaching is not just about telling stories however. Ultimately it has only one justification, a justification that allies teachers the world over, in every culture, of every time and place. Teaching and learning are about enlightenment, a word that invokes the double meaning of bringing light to a situation, and of lightening the burdens of human experience. This of course was the great dream of the eighteenth-century European Enlightenment, but that particular dream may have turned into a nightmare, through a mistaking of a *particular* cognitive modus for a universal method of being. In the contemporary context, one senses this in the example of free market economics wilfully turning into a (pseudo) rationalist science then attempting to impose its logic on the whole of humanity. In North America, education is becoming, or has already become, a "business".

The task of enlightenment which legitimately underwrites the work of teaching must find its own character in its own specific context. This is not an appeal to the relativism of all values but an acknowledgement of the way human burdens are always context-specific, and that the lifting of them through understanding always requires specific attention to that concrete specificity. The unique disease of the West may be the tendency to abandon the specific in the name of the general, usually in the name of theory, a mask for the desire for transcendence. We speak of "children" instead of Jane, Mary or John, so that John's particular reading problems are deflected into theories of reading difficulty rather than attending to the specifics of John's life. Coincident with this is an evacuation of the interiority of persons in favour of externalized abstractions. As the German philosopher Max Scheler put it, for Western civilization, "the entire development has been a one-sided and overactive expansion outward",[21] with the consequent emptying of individual identities into a vast ocean of personality constructs constructed by ideological orders of politics and commerce. For teachers in the West, the deepest challenge may be to learn how to reclaim senses of the Self that are not dependent on manufactured images or commercial summoning. Instead, in the face of shrill prescriptions, let deep down reverberations of the soul now emerge pedagogically from a new kind of meditatively centred self-assured autonomy, and let young and old join hands in a hymn of joy that celebrates a space of common interest and free intelligence.

To conclude: In this paper I have chosen to proceed not so much by working through, in a labour of metaphysics, the application of hermeneutic theory to educational reality. Rather I have attempted to show the educational world as always everywhere interpretable especially in so far as educational practices open up onto their broader cultural context. In the contemporary situation, the interpretive frames by which any phenomena might be more clearly understood I have taken to include as postcolonialism/postmodernism, videoism and the culture of representation, and speculative hints about a hermeneutic pedagogy. In the last instance, it is my hope that hermeneutic pedagogy will find its identity in a full and creative engagement with the broader culture in which it finds itself, and that it will share with teachers and students everywhere a common interest in human enlightenment.

6

Modernism, Hyperliteracy and the Colonization of the Word

Common opinion has it there is a crisis of literacy in the West on at least two fronts. The first concerns the rising phenomenon of "functional illiteracy" whereby increasing numbers of people are incapable of reading even the simplest words, signs and instructions. In Canada, government statistics for 1990 indicate that about sixteen percent of the population "fell" into this category.[1] The second phenomenon has been referred to by Yale professor Alvin Kernan as "the death of literature." This is a complex issue, but it devolves primarily on the delegitimisation of the Western canon of great books as Eurocentric and dominated by the partriarchal ideology of "dead white males". In the nineteenth century, Matthew Arnold's "timeless best that has been thought and written", and later T. S. Eliot's "unchanging monuments of the European mind", well reflected the lofty sentiments of this grand tradition which sought to articulate a moral high ground for civilization.[2] The unseating has not meant in any way the demise of literary activity *per se*, especially not in the academy. But the condition contains an important echo of a much deeper problem for the West, namely the crisis of its epistemic authority. The new literary activity is primarily driven by a concern for what Jonathan Culler calls "the conditions of meaning",[3] and the question of what authorizes ideas (gives them authority) when the old valuational authorities of, say, Church, State and High Culture can be shown as players complicit in the formation of some of our deepest problems.

In this paper I wish to take up the question of literacy in a different way: through a kind of genealogical, phenomenological, deconstructive exploration of three contexts within which any discussion of literacy today may need to be located. In the themes which follow, put into play is a series of voices not heard often enough in current debates. And here I am not so much concerned to argue a linear case about the matter as to explore the way in which the meaning of what is at stake is connected to a whole constellation of issues that cannot be unravelled in the usual discrete sense of Western analytical thinking. The influence in this approach is undoubtedly that of the great hermeneutical scholar H-G. Gadamer, who used to speak of the way an understanding of any text or situation is best achieved not by frontal attack but by an attending to how meaning "floats" in, out, through and around the specificities at hand.[4] So it is too that throughout the paper, in discussions about "literacy", the four different terms usually associated with it, namely reading, writing, listening and speaking, are intermingled fairly freely, even though in the field of English language education, for example, each of these aspects has separately associated with it a considerable mass of scholarly literature.

For us in the West, I wish to suggest that the various crises of literacy currently at work force a question about literacy itself as a kind of cultural artifact. The questions about *conveyance* underwriting the massive preoccupation with technologies of communication in our time are really secondary to the more primary matter of human language itself, within which speaking, listening then writing and reading articulate within a dense cultural coalition. Any concern about language must point eventually to a concern about human relationships, to a concern for how we have come to be organized and structured as a human community. I mean, maybe the sixteen percent of functionally illiterate persons represent a new homeless class of those disenfranchised by a hyperliteracy of politically correct thought and action at the top. Similarly, there may be something quite appropriate about "postmodern," deconstructionist work which has inspired so much the new literary criticism aimed at de-anchoring the author-ity of traditional Western literature. Taken at its best, deconstructionism may open a way for new forms of expressive activity, both linguistic and aesthetic, which in turn are more responsive to the inevitable pluralism of our contemporary situation. The kind of literacy invoked may also inspire less mania for, say, pure production, and point toward a more contemplative, hermeneutic appreciation of the operation of the Word in human affairs. Such an appreciation is well understood in all Wisdom traditions, north and south, east and west, and in this paper I am led to an understanding of literacy which holds much in common with mystical traditions focussing on sensibilities like attunement and attention rather than on, say, production and display. In our present context, learning to "read the world", as Paulo Freire once put it,[5] involves a form of literacy which is dependent not just on a command of surface cultural codes, but on an ability to reach one another across conditions of time and space through gifts of interpretation and translation. But this is to get ahead of things. First, a consideration of the following contexts.

Context One: Gunpowder, Protestantism and Printing

In the nineteenth century, Thomas Carlyle identified three events which, in his view, have shaped the modern character of the West. These are *gunpowder, Protestantism and printing*.[6] It is an interesting little list, with the items each inextricably linked. Gunpowder, for example, has to do with the technology of power, and as the contemporary French philosopher Jacques Derrida has helped us to understand, the relationship between *language* and power gains particular focus in the nuclear age.[7] Nuclear weapons and their deployment share a link with the apocalyptic, interpretive question of finality and the judgement as to whose particular interpretation of the human story, whose word, shall be taken as final or authoritative. In so far as wars are wars of interpretation, in the current global dispensation in which we live, the privilege to arbitrate the final word may not rest with those most literate, in the usual sense, but rather with those in charge of the gunpowder so to speak, those who have been able to secure an alliance between their interpretations and the necessary technologies for the destruction of others'.

As the second great defining movement of modernity in the West, Protestantism also has to do with the matter of interpretation, but in a special way. The problematic, which Protestantism has never resolved, is the relationship between authority, tradition and what might be referred to as "creative, responsible interpretation." In the West, Protestantism opened the door for personal and individual freedom in interpretation, but in a way it has failed to recognize how freedom understood in the protesting sense still always lives symbiotically with what it rejects. Any freedom purchased as a rejection of something is not a real freedom because it still needs what it rejects in order to sustain its self-identity. In a way, the kind of personal autonomy which Protestantism inspired in the West (enshrined, for example, in the ideals of the French Revolution and the American Constitution), still operates in a profoundly adolescent manner because the full tensionality at work between individual and community, autonomy and tradition, has never been adequately theorized to show the fundamental inextricability of the one from the other. The language of revolt is still a language, which to be understood must presume an even deeper resonance with a common realm. Pierre Bourdieu has referred to this as the "consensus in dissensus".[8]

In the case of Carlyle's third key aspect of modernity—printing—many historians have made the point that the Protestant revolution would have been impossible without the printing press.[9] It is printing that provided the technology of dissemination necessary to the libertarian advance across Europe in the sixteenth century, and it is within the discursive nexus of printing, dissemination and emancipation that we can look, I suggest, for a sense of the deep valances operating in current preoccupations about literacy. Problematizing Protestantism's role in the history of the democratization of reading, for example, forces the question of reader responsibility. I mean, why do we read? Is it only to feed private visions, to privately join a text-dependent community at the expense of something deeper, more fully communicative? Could reading and reading pedagogy not be charged with a profound sense of public responsibility?

In the modern context, too, one seldom discussed but important phenomenological consequence of mass literacy, which the Protestant democratization of literacy sponsored through printing, may be described as a forcing of human conversation into a realm of increasing abstraction, increasingly disconnected from its necessary human substrate, its situated ground [<L. *humus* ground]. In phenomenological terms, this could be called "the crisis of intentionality" in literacy, that is, the crisis of literacy's purposes, the question of to what, *in the world*, does a commitment to reading, writing and speaking refer. George Steiner once suggested that Shakespeare and Milton, who wrote at the cusp of oral and print culture, belonged to the last moment of Western history when "words were in natural control of experienced life". As Steiner argues it, the modern writer uses fewer and simpler words because in a mass technical culture like the West, not only have the very boundaries of the concept of literacy become radically constrained, but also the range of experiential realities for which words can give an adequate account has been profoundly diminished.[10]

Printing may be the perfect delivery system for Platonism. Human ideas are given the capacity to circulate without face to face dialogue; ideas can be labelled "interesting" or "uninteresting" without reference to the specific location or lifeworld groundness of their original speaker. Ideas can also turn into a form of cultural capital, feeding into all of the attendant systems of a capitalist economy, without any necessary concern for how the ideas may impact on the lives of people. It is in this sense that we may understand *hyperliteracy* as an exaggerated investment in the power of literacy to the detriment of attention to how life is lived. Paulo Freire's pedagogy aside,[11] the inordinate attention given to the literacy crisis in the West inevitably begins by turning the concept of literacy itself into an abstraction, with literacy campaigns serving often to deflect attention away from those ways in which people are kept in the dark about the deep structure of their lives.

Far more important than high literacy rates, it seems to me, may be an *interpretive ability* that requires not just a sense of charge over the surface structure of print, but also an ability to read the symbolic capital at work *through* print, and to refute its control over one in any definite way. There may be a need to understand the jeopardy involved in a world that takes print too seriously. A fuller understanding surely requires an attention to everything non-print, or at least an attention to the deep dialectic between print and non-print. So, for example, illiteracy in the West is not just a function of persons being ill-equipped with print *per se*, but of being situated in circumstances where either print is not valued or where induction into reading is retarded by specific lacks in human relations. And such deficits are linkable not to books but to social and economic conditions.[12]

There are several other elements to the relationship between Protestantism and printing that bear examination. For one thing, given the link of mass literacy with the Reformation, there may be need for closer research into the social schizmatics inherent in the power to reproduce ideas through printing technologies. There is, I would argue, something latently schizmatic about an infinite availability of the written word, related to something Plato recognized, namely the inexorable vulnerability of the written word to misinterpretation. Plato described this quality as "writing's greater helplessness".[13] Once I have put my ideas on paper, anybody can have access to them and interpret them in any way they want. Such is the consequence of publication, making writing public. But in the physical absence of an author, which publication affords, the way is clear for a reader to become the architect of her or his own ideas of what is meant in any text, and it is precisely the capacity for misinterpretation that inspires, I suspect, much of the publishing frenzy responsible for the ecologically disastrous proliferation of the various print genres. It has something to do with the need to justify (or clarify, or extend) oneself vis-à-vis the opinions of those one has never, literally, faced.

When printing avails itself of all the latest technologies of reproduction, such as photocopy machines, desktop publishing, word processors and so on, the question of the social responsibility involved in the dissemination of the word comes to the fore in important ways. For example, the availability of more information, more text, may actually reduce commitment to the common good by fostering a certain paralysis or postponement of commitment with respect to the resolution of social problems. This paralysis resides in the suggestibility that the answer to our difficulties always awaits more information or another formulation. We learn to await, not Godot, but Data. There is a wonderful cartoon series by Matt Groening entitled *School Is Hell*, depicting some important lessons to be learned from experience in school. Lesson 19 concerns "Graduate School", with one frame given to the question of how to avoid finishing one's thesis. How? "Read another book; Repeat when necessary".[14] There may be a relationship between an exaggerated concern for literacy and the avoidance of public responsibility that, in the realm of language pedagogy, should not be ignored in favour of sentimental notions about, say, reading and imagination. Those convinced of the soteriological power of the contemporary cult of information would do well to be balanced by the Chinese sage Lao Tzu: "Whoever seeks to rule a country with knowledge alone is harming the country".[15]

Context Two: Postmodernism, Deconstruction and the Achievement of Meaning

The first context for this discussion was "gunpowder, Protestantism and printing". The second context is the critique of modernism by the so-called postmodernists like Jacques Derrida, Michel Foucault and Jean-François Lyotard—the French gurus, as they are sometimes referred to.[16] The main contribution of the postmodern thinkers to questions concerning literacy devolves, I suggest, on two points. One has to do with *the meaning of meaning*, involving a reconsideration of the way meaning is achieved in texts and of how claims to understanding what a text means are possible. A second has to do with the consequences of a cultural self-consciousness becoming decentred. What happens to the way one "reads the world" (to use Freirean language again) when one realizes that one's personal and collective position in the world has been radically relativized?

Jacques Derrida has characterized and criticized the Western tradition as being *logocentric*, that is, driven by a desire to establish human meaning through an anchoring of it in constructs and categories which can then be taken to "represent" an original reality. The representations in turn accrete to form the stable capital of culture which then can be manipulated, taught, disseminated as the pure sediment of a people's organized life. This is the style of the *modernist* modus against which postmodernists identify themselves, namely an *establishment* of truth linked to a technology of dissemination and control. Under the influence of linguists F. de Saussure and C. S. Peirce, and perhaps more profoundly, phenomenologists like Husserl and Heidegger (linkable to

Nietzsche), Derrida and the postmodernists have shown that the meaning of any word, concept or idea is *not* anchorable in any definitive sense. The meaning of something cannot be "defined", only derived referentially. Furthermore, the surfacing of meaning in any given context, such as in reading and interpreting a text, always involves an act of suppression, so that in any presented interpretation, something is inevitably lost, although in Derridean terms, not really. What is lost continues to "play" (one of Derrida's favorite words) within the present interpretations as a "trace", which can itself be archeologically recovered through a process of "deconstruction". A deconstructive approach to reading, then, asks not the logocentric question "What does this text mean?"—the answer to which results in a form of cultural capital linkable to the politics of social control. Rather, deconstructively one asks "What is at work in this text for its statements to be meaningful? How is the sense of meaningfulness achieved either in the text, or between the text and the reader?" Framing the question in such a way opens the door to the lost "Other" voices at work in the construction of meaning—the silent partners in the play of meaning, we might call them.[17]

It is not difficult to see how a deconstructive approach to reading smokes out the profoundly political quality of the infrastructure of any culture of literacy. The meaning of texts is not only highly unstable but always, inevitably, waiting in the wings where all the supplementary actors are literally ready to burst onto the scene at any given moment. A postmodern orientation to reading and writing has a particular interest, inevitably, for persons, groups, ideas that are marginalized within the reigning dispensations of knowledge and control—women, aboriginals or the once colonized peoples of the Third World. Indeed, it is precisely writers from such groups that have captured major literary awards in the West in recent years.

The point of deconstruction is not simply to replace one interpretation with another, but to show how a fuller range of interpretive possibility exists within *any* text, and that a really responsible kind of reading works, not so much in defense of particular interpretations, but in defense of interpretive possibility itself, which, in its most radical form, involves the right to read my life in relation to any text, to see how I am situated within it or without it. Modernist defenders of what can be termed "logocentric literacy", like, say, E. D. Hirsch and Allan Bloom,[18] seem inexorably deaf to the deep politics of exclusion that resides within the culture-management *eros* of the logocentric tradition. To say this is not to fuel the flames of anarchy, but only to legitimize the right to speak of all voices suppressed within the dominant dispensation of things.

Again, too, the critique of logocentrism is not to be taken as an invitation to suggest that if any interpretation is possible then no interpretation has any particular value. The critique of logocentrism is not nihilistic in the sense of denying the value of any value; it only serves to protect the full play of possibilities at work in any situation and to uphold interpretations that within larger or re-evaluated schemes of things are more just, more comprehensive. The link between interpretation and justice requires more elaboration than can be given here but it has to do with recovering a sense of the narrative structure of experience and an ability to read one's life against the silent macro-narratives of contemporary life, which macro-narratives I have elsewhere discussed as *colonialism, science and secularism.*[19]

Literary activity in the postmodern mode (primarily theory and criticism) is caught within a particular kind of difficulty, however. Where does one go, how does one proceed, after the meaning-drivenness of the West has been radically critiqued? Write another article on the meaningless of meaning, or a play on the modern futility of purpose? Interpret a simple poem to the point of absurdity? In a way, such activities merely contradict themselves, letting in by the back door what is kicked out through the front. I suspect that what the postmodern discourses are reaching for is a way of articulating an intuition of a certain global transformation of consciousness, one allied with developments in both the new biology as well as with oriental Way philosophies. Such a claim leads naturally to the third context to be discussed.

Context Three: The Cultural Implications of the New Biology

As a third context for responsible discussion of literacy, I would like to consider what William Thompson has described as "the transition from ideology to an ecology of consciousness".[20] Thompson can be named as one of the most luminous and articulate voices in the now fairly well known tradition of "new biology", which has problematized the old Enlightenment assumptions about rationality, orderliness and the mechanical quality of nature. In a manner sounding remarkably similar not only to the deconstructive critique of logocentrism but also to the ancient Wisdom traditions of the Tao and Buddha, the new biology proposes that human consciousness, indeed like all of the natural world, operates not like a rational predictable machine oriented towards solidity and stabilization, but rather more like a vibrant network of nodes in which each node is linked to others through a myriad of connectors. Such a conceptualization increases our awareness of the gargantuan range of possible combinations that can exist between different entities, at the same time as it, in a sense, humiliates (makes *humble*, more *human*, better *grounds* >L.humus, earth) the Western privileging of those forms of reason, which as modern experience shows, are actually forms of ideology, that is, interpretations masquerading as a form of certifiable truth backed up by political, military and economic technologies.

Within an understanding of the ecology of consciousness, two things happen to the way we look at and appreciate things. One is to begin to sense how everything is related to everything else (Commoner's *First Law of Ecology*),[21] and then secondly, there is an appreciation of how it is that we live within a living web of meaning, not in a static, linguistic museum. It becomes impossible to view the world confidently, arbitrarily, in terms of the old categories of truth and falsehood, knowledge and ignorance, just as one must come to terms with the transience of one's securities.

Transposing this ecological understanding to a consideration of language and literacy it must be acknowledged that an appreciation of the webbed character of language has been well understood for some time, expressed in such formulations as Heimlich and Pittleman's "semantic mapping" and, say, Umberto Eco's conceptualization of words as "rhisomes".[22] Here, however, I want to move directly to a consideration of the implications of the ecology of consciousness model for language pedagogy.

When honoured recently by Washington University, St. Louis, for his life-long contribution to the study of language and literature, Walter Ong made the following comment: "The older I get, the harder it is to write, because the more I realize how everything is related to everything else".[23] Apart from the fact that the remark is a pure restatement of Commoner's Law, three important themes inhere in it. The first is an honouring of the genuine difficulty of writing; second is the suggestion of what it is that *makes* writing uniquely difficult; and third is the timing of the remark. After a lifetime of writing (often on the subject of writing), there is, in Ong's words, an air of resignation, verging on a mystical vision of that unity in reality which cannot be named simply by describing its component parts.

The sequence may be described as follows: Writing leads to a careful attending to the details of experience carried in words to a kind of comtemplation. Such careful attention in turn leads to a deeper awareness of the profound interconnectedness of everything and to a mode of insight more in line with what might be termed "mystical appreciation", rather than say, premature declaration and annunciation. Writing leads to a sense of the ecological fragility of experience and to a contemplative awareness of the foolhardiness of saying too early what the world is like. It is not a far leap to say that, in a way, writing leads to the end of writing, or that writing serves its unique purpose when the writer is led to a shore of silence issuing from a profound respect for the integrity of the world, an integrity which must be preserved for us to say anything about it at all. And so it is that Canadian writer Margaret Atwood once commented that "mystics don't write".

These remarks should not be taken as an exhortation to anti-writing or anti-literacy, but to a view that writing, and everything involved in it, should not be trivialized for purposes of pedagogical expediency or economic or political gain. It is not incidental to the argument that in pre-printing societies, before the democratization of writing, writing was primarily associated with the priestly classes. Even in classical Greece, dramaturgy, the writing and staging of dramas, was linked to theology, a connection carried etymologically in the word theatre, meaning a "beholding" of the action between the divine and human realms (>Gk. *theaomai*).

The point is that before anything can be written, something must be seen, and because insight is the necessary condition for good writing, preparation for writing inevitably lies as much in the realm of existential preparedness than in the practice of the "writing process" or "word processing". Being prepared to write involves an attunement or attentiveness to reality most closely allied not to epistemology (knowing how to write) but to Wisdom (knowing what should be said). Writing is a holy act, an articulation of limited understanding oriented to a pre-existent Whole. Anything else is a cultural fetish, driven by and towards secondary aims.

Conclusion

The first inkling that something bizarre might be at work in the so-called "Crisis of Literacy" came to me not long ago in, of all places, *The World's Biggest Bookstore* in Toronto. It suddenly struck me how odd it was that we should be preoccupied about a crisis of literacy in a culture virtually saturated with print of all types, hues and genres. As a Gutenburg Society we are completely surrounded by everything from books to bus tickets.

Such a contradictory state of affairs seemed even more odd as I reflected on once being an elementary school teacher and discovering that, technically and pedagogically, teaching young children to read is not a particularly difficult task. Put children and their natural curiosity together with a competent reader (parent, teacher, peer) with the time and inclination to watch over the children as they come into contact with books, magazines, stories, comics, signs and so on, and almost unawares youngsters will confidently declare: "I can read". Like any other form of learning, learning to read is a relational activity—it depends upon a relationship. Any crisis in literacy is, then, preeminently a crisis of relationships. It may be one of the great ironies of history that because printing has been such a deep contributor to the shaping of our present arrangements, understood in a certain way, literary activity itself could be seen as complicit in the current crisis of literacy. The culture of literacy, which Western culture is, has created its own crisis in the sense that a culture oriented by print is one oriented by a particular way of arriving at what should be valued, and how.

The use of the term "crisis" in the context of the current public debate about literacy is interesting because it does not suggest a pathology, *per se*, but rather a turning point, a moment of decision (>Gk. *krisis*, decision). In fact, because of the link between printing and paper production, de-pathologizing certain forms of literacy deficit and profoundly pathologizing certain other orientations may be one of the most important and difficult challenges facing our survival on the planet. My concern about "hyperliteracy" has emerged from an increasing unease with the relentless proliferation of print materials consequent to the inauguration of word processing and word reproduction technologies. In my own work context as a Western university educator in a teacher preparation faculty, the increased production of books, journals, curriculum proposals and educational reform agendas is matched in sheer volume only by the kinds of demands contemporary educators are making on students to write, write, write (produce, produce, produce). In both schools and universities, however, one cannot help but be struck, not just by the sheer amount of literary production, but also, in some deep, barely acknowledgeable sense, by the amount that did not need to be produced.

I suspect that if there is a crisis of literacy in the West, it is the result not of the lack of educational opportunities, nor of deficiencies in literary materials *per se*, but of a difficulty deep in the heart of Western desire. What postmodernists have named logocentrism or meaning-drivenness must inevitably come up against what mystics and sages have understood for a long time, which is that genuine meaningfulness always contains an absence as well as a presence, silence as much as declaration—a dialectic of "protention and retention installed in the heart of the present", as Derrida once put it. [24] Logocentrism, translated into forms of cultural production and reproduction suffers a deficit that cannot be identified from within its own lexicon, namely the lack of a creative logic of the negative, the Zen *mu* (nothingness). Western desire understands fullness and completeness only one way, as a subsumption of everything under its own rubric in the name of progress. As a consequence it cannot stop; nor can it abide an unnameable Other as bearing a creative word for its own transformation. So it is, for example, that if the new burgeoning literary activity, with the consequent re-alignment of the Western canon, does nothing to reassess the very grammar of literacy itself, then what takes place is a mere replacement of one version of political correctness with another, with the new functionally illiterate maybe being only the most recently colonized ones under "new literacy" elites.[25]

I suspect though that what is really called for is an attention to what Canadian musicologist R. Murray Schafer has called "the tuning of the world",[26] involving an aspect of truly literate and humane relations which has not even been mentioned here so far, namely listening. It is a breakdown in the necessary reciprocity between speaking and listening, written production and careful attention to what is being written about, that produces a condition Thomas Berry has identified as "cultural autism".[27] A culture of science and technology, like ours in the West, is inspired by a Cartesian subject/object dualism which, as a long-range cultural prospect, imprisons more and more persons within the cages of their own subjectivity, reducing all others to the status of objects. Others are seen as simply unnecessary to the pure functioning of my own cognizing ego.[28] The result is that the very metaphysic from which the modern West draws its deepest inspiration is also the one that is killing it, depriving it of all pleasures of intersubjective discourse. Genuine literacy is most creatively a discursive activity which does not rest with a pedagogic literalness putting language purely at the service of the will. Reading the world, inscribing and being profoundly inscribed by it, has to do more with deep attunement or hearing, and involves a kind of obedience to life's deepest resonances [<Fr, *obeir* , to obey >L. *o b audere*, to hear from]. The ancient Chinese sage Zhuangzi provided a hint: "Show me someone who has had enough of words that I may have a Word with that person".[29]

7

On Discursivity and Neurosis: Conditions of Possibility for (West) Discourse with Others

Wherever one is situated today, but perhaps most especially in the West, there's a feeling of living through an interregnum, a time when old political, economic and social confidences are evaporating, yet it is still not clear where firm new directions may lie, should they be so desired. Certainly the new politics of identity[1] makes it clear that all those voices that once were only subterranean, or off-stage, to the main play of dominant orders, well, those voices now expect to be heard. Yet for the very possibility of being heard to exist, there has to be a kind of deep facing of the implications of what really hearing another person or group means to the way one lives, or, better, to the way we live together. The new technologies of communication may make possible all sorts of new modes of contact between people, but, as anyone with *Internet* experience quickly learns, just being able to talk with more and more people is no guarantee that the talk is any more profound or intelligent or insightful, that indeed for all our expanded abilities to communicate with others the basic quality of our lives may be no better. So somewhere in the middle of these new circumstances there needs to be a thinking through of those conditions unique to our times under which speech and hearing are connected to questions of life practice. Otherwise talk just goes on and on, becoming increasingly neurotic because of being unable to speak directly to or from the conditions out of which it arises.

In the title of this paper, then, linking discursivity with neurosis, followed by an exploration of new conditions of possibility for discourse (conditions now self-consciously denoted as "West"), gives notice of a certain disillusionment I feel with my culturally received, monotheistic valourization of the power of word-ing (understood as reasoning, dialoguing, discussing, conversing, etc.), and my sense that the problem is not discourse *per se*, but the way my understanding of it is, or has been, too stuck within its own cultural self-enclosure, within the compound of its own cultural grammar, one might say. In taking up these issues within the context of a conference convened to consider "Fragmentation and the Desire for Order/Unity", I wish to declare that, for me, the issue of the theme is not in the way "Fragmentation and Order/Unity" play off each other relationally or symbiotically (which they probably do), but how so inevitably and incidentally in the West that play-off has a neurotic tail-chasing character that is inspired precisely by Desire. My remarks, therefore, about the possibilities of new conditions of discourse for the West, turn most profoundly on a problematizing of Desire itself. The deep neurosis in our communicative practices may issue, I suspect, from a form of constant craving, the satiation of which we are culturally predisposed to believe is pre-eminently possible only through an act of language, even language translated into action as policy, or social change. In Hebrew, the word "word" (*dabhar*) means *event*, and in the Greek gospels we are told that we live by "word" as much as by "bread"; which goes to show that in the Hebrew-Christian tradition anyway, word-ing is somehow linked to an interest in power (agency) and to appetite. Our orientation to language and its various modalities is inevitably meaning-driven, deeply purposive, or logocentric, as Derrida would put it, so that any investigation of sickness in our discursive practices may necessarily have to begin with the matter of our primary expectations, linguistically mediated.

That it is possible like this to have a discourse about discourse is a relatively recent phenomenon in the West. The turn to language in social science is traceable to Wittgenstein, and also to the Vienna Circle of the 1930s which precipitated the Frankfurt School of neo-Marxist critical social theory. But in the contemporary period it is to Michel Foucault that the largest debt is likely owed for illustrating how social practices are made topical and sustained through forms of discursive community that in turn must be sustained for the social practices to go on.[2] And then to Jacques Derrida we are indebted for so strongly resurrecting the pre-Socratic notion (also well understood by Kant and Marx) that presence always implies absence, that in present practices there lingers the suppressed "trace" of what makes them possible.[3] So the Greek valourization of dialogue through the symposium, for example, *requires* a silent slave class to do the dirty work of life-support, and it requires the silence be safeguarded.

This new discourse about discourse eliminates forever the possibility that our talk and action can go on naively, innocent of the political realities that sustain them. The orthodox canon of English literature has to acknowledge its patriarchy; talk of the "humanities" requires admitting to the global empire of capitalism which inspired the confidence to speak for the entire species; Enlightenment principles of Truth and Reason underwriting the contemporary hard and social sciences are being forced to respond to the cries of those refusing to be subsumed under scientific accounts.

Entirely too presumptuous an undertaking to be sure, but in what follows I wish to explore conditions that may mark the limits and possibilities of discourse within the contemporary situation of the West. Inevitably, I speak as a white Western male, but one formed through a personal biography of displacement from non-Western domains. I was born in China during the Maoist revolution, then ejected with my family as a foreigner. I grew up in Central Africa (Northern Rhodesia/Zambia), but after political independence it was clear that my skin colour, and all reflected through it, had little place within the new social agenda. So now I speak as a white male academic, profoundly sensitive to the ways my training in the codes, contents and protocols of the good liberal Western tradition bears only tainted currency in many other realms of our shared planetary home. I search for ways of speaking and acting that may make possible for the West forms of encounter with others that are more friendly, less violent, more self-reflexive and not condescending. In undertaking this task, I repudiate any postmodern claims about the end of grand narratives, or even the end of narrativity.[4] The challenge is to reinterpret the grand narratives from within the space of our postcolonial understanding of the modern world system, to move away from triumphal declarations about Truth into an acquaintance with the way human beings find their deepest companionship in the action of telling stories to each other, of giving accounts of their experience, that is, precisely in the practice of narrative out of which good theory comes.

Before proceeding, I might note that my disillusionment about the possibilities of what can be rendered through discourse began with reading Tibetan Buddhist teacher Chogyam Trungpa.[5] In *Cutting Through Spiritual Materialism*, Trungpa undertakes a meditation on the works of Nagarjuna, the 2nd–3rd century A.D. founder of Madhyamika (Middle Way) Buddhism. The word "neurotic" is used to describe the action of ego, which manifests itself as the Three Lords of Materialism (the Lord of Form, the Lord of Speech and the Lord of Mind). Trungpa explains:

> The Lords use discursive thought as their first line of defense, as their pawns in their effort to deceive us. The more we generate thoughts, the busier we are mentally and the more convinced we are of our existence. So the Lords are constantly trying to activate these thoughts, trying to create a constant overlapping of thoughts so that nothing can be seen beyond them.[6]

One witnesses here a primal critique of everything assumed to be good in a Word tradition such as that of the West. The very desire to generate thoughts and concepts discursively is not only linked to a phenomenology of deception, particularly to a deception about identity (existence); so also is the activism at work in this deception linked to an ever-deepening myopia. Here, then, are illuminated the seeds of hyper-production so characteristic of capitalist versions of literacy. Also clarified are the exaggerated vanities of Christian ideas about proclamation ("Here is the news...."), to say nothing of the oppressive officiousness of the activist mind. All these lead to a hardening self-enclosure, ripe for xenophobia and parochialism, the death of openness. So it is that there seems to be a widening despair in the West about what can be achieved through wording, through talking, through writing: an implosion of the democratic ideal, of consensus seeking, and even of the literary ideal as a form of social discipline.[7] Of course, we are not talking here of the end of discursivity *per se*. After all, even a Buddha has to talk to critique talk. Instead, the aim must be two fold: to show the limits of conventional West phenomenologies of discourse at the same time as refract them through understandings that may open them up and rejuvenate them through reformulation.

Herewith, then, is an exploration of conditions of possibility for (West) discourse with others, considered through three clustered themes: 1) Post-colonial theorizing of the other, enantiomorphism and a recovery of the logic of the negative, 2) The homocentric fallacy and a shift from ideology to an ecology of consciousness, and 3) Meditation and the pedagogy of presence.

Theme One:
Post Colonial Theorizing of the Other, Enantiomorphism and a Recovery of the Logic of the Negative

Enantiomorphism is a term derived from Greek describing how Truth cannot be expressed except in relationships of opposites (> Gk *enantios*, opposite + *morphe*, form).[8] Sometimes what is denoted is the tendency of things to actively turn into their opposite, as in the case of the word "socialism", which, as Vaclav Havel has shown,[9] in Eastern Europe turned from being a word of celebration to a swear word in about fifty years. American democracy requires the practice of fascism to protect its interests in Brazil, Chile and Mexico. In teaching, it takes a monster child about two weeks to turn a meek teacher into a monster.[10] Generally, the degree to which this dynamic holds true depends upon the degree to which polar identities fail to recognize or appreciate how such self-identifications stand in a dependent and continuous relationship with what they reject. This resonates with postmodern formulations that any identity requires an Other by which to define itself: that I understand who I am through whom I am not. As well, the play of opposites is articulated in Asian wisdom traditions where virtue involves maintaining a harmonious balance between the pulls and tugs of opposition, and that to fall in love with extremes is to undermine the grounds of genuinely creative existence.

Why this last understanding is so often given a pejorative twist in the West (Aristotle's Doctrine of the Mean, notwithstanding), to mean quietism, non-action or even moral cowardice, is itself a matter worthy of consideration. Ashis Nandy has noted, for example, that in the context of British imperialism in India, the British interpreted the ease of their conquest as a revelation of a certain moral and intellectual deficiency of the Indian people. In fact, a more accurate interpretation would show that it was Hindu virtues of tolerance and openness that enabled the British to establish themselves.[11] It is only the deep hubris of capitalism that can afford a view that its global successes are due to some inherent trait of strength and superiority.

Now certainly, enantiomorphism itself can be read as standing in a relation of opposition to all formulations oriented to final resolution. But such is the point: orientation to finality, closure and fixity always ends up revealing a condition of lack, and usually the result is violent because the requirements for "finalization" are inevitably political, with arrangements of oppression required toward nay-saying. So enantiomorphism should not be taken as a fixable concept, but rather as a descriptive device for the way in which things naturally unfold. Call it a reminder never to take any one thing, idea or person with ultimate seriousness: even here, the word "never" requires a gloss, but that is a task for another time.

The beckoning, then, is for a language which can articulate the phenomenology of living "in the middle" of things, a language not determined to have the final say, but one that can show the way of the condition in which we always already find ourselves, namely in the condition of perpetual non-resolution, yet one in which we are mysteriously, even mystically, sustained. There is a resolution already, always at work in our non-resolutions, but one that cannot be named from within any one lexicon or grammar, also without which the possibilities of human language cannot exist. Pierre Bourdieu has referred to this as "the consensus in dissensus".[12] The great hermeneutical scholar, H-G. Gadamer, after a life devoted to inquiry into the grounds of human understanding, was prompted to ask: "Does what already sustains us require any grounding?"[13] It seems such a plaintive remark from someone in the sunset years of a distinguished career in Western metaphysics, but it points to an important insight, namely that the search for a theoretical "grounding" of human life belies the truth that human life is already sustained without such grounding. There is a homocentric fallacy at work in most Western attempts to explain its actions, another theme to be examined later.

The following illustration can be taken from the realm of pedagogy, one showing not only the way in which Western pedagogies so relentlessly construct the delusion of resolution, but also how, in that process, they simultaeously shut down the possibilities of enantiomorphic insight by hardening the borders of self-definition. The conditions of creative interpretation are thereby foreclosed.

Augustana University College is a fine liberal arts institution which traces its identity to Martin Luther and the Protestant Reformation. Like any well-intended academy, the college is dedicated to inspiring its young with the noblest ideals of Western culture, and in this case the hero is the Augustinian monk from Wittenburg. It is understandable, therefore, that the most striking icon on the open campus commons should be a statue of Luther. But here one might ask, what representation of Luther would constitute the most pedagogically responsible one? Or, in the context of the present discussion, how might Luther be depicted to show the character of Lutheran Protestantism in its most whole-some sense? How should the students at the college be taught to "read" Luther in a way that might avoid a plunge into one-sidedness?

Inevitably, perhaps, the college elders elected the high road, choosing to depict Luther at his young, virile best. Eyes clear, skin smooth and taut; the sheer force of the bronze truly gives pause. But one must ask, what of the older Luther, the scrofulous one, the man drinking four gallons of beer a day whose later writings may show signs of paranoid alcoholic psychosis?[14] And what of the downside of the Protestant Reformation as a whole, as it can now be read in retrospect from the point of view of our present experience of it: its propensity for schism and divisiveness; its ability, in the name of purification, to produce not just intolerance for ambiguity, but also an exaggerated imaginal literalism through the death of symbol. Of course too, one must give account of the deep pessimism about human nature that Luther inherited from Augustine, subsequently willed to the future, a pessimism with its own self-fulfilling character, whereby if I feel doomed my only comfort is in making others feel the same. What about all this?

Enantiomorphically, it is necessary to affirm that the young Luther and the latter share an immutable continuity, and that the truth of Luther, including the deep Lutheran legacy in the history of the West, must be found in acknowledging both sides of his character. Pedagogically speaking, to hold up only the young idealist as a hero, to the neglect of acknowledging his imbalances and exaggerations, ensures an induction of the young into a cultural interpretation full of repression, producing a stance toward life that must be inevitably paranoid and defensive, determined to keep the devil at bay. The Luther curriculum then degenerates into debates over which interpretation of his character is "correct", instead of trying to creatively discern how all aspects articulate one unity. When God and the Devil are set up as two identically different players within a cultural architecture of dualism, it becomes virtually impossible to learn how God can so easily turn out to be the Devil, and the Devil may be God in disguise. Any attempt to create "pure" identity, whether in the name of religion or ideology, inevitably falters from the discovery that purity, as the possibility of life-without-difference, is a vain hope.[15]

In terms of contemporary global reconfigurations of influence and order, one of the most difficult challenges facing the West is the realization that the West itself is not a pure identity, a sign to be held up as a clean example of development, progress and civility. The debts, both economic and cultural, to Others, especially to peoples of the former colonies, are too large[16]. Too, the demographic shifts whereby the people of India, Pakistan, the Middle East, and so on. have taken their places on the home soil of their former colonizers only show how the colonial past has to be "faced" in real terms.

Actually, from an enantiomorphic point of view, that facing is a responsibility of all players. For one thing, the myth of pre-contactism presumes to insinuate that before the arrival of Western colonizers, life was unproblematic for non-Western peoples, but the most cursory examination of pre-contact conditions in any colonized country simply does not bear this out. Pestilence, famine, internecine strife, ritual slaughter, tribal warfare were common features of many landscapes.[17]

The new massive interfusion of cultures, then, one of the long-term legacies of the modern colonial period, brings with it the inevitability of tradition-boundedness being challenged to reassess itself. However, whether this is understood positively or negatively, that is, whether it is a loss or gain to have one's stable structures of belief relativized (made relative by showing a relation) by encounters with Others, is not simply a hermeneutic option that can be decided completely, purely, by those in charge. There is always more at work through interfusion than can be disentangled by means of the languages and lexicons of pre-contact conditions. Contact, or "facing" the Other, always means examining the ways I am now inexorably different than I was before contact, and things can never be the same again. In the case of Islamic tradition, for example, Abdullahi Ahmed An-Naim has shown how the traditional Muslim concept of *sharia*, or the pure, exclusive tradition of Islamic law, is being re-worked through new interpretations of the Koran to provide a language for Muslim practice that is more tolerant and open.[18]

In summary then, post colonial realities point to ways in which linguistically mediated Western assumptions about identity contain an *aporia*, or perplexity, which can only be addressed by acknowledging how identity means nothing without a set of relations, and that historically it can now be seen how Western identity in particular got constructed through long-standing dependencies with silenced Others, Others now claiming their debts. In terms of the new possibilities of discourse, there must be a facing of the exaggerations implicit in one-sided interpretations and an owning-up to the consequences of operating out of a fiction of purity; a thinking through of how purity may not mean one thing (pejorative monotheism), but a full plenitude of the Many (unispheric polytheism), articulated as a coming to terms with a logic of the negative implicit in all speech and action, whereby there is a silent partner in all conversation. It implies the end of unity in any secured sense, but maybe also a sense of relief to be gained from shedding those defensive weights that a belief in pure identity requires to sustain itself. At the same time, a new invigoration becomes possible from acknowledging how that which once had been held at bay contains at least part of the answer for a shared future. This may lead in turn to an understanding of unity that is not dependent on the usual Western assumption of identity as difference. I do not need to keep you in your place in order to be me if I understand the concept "me" itself to be a fiction. This will be explored later under theme three.

Theme Two:
The Homocentric Fallacy and a Shift from Ideology to an Ecology of Consciousness

It is we humans who take all these phenomena of Nature as having some definite design in relationship to human destiny and welfare, but this homocentric interpretation of the world always ends in tragedy, if not in an utter confusion of thought.

So says the great Zen teacher D.T. Suzuki.[19] The roots of such homocentrism in the West are not difficult to trace. That Man (*sic*) is the crown of the created order, destined to rule over it as a duty, if not pleasure, is the central myth of *Genesis*, and it is the myth that made possible the vast confidence of science in both exploring and unlocking the secrets of the natural order without fear.[20] In the social realm, Marx's scientific materialism, applied to the engineering of social space, is only the most obvious of serious attempts to live as if human will and intention are the final arbiter of the destiny of human affairs, a view most notably contraindicated by Chernobyl. A more subtle form of the same disposition can be found in the "social construction of reality"[21] myth which dominates Western social science. It provides a language for being able to claim that we are who we think we are, without extra-human contingencies, and that the self-enclosure of our cognitive constructs represents a triumph of some sort, something worthy of cultural applause, even though phenomeno-logically, in terms of how we live, it may be a form of imaginal and egological imprisonment of the darkest kind.[22]

The critique of homocentrism can be taken up in two ways. In the most elementary sense, human vulnerability is easily named by pointing to all the ways our securities so easily fall victim to natural forces over which we do not have, nor likely ever will have, any real control. The fallout from Mt. Pinatubo's eruption in the Philippines has exceeded, in terms of negative influence on the ozone layer, all human pollution since the beginning of the Industrial Revolution. An earthquake can easily wipe out in a few minutes a human population the size of Hiroshima. In a family, the different personalities of offspring, quite apparent from birth, are simply not explainable in any absolutely reductive way by Learning Theory.

As a teacher of teachers in a university faculty of education, I am often appalled at how virtually none of the languages and constructs of teacher education give even a nod to this deep lacuna within human experience. On the contrary, every space is required to be filled with either action or explanation, almost as a denial of death, a determined evasion of the inevitable news that no matter how complete one's plans, things could very easily fall apart. Homocentrism is haunted by a heavy, ghostly demand for complete human responsibility in everything that happens, and it is a demand that can never be satisfactorily fulfilled precisely because it is impossible to have a plan that could anticipate every contingency. Homocentric pedagogy is a serious, joyless business, and distinctly anti-pedagogical in the sense that there is no place for that-which-cannot-be-named, no awe or reverence for all those forces that surround us every moment and which at any moment might betray our false confidence. An attunement to such things leads inevitably to forms of relating to the world which have largely been banished by science and secularism, but without which there can be no wisdom or understanding. Homocentric pedagogy is inevitably a pedagogy of despair.

A second line of critique against the homocentric fallacy involves acknowledging the way the natural world has its own subjectivity. As Thomas Berry says,[23] the world is not just an object to my subjectivity; rather it has its own set of response abilities to human conduct. The species death of birds, fish, reptiles and so on as a consequence of human pollution is a *response* to what human beings do, not just a vacant termination. Thus we can look to the natural world as a kind of interlocutor with the capacity to pass judgement on human affairs. The injunctions of Jesus, "Consider the lilies of the field...; Behold the fowls of the air...",[24] point to an insight well understood in Asian Way traditions, especially Taoism, that there are important lessons to be learned from deep meditation on the natural world, particularly with respect to the balance of relations among emergence, nurture and decay.

Most social theory in the West, especially since the turn of the century, has been generated in urban, highly industrialized environments, places where the only trees and plants available to human observation are products of hyper-cultivation, and the only visible animals are profoundly domesticated. Such a site for the generation of theory and policy must inevitably ensure social outcomes that are driven by the ambiences, rhythms and tones of their situational origin, characterised most clearly by prediction, control and rationalization, to say nothing of an embeddedness within a sonic environment echoing primarily the noises of machines. Canadian musicologist and composer R. Murray Schafer says one of the first prerequisites for learning to hear the world in new ways is to undergo "ear cleaning".[25]

Another aspect, then, of interlocution in earth-human relations, and the critique of homocentrism that such interlocution entails, concerns an attention to the necessary geography of all human thought and action.[26] Our ideas and actions are inspired just as much by physical landscape and "geophysical memory"[27] as by Platonic notions of pure thought, for example. William Thompson suggests that fairytales such as *Snow White and the Seven Dwarfs* are best understood as reflecting human memory traces of prehistoric geophysical activity. The dwarfs are a subliminal reminder that underneath the sunlit surface of human affairs there is the constant subterranean agitation and tumultuous work of geophysical forces that could erupt at any time. In a different turn, David Campbell,[28] explores how the identity, "United States", is a construction that privileges the spatial over the temporal because Europeans who encountered the New World went out of their way to deny its historicity. In American experience, history developed into an "eternal present", a condition emerging from the experience of rupture from, and discontinuity with, the Old World. The Puritans turned "geography into eschatology", a move that justified the genocide of native American Indians and the enslavement of the African-American as embodiments of the Anti-Christ. The imaginative geography of the United States, then, is "iconic" and "ideational", with politics privileging the "symbolic". Underdeveloped in the American psyche is what could be called a narrative phenomenological sensibility, which pays attention to the complexity of human experience in its lived conditions of place, story and family, and so on. Solutions to human problems always begin with abstract theorizing rather than with an attention to life as it is lived in its specificity.

These examples from Thompson and Campbell point to the obvious, but under a homocentric dispensation, suppressed truth that there is always more going on in the world than human beings could ever dream of; that indeed even our dreams are shaped and moulded by the ways our experience is conditioned by relations to particular temporal and spatial situatedness on the planet, both socio-political and otherwise. Thompson suggests that such dependencies invite a reorientation of thinking about thinking away from orthodox conventions which regard the purpose of thinking to be the securing of metaphysical, social, political or scientific truths, truths which always end up being found out as "ideologies", or hyper-extended imputations of the specific being the general. Such renderings, when turned into institutional forms, must of necessity close an eye to their own dependencies in order to remain stable. What is required, says Thompson, is an understanding of consciousness itself as "ecological", always in a state of reverberation and transformation as a consequence of its broader connections. This understanding not only reveals the conditionedness of our imaginal life, but also our potential for re-imagining, should it be possible to cultivate new ways of paying attention. Paying attention in new ways can best be named as the practice of meditation, the last theme to be taken up in this paper.

Theme Three:
Meditation and the Pedagogy of Presence

The contemplative life must provide an area, a space of liberty, of silence, in which possibilities are allowed to surface and new choices—beyond routine choice—become manifest. It should create a new experience of time... not a blank to be filled or an untouched space to be conquered and violated, but a space which can enjoy its own potentialities and hopes ... open to others—compassionate time, rooted in the sense of common illusion and in criticism of it.[29]

Facing the General Assembly of the Council of Europe in Vienna, Vaclav Havel recently issued a lament for the dismal prospects of a new Europe emerging from the ashes of the Cold War.[30] Currently, too many Western states are trying to "outwit history by reducing the idea of Europe to a noble backdrop against which they can continue their petty concerns". Attempts at unification around principles of democracy and pluralistic politics seem doomed largely because of an erroneous belief that the task ahead is a purely technical, instrumental and administrative one, involving nothing but "endless" discussion and debate. What is neglected, he suggests, is a new kind of common moral obligation between peoples and states that can incarnate the full potential for creative change that the present moment holds. Speaking self-reflexively, Havel suggests that such potentiality has little chance, however, "without ever attempting to change anything in ourselves, or in the habitual motives and stereotypes of our behaviour".

The question of how we come to change our social, political and personal habits is of course critical to any proposal for collective reform. It is an issue of special relevance in the contemporary period when the technology for manipulating both public and private consciousness is so well developed. People everywhere suffer the irony of being offered a ubiquitous promise for individual expression while that very promise is manufactured by others through a dense and largely hidden network of sophisticated marketing and media technologies tied to corporate capital interests. Even public education, once venerated as the primal hope for shaping public will, now shows itself too often as a hollowed-out site of "culture wars",[31] incapable of anything but the most banal and washed-out renditions of human reality, an induction into "know-nothingism," as Gayatri Spivak recently described the American university educational system.[32] Religious groups and other traditional sources of inspired morals too easily reveal their complicity in regressive politics, or a commitment to narrow sectarian interests which are entirely inappropriate for a time when the positive fruits of the new cultural interfusion require, more than anything else, a spirit of openness, generosity and care.

The widespread cultural confusion in the West, now very close to the surface, and signified most obviously in the postmodern move to show the inability of language to contain a call to action which could be held in common, such confusion may be a prelude to a new enlightenment. Again as Trungpa says, "Confusion is part of the path",[33] but for the next stage to be realized, there has to be a cleansing of the old rationalities, all those rationalities linked in the West to a conception of the Same named, say, as capital interest, an interest in turn linked to the reduction of most forms of cultural capital, from "higher" education to the use of "manipulatives" in kindergarten, to the language of power. There needs to be an attention to what David Loy calls "the repressed shadow of rationality",[34] which is meditation, or meditative consciousness, an attunement to the world which is not dependent on the ravenous pressures of the market or on all those other forms of interference which get in the way of the genuinely new.

It is not the place here to lay out a program for the practice of meditation, with all the permutations and possibilities articulated by its many traditions in the world.[35] Let the aim be simple: to evoke its primary purpose and show its value in the present discussion. Etymologically, meditation has to do with gaining the true measure of one's situation (>L. *med-*, measure), which is achieved through a stopping of all those daily rituals and habits which inevitably act to sustain status quo conventionalities. Most traditions of meditation emphasize the importance of understanding breathing, and this is not just another piece of exotica, but an acknowledgement of how the simple practice of breathing reflects the character of our connection to the outer world. The lungs are the door through which the outside world is taken into the inner world and transformed into a response via the cardiovascular system. Stress responses to environmental pressures are most often connected to breathing difficulties. Wisdom traditions understand this very well. In Hebrew, the word for "breath" is *ruach*, which is also the word for "spirit". Spiritual difficulties are breathing difficulties, and vice versa, problems in our understanding of the necessary conditions for good relations between Self and Other.

Meditative stopping makes possible a new kind of stillness in which can be heard or recognized, maybe for the first time, all of those voices, intuitions, dreams and aspirations (another term connected to breathing) which have been suppressed under the dispensations of the dominant order. Meditation disrupts the grammar of received consciousness to make consciousness available to its wider purview, which is the ability to think freely, in a way not dependent upon concepts determined by essentialist thinking to be the neccessary tools of thought. It invites an orientation to language and thinking which is no longer dependent on this or that (postmodern relationalism) but acts out of a forgetfulness of language as self-consciously appropriated ego-identity, working instead in a condition of "non-abiding" (>Skt. *sunyata*). To become forgetful in this way is not self-induced amnesia or escapism, but rather an emergence into recognition of the deep interdependency of any identity, and a full owning-up to the way in which I always already am that of which I speak, even when I speak of the world and others as object. This is the famous *tuam sat asi* of Hinduism, "that thou art".[36] The subject/object dualism that underwrites virtually all of Western metaphysics, relegating conversation to a form of power negotiation arising from arguments over concepts, is shown meditatively to be a fiction, because, as David Loy says, "To forget oneself is to wake up and find oneself in or, more precisely, *as* a situation—not confronted by it but one with it".[37] And so, as Martin Buber once put it, "all real living is meeting".[38]

Approaching the world meditatively or contemplatively is a living form of saturated ethics whereby the discipline of meditation produces what can be called a "condition of unthinkability." When I begin to understand that everything is interpenetrated by everything else, it becomes, in a very literal sense, quite unthinkable that for the sake of my own fictional identity I should deliberately perpetrate violence against another. To kill my brother is to engage in my own destruction; to wound the earth through willful negligence is to destroy the means of my own survival. If, as Gandhi once said, I am wealthy, it is because I am a thief.[39] Putting the matter positively, Thomas Berry says that when I heal myself, I heal the world,[40] and it is this inspiration (another breathing term) that is the true point of meditation, namely healing—healing oneself of all those cultural diseases that are mediated precisely through forms and constructs that one's cultural grammar predisposes one to live out as natural. For Western civilization, said Max Scheler, "the entire development has been a one-sided and overactive process of expansion outward",[41] with a coincidental evacuation of the inner life. The evacuation itself contains a double bind, full of haunted memory and desperate to fill its lack, but frustrated at every turn, because what is craved is a "something", something like everything else already in possession; an evacuation still full of the grammar of consumption whereby every void must be filled, every space made replete as a sign of Divine presence. Meditative consciousness, therefore, in its true shamanic character, must precisely be none of this, a process instead of "de-reflection", as David Loy describes it, whereby "the legacy of the eighteenth-century Enlightenment project—in social and scientific terms, that which liberates us from absolutism, dogmatism, and superstition—must dovetail into the enlightenment that frees me from *me*."[42] Ego-identity in its most dogmatic forms is the full binary of pejorative monotheism, the concept "God" being the logical extension of Me/Us, so that a process of dereflection which frees me from *me* can at the same time make possible a true resacralization of the world, or, to put it better, dereflection can inaugurate a human discovery of the world as already sacred, already whole. As Derrida has said, "the death of God will ensure our salvation because the death of God alone can reawaken the divine".[43]

If the times are dismal, if at every turn there is cause for doubt about the possibility of basic human decency being translatable into sustainable social policy or good politics, it may be important to remember how the link between pessimism and utopian fantasy may itself be sustained by a neurotic symbiosis entrapped in particular interpretations of time and space. Marx knew the pessimism well: "The tradition of all the dead generations weighs like a nightmare on the brain of the living", he said in *The Eighteenth Brumaire*,[44] where he grappled with the issue of how, at the precise moment in a revolution when people are at last free to choose a new future, they always inevitably end up framing it in languages and customs borrowed from the past, thereby ensuring a quick return to old problems, rearranged. The contemplative life, more than anything else, turns away from backward or forward visions to a disciplined practice of living in the present, such that the true character of morality is well understood for its ordinariness and simplicity, not its grandiosity, and wherein the really revolutionary challenges of life, including genuine pleasures, are never "over there" or "back then" but always everywhere mediated in the here and now. Wendell Berry has warned of "the futility of global thinking",[45] whereby, particularly in a (Western) culture framed by Fall and Redemption mythology, the temptation is always to look for a saviour, in the form of the one big solution, one program that can solve all problems. Such is the nature of fundamentalism, and it can come in the guise of science and technology, or the cult of information, just as much as in the swaddling clothes of conservative religion.

"The purpose of meditation", said Trungpa, "is not to get higher, but to be present". It involves "the continual act of making friends",[46] with oneself and with the world. In the first instance, from my privileged place as a teacher of young children, I can testify to the devastation caused by a Western educational system constructed on an Aristotelian assumption that knowledge compounded leads eventually to God. Not only does this end up as a fast track to ambition, careerism and other forms of cultural "high", so also does it lead to an abandonment of others in the name of seeking or desiring transcendence, transcendence usually masquerading as theory. It is in the lives of children that the lived implications of broader social values are to be seen most clearly, and today the most obvious social diseases of the young can be traced to their being abandoned to theory, be it social, political or pedagogical. As Ashis Nandy has suggested, in technical industrial cultures, the real child is supplanted by the idea of childhood.[47] The particular needs of particular children are never addressed because they have no currency on prevailing registers of research or policy.[48] One does not have to look far for the absence of presence, or rather both absence and presence badly understood. The most serious need in any educational reform today may be for adults to simply be "present" to children, although what is meant here is not cloying, earnest concern, but a deep attunement to the valence between genuine intimacy and detachment. My favorite icon of the Buddha shows him literally crawling with children, and there is unadulterated joy on everyone's faces. It must be asked here how a life based on detachment seems to afford such an opportunity for children. In Buddhism, the practice of Presence implies the practice of Absence, leading in turn to Wisdom (>Skt. *prajna*), and it is this last which is the real home to which children are most naturally drawn and where they find their deepest companionship and happiness. There is a Christian parallel to this insight in the Gospel of Mark: "and the children came to him...."[49] The attractiveness of Wisdom for children is a subject worthy of further research.

To conclude: this consideration of the relationship between discursivity and neurosis began for me with a worry that, in the West, in the context of massively increased powers of linguistic production of various modalities (print, different media capabilities, and so on), language is losing its ability to convey anything except artificial constructions. Or, in the midst of an incredible inflation of the word through the new technologies of linguistic production, the ability of "yea" to mean "yea" or "nay", "nay" has become almost impossible. For the West, I believe this condition is largely a consequence of science, whereby, in the Cartesian version anyway, which has roots deep in our various monotheistic sensibilities, language itself becomes an object of science, an object for personal manipulation by an Ego separated off into a shell of pure identity from which to make statements about a now-separated-off world. The long range effect seems to be to render human experience of communication as profoundly hallucinatory because that to which any speech (for example) refers, loses its ability to reference a common world. A recovery of a sense of a common world may be the first prerequisite for a more relevant understanding of humanity for the West, although as Goethe once remarked, "you can only understand what you love". So at least we know where the true challenge lies.

8

Teacher Education as a Form of Discourse: On the Relation of the Public to the Private in Conversations About Teaching

I

One of the great contributions of postmodern thinkers like Michel Foucault and Jacques Derrida to the human sciences generally, in which Education is situated, has been the concept of "discourse". To call a particular way of thinking and acting a discourse is to reference the way meaning is achieved amongst actors by a mutual agreement, direct or tacit, about key terms and actions. A discourse is a kind of self-enclosed semantic and practical universe within which people operate "as if" everyone knew what everyone else is talking about.

Teacher education is a form of discourse in this sense, namely it has, over time, developed its own in-house language and sets of procedures which define it, and within which the various stakeholders feel at home. There are, for example, the easily identifiable roles of Teacher Associate, Faculty Supervisor, Student Teacher, School Administrator, the students in the classrooms, and so on. These roles have certain variances depending on how the different actors characterize their work, but, as anyone who has tried changing or reformulating anything in Teacher Education quickly finds out, all the variances have definite limits to which they can be pushed, because otherwise a systemic crisis occurs, raising the prospect of a fundamental re-ordering of the whole system, or discourse universe, a prospect which, in the most literal sense of the word, is "unthinkable". The French educational philosopher Pierre Boudieu has suggested that the essential conservativism of education has to be addressed at this level, namely appreciating the unthinkability of things being otherwise.[1] To think a different way, and to live it, requires an accessing of concepts and insights that are free of those kinds of dependencies upon which an institution might depend for its self-survival.

The general homogeneity of the discourse of teacher education is what I wish to problematize in this present discussion of the relationship between the public and the private. Anyone involved in teacher education engages in those practices typical of the profession, such as teaching methods courses and supervising students in their teaching practice. We know most of the jargon, the buzz words and what it takes for actions to be judged successful. "Journaling", "collaborative teaching", "consulting", and so on, are terms with which we are familiar, and we know how to use them publically, to make it seem "as if" we know what we're talking about, and certainly to satisfy our various constituents that we do. But each of us also knows, and we may even have confessed this to each other in private, that things are not as smooth as they seem. I, for example, as an instructor in an "Introduction to Teaching" seminar, experience increasing unease with the teacher-education lexicon and corpus of literature precisely for its smoothness. It operates so much "as if" everything was really quite understandable and "as if" all problems were simply problems of implementation rather than, say, events characteristic of a deep contradictedness inherent in human experience itself—a contradictedness that can't be easily dissolved by facile exhortations to "try this and/or that" as a way of remedy.

When I first vetted some of these ideas with a colleague not long ago, his response was to say that the kind of issues I was raising were "philosophical" in nature but that, in teacher education, there was "a whole other dimension" that was ignored in my remarks, especially in the realm of "helping students to become productive members of society". Well, maybe so, maybe not. What it means to be a creative productive member of society, as a teacher, is exactly what should define our work. But how we might proceed in the context of our present situation still needs exploring. I mean, surely as teacher educators we have to recognize the abysmal failure of our schools with Native people and take that failure as a deep comment on *our* procedures and assumptions about life and knowing. And then too there is all the important research that has been done concerning the relationship between school and work, reminding us that under the rhetoric of providing an equalization of opportunity for life prospects, the school actually functions as a giant sorting mechanism which operates precisely against equality by establishing cognitive and existential sieves that serve the values of the middle and upper classes of our culture.[2]

Or, on a more mundane level, I realize that so much of my talk with students is focussed on their *performance*, such that whether things go badly or well is taken to be largely a function of that performance, when in fact I know that very often this is not the case. So, for example, a class that goes well is usually one in which good classroom routines and expectations have already been established by the cooperating teacher over a period of months, and the student looks good to me as a drop-in observer precisely because of his/her being able to operate with a minimum of fuss. Or, as sometimes happens, a general leadership core of students in a class comes from stable, literate families, so that they do not have inordinate emotional and material needs which have to be met before formal teaching can proceed.

The point works the other way too. Student teachers who do badly are often in classrooms already full of troubles, and as we all know, even effective, seasoned teachers have miserable experiences with some classes. These remarks only reinforce the point that classrooms are crystallization centres for the broader tensions at work in the culture and it may well be beyond the power of one teacher or school to deal with them fully.

Naming teacher education as a form of discourse, then, opens the way for an examination of it as a language activity, or set of language practices. As such, we can explore our practices by accessing much of the philosophy of language work now available to us from the so-called postmodernist movement. This enables us to see the way in which what are so often referred to as personal difficulties of students we encounter are in fact symptomatic of much deeper, basically unresolvable, contradictions lying at human experience itself, framed and carried in the culture by linguistic practices. A key point to be made will be that it is one of our firmest assumptions about language itself that needs to be interrogated, namely our assumption that it is possible to name completely what is happening in any situation. Or, to put it another way, maybe we should begin with a problematizing of our desire for smoothness in teacher education, and open the possibility that an over-determination for certain things to happen in a certain way for, say, certification purposes, is itself a form of cultural prejudice which may in fact get in the way of genuine creativity in teaching and may, in the name of certainty, actually exercise a kind of violence against children as well as against our students and ourselves. I often invite my students to respect the mystery that lies at the heart of teaching, a mystery carried through children, who embody that which is yet-to-be-revealed. Much of what constitutes good teaching simply cannot be known in advance of a genuine encounter with children. But this is to get ahead of ourselves.

II

Each of the three movements in contemporary language theory explored in what follows is oriented by questions that postmodernist formulations have opened up, although each is oriented to language and life in different ways.

Modernism/Logocentrism/Representationalism

Modernism, logocentrism and representationalism are key terms in the critique postmodernists have made against what is perceived to be the dominating motif of language and action in the Western tradition.[3] Driven by a preoccupation with essence, being and substance, Western thinking since the Greeks (Plato and Aristotle) has been underwritten by a desire for stability and security through the naming of things in the world and an anchoring of the terms as if they bore a fixed relation to something Real. Words are taken to *represent* the real world, and the real world is invoked by our very speaking about it. If there is doubt about this, the failure is understood to be one of incorrect interrogative procedure or bad science, with greater attention needed for the defining and clarification of terms, and an atomizing or analyzing of experience into manageable order. Indeed, keeping one's house, one's papers, in order is taken to be the chief mark of virtue. The basic gesture of logocentrism is the search for the meaning of something, some experience, then an anchoring and stabilizing and storing of it as the cultural sediment of personal and collective life. The *dictionary*, along with other disciplinary canons, i.e., classical foundational texts, is the noblest icon in the logocentric display, because in the presence of doubt it provides an orthodoxy to which to refer.

In teacher education it is not hard to see how this operates. We have checklists of essential student competencies, generic teaching skills, instruction modules, teaching styles inventories, and so on which provide a sense of security both to us as faculty and to our students by suggesting that what counts as good teaching can be somehow anchored "really". Real teachers are thought to be identifiable through these indexes, and if not, then the indexes are recommended for change to more accurately reflect what is known to be true. Or if a particular student's behaviours are not reflected in the indexes then the student is deemed clearly not suitable for teaching (Socrates beware).

Equally well known is the genuine practical difficulty of translating the indexes in concrete situations. Our teacher associates are always complaining about "the forms" we use to evaluate practice teaching, and the complaints have not been assuaged even though we are on our third form revision in five years. Similarly, recently we spent hours and hours trying to establish a workable definition of "outstanding" for use in practicum evaluation. But the harder we try the more frustrating it gets as we realize that, not only are there so many different variables involved in any situation, but the variables are all related to each other and cannot simply be singled out for purposes of control. So we usually end up with some broad categories and then recognize that "it's all a matter of interpretation". That we might sometimes feel guilty about interpretively using our subjective judgements in matters like these is itself a topic worthy of serious historical examination, having to do with the rise of science, and the cultural schizophrenia inspired by Cartesian dualism regarding subjectivity and objectivity, but that is another story.[4]

No, the problem of trying to establish definitively the nature of the Real—the real teacher, the real teacher associate, the real student teacher—the very desire for such establishment may itself be the problem. It's a deep cultural hoax, as Derrida and the postmodernists might put it, although to call it *that,* to call it *anything,* is only an extension of the same difficulty. So the question is not how to put an end to such indeterminacy, which is only another logocentric form of determinism in a new guise, but rather how can we live with indeterminacy creatively. It is this project that the postmodernists have attempted to take up. If our practices and actions are not fixable in any final sense, then how can we proceed at all, how can we describe, evaluate and share our experiences? It is here that the languages of play, dance and aesthetics come to prominence, and we are led to the second language modus for considering teacher education today, that of postmodernism/deconstructionism.

Postmodernism/Deconstructionism

Whenever the terms postmodernism and deconstructionism are invoked in educational circles it is usually as a form of swearing. People see in the self-conscious de-anchoring of tradition a powerful threat to many of the positions and ideas we have long held dear, especially, perhaps, the dearest tradition of all, that of Truth. Postmodernism is seen as an invitation to relativism, even nihilism, whereby, because the foundational Real cannot be secured, everything is reduced to flux. In the next section of the paper I will attempt to address these concerns through a consideration of what can be called "contemplative/hermeneutic" modes of inquiry, but before doing so, certain other aspects concerning postmodernism need to be discussed.

The first is to say that, in my view at least, the questions which postmodernism has articulated are not simply philosophical or intellectual challenges that some foreign university professors have dreamed up to disturb the unenlightened. Rather, the postmodern formulations only serve to articulate what, in a deep and subtle way, is already everywhere the case, namely that there is a crisis of epistemic authority at work in the Western tradition which cannot be denied or overcome simply by trying to go "back to the basics". As we have discovered, trying to establish what the "basics" are is exactly the problem. So when I go to visit one of my student teachers in his or her school placement setting, I do not ask myself the academic question of "what would postmodernism say" about this or that practice. Rather, I find the contemporary classroom *already* postmodern in character. Even though a school may have its "statement of philosophy" and teachers' plans are underwritten by "clearly defined goals and objectives", the relationship between these documents and what transpires in actual practice is tenuous at best. This is because there is a cultural grammar at work which is much more powerful in its influence than any self-consciously derived good intentions of this or that school, teacher or classroom.

Perhaps the best analogue for postmodern consciousness in the common realm is remote-control television watching, whereby consciousness is shaped no longer by a linear textual imagination of authors and books, or by a shared sense of community, but rather by flashing icons and storylines that last no longer than an hour. Furthermore, the power to decide whether or not to meaningfully engage what is presented on television is radically concentrated in the hands of individual viewers through the remote control device which enables the viewer to shift attention to this or that "channel" at will and whim. The cultural consequence is a kind of rarefaction and radical atomization of the influence of the external world—the break-up of received tradition, we might call it—in favor of individual choice and action.[5]

Today's classrooms, particularly at the elementary level, are postmodern places in the sense that the dizzying array of projects and activities that prevails everywhere constitutes a kind of cosmic dance which has its own justification and animus and does not ultimately depend on formal curricular mandates from the ministry of education. In other words, whether one is studying dinosaurs or math problems seems secondary to the more primary interest of being engaged in activity itself. Indeed, like "dead air" on the radio, the possibility of students having nothing to do is the inspiration for many teachers' worst nightmares. Planning is taken to mean assuming full responsibility for filling up time and space to full capacity—giving taxpayers full value for the dollar.

The result is a certain air of distraction, and a rather compulsive quality in the actions of both teachers and students. Even more serious, though, and this leads us to further insights from the postmodernists, especially J-F. Lyotard, is the consequence of a kind of cultural amnesia taking root in the midst of everything, a certain forgetfulness of purpose, or a deepening difficulty in identifying how or whether the activities fit together in any meaningful way. Discernable in some quarters is even a certain loss of care for the project of integration itself. In Lyotard's terms, this is precisely the character of the postmodern condition, namely the loss or the end of "grand narratives"[6] which in former times united all human action in the Western tradition around great themes such as Truth, Redemption and Enlightenment.

Some postmodernists, particularly J-F. Lyotard, entertain an acceptance of this particular condition as not only inevitable, but desirable. It speaks of the end of ideology and dogmatism in the human realm and a radical acceptance of human differences without the burden of moralism masquerading as certifiable interpretation. In a way, I agree that this is desirable. The postmodern movement holds great promise for a surge of creative activity by affording new kinds of co-incidence between human beings. In the context of schools and classrooms, one positive effect of the freeing of students and teachers from the burden of dogmatic authority (a dogmatism carried powerfully and subtly in, for example, the way Piagetian psychology is prescribed as a form of pedagogic truth without consideration for its Darwinian deterministic undertones[7])—is a new kind of pedagogic relation, one based on genuine reciprocation between teacher and student rather than on the former logics of transmission and control. In many ways, today's classrooms are friendlier, nicer places to be than they were fifty years ago because there is a deeper acceptance of the differences in children, for example, and a diminishing desire to banish all children under a rubric of the Same.

In my view, however, it is premature to rest with a simple acceptance of the polyphony of curricular and pedagogic voices in teaching today, or within the culture generally. This is because pure acceptance of difference without a consideration of the meaning and implication of that difference for all concerned only intensifies the isolation of individuals in their difference. If I merely accept you in your difference without exploring *how* you are different and how *your* difference reflects *my* difference from you, that is, how knowing you invites self-reflection on my part—without such a conversation we merely exist as two solitudes. And that is what strikes me as the chief danger in the postmodern condition, namely the increasing isolation of persons within the cages of their own subjectivities without any historical, philosophical or linguistic means for establishing deep and meaningful connection with others. A loss of capacity for intimacy is one way of putting it. In teaching it may even be characterized by teachers being enfolded in the mannerisms of generosity and care for students in the name, say, of good reinforcement psychology or the student teaching evaluation category of "Displays a positive attitude". Because of a deep incapacity to be affected by the difference of the Other embodied in one's students, however, this positive manner often has more the air of an affectation and it contains its own pedagogic violence. It is in this relationship of "difference" to "same" that I wish to explore living creatively with our differences *together*.

When Derrida says "there is nothing outside the text"[8] he locates his interests as a scholar primarily concerned with texts and problems of language, particularly the relationship between speaking and writing. But if, as Paul Ricoeur[9] has done, we extrapolate the notion of text to mean the text of life, life as it presents itself to us, then we are in a position to gain insight into the teaching relationship in new ways. To say "there is nothing outside" is to problematize the outside/inside public/private dualism of Cartesian self-enclosure which underwrites the myths of subjectivity and objectivity in our culture, and which renders our relation with the external world, the world which is object to my subjectivity, as essentially antagonistic.[10] The phenomenologies of control that dominate educational discourse seem to me to find their origin precisely in that relation.

"There is nothing outside" does not mean, however, that we are now banished into an amorphous glue of collective subjectivity with everything now "inside". It simply means that everything that is required for a full expression of our situation is already, everywhere, always present. There is no external Archimedean reference point from which we might objectively observe ourselves, or in relation to which we might register our virtue. Neither is the Derridean formulation simply an invitation to self-satisfaction, because full presence also implies full absence, that is to say, everything I understand myself to be *now* must also include everything that I am *not*, everything that I have denied or neglected in order to be the present me. This kind of sensitivity to a vibrant dialectic between presence and absence, self and non-self, visible and invisible is well understood in oriental wisdom traditions, not just postmodernism. In the West too the medieval mystics knew it well. Consider for example the words of John of the Cross:[11]

> To come to the pleasure you have not
> You must go by a way you enjoy not
> To come to the knowledge you have not
> You must go by a way in which you know not
> To come to the possession you have not
> You must go by a way in which you possess not
> To come to be what you are not
> You must go by a way in which you are not.

In Derridean terms, absences play within me as a form of "*trace*",[12] residual in my present practices. This is true of cultures just as it is of individuals. The fact that Canada's classrooms are now made up of immigrants from all over the world is a reminder that the self-enclosed identity of the former imperial European powers was indeed permeable. The presence in our classrooms of refugee children from Africa, Asia and Latin America is a form of *visitation of an absence* in the sense that they represent a Derridean trace within the imperial white bosom, a reminder of the plundering consciousness of the logocentric imagination. Gregory Ulmer[13] refers to the "imperial dispensation" of logocentrism.

The refugee example points to another feature of the trace, which is its agentic quality, its sense of agency. As Harold Coward[14] has described it: "The trace is not simply a passive past for it proclaims as much as it recalls—it has impulsive force, the force of articulation or differentiation". One's personal or collective past can never be cocooned, therefore, into sentimentalized history or nostalgia, but must constantly be "faced" within a dialectic of "protention and retention that one would install in the heart of the present".[15]

Nor is the trace simply an artifact in or from the *past*. It also has the character of that-which-is-yet-to-come. This is what Derrida[16] calls "the as-yet-unnameable which is constantly proclaiming itself", held for us in silences and spaces and in our senses of "lack" (another Derridean term) and desire. But again, what we think we lack is not "outside", but always everywhere already present. To paraphrase David Loy,[17] "What I have sought I have never lacked".

These formulations lead naturally to the third modus I wish to address, that of the *contemplative/hermeneutic* traditions, and it is within that discourse that I will attempt to ask for the shape of teaching and pedagogy responsible to our times.

The Contemplative/Hermeneutic Imagination

David Loy again has put it well: "Perhaps this is what we have always sought: not to become real but to realize that we don't need to become real". Instead of lamenting the loss of the Real through the postmodern critique, we can begin with an acceptance that "Reality" itself is a cultural, categorical artifact that has left us chasing our tails. There is no purely distinct reality "out there", such as "out there in the schools" for education faculty members and for student teachers. We can begin by accepting that we do different kinds of work but to label one "real" and the other not so is simply artifice. All of us and all of our constituents share the same deep reality although we find ourselves in it at different points and moments. The question is how to orient to that which we already are, together.

> The epitome of the human realm is to be stuck in a huge traffic jam of discursive thought. You are so busy thinking that you cannot learn anything at all. The constant churning out of ideas, plans, hallucinations and dreams is quite a different mentality from that of the realm (of Wisdom).

So says the great contemplative teacher Chogyam Trungpa.[18] The ability to attend to ourselves, to our students, to our collective lives depends first and foremost on a form of *stopping*, and the creation of a space in which we can truly listen and hear ourselves. In our own teacher education program at the University of Lethbridge—and it has a reputation for being a good one—the most appalling aspect to me is that it is so full, so busy, so noisy. This is usually taken as a sign that "real" things are happening, that there is no "wasted" time, that "standards of performance are maintained at a consistently high level". Again, this reflects the modernist three-fold impulse to *name, anchor* and *accrete*, so that fullness is understood only one way—as an absence of space. And it is precisely that mentality which gets transposed and reproduced in schools, just as it underwrites the rhetoric about success in the worlds of business and politics.

The problem is that such an approach is simply unsustainable. It produces exhaustion, to borrow a term from industry. It is also unmindful of its lack, the awareness that fullness also includes emptiness. Whole language, for example, cannot just mean a full bag of words, constructs and grammars, or even "open approaches" to the question of language acquisition. I mean, in what way is language not always already everywhere whole? Of course, if we ask in what way language is broken such that it needs to be put back together, we can say quite clearly that it was broken by the self-consciousness of science, and the dominating language of technology which reduced language to object without attending to the matter of its own pre-existing language. No, language will be whole when we stop attending to language as such, instrumentally—when we stop being so self-conscious about it—and when we attend more directly to how we use it in the manner of our living.

In the teacher education context this means attending to how we conduct ourselves, here and now, just as much as it means taking responsibility for specific knowledges we feel our students must have before they "go out". It means learning to be whole ourselves, attending to our wholeness, which means attending to our suppressions, our denials just as much as to what we already celebrate publically about ourselves. In deconstructive terms, our suppressions, lacks and so on are made most transparent in the faces of those most different from us. Others always serve initially as a reminder of what we are not. So it is that the fullness of my person requires for its genuine maturity a full openness to others, rather than a strict self-enclosure within, say, a predefined identity as "Teacher". Genuine growth in self-understanding is the consequence of an ongoing four-fold action: an opening to others, an engagement with others, followed by a form of self-reflection implying self-modification, followed in turn by re-engagement. It is this four-fold action within the dialectic of self and non-self that affirms the profoundly ethical character of the deconstructive project, providing the basis of a genuine meeting between people.[19] At once, too, it locates that project within the deep structure of the contemplative/meditative Wisdom traditions of the world, providing a means through which positive human integration is possible without the violence of the ego-logical self-understanding of the modern West within which so much of our teacher education efforts are practised.

The deconstructive dialectic of self and non-self also contains a hermeneutical/interpretive dynamic which acknowledges the way in which one's concept of self emerges constitutively within a storied horizon of past, present and future.[20] It is this hermeneutical dimension which is most profoundly lacking in the more exaggerated postmodern formulations, and which lack accounts for the clear signs of evasion and irresponsibility that haunt much of that work. Human consciousness is constituted through the storied quality of its affairs much more powerfully than through, say, abstract ideas or intellections which are in any case a fairly modern invention. The opening of self to the non-self involves primarily an opening of our stories to each other, an acceptance of how we are always everywhere already living in the midst of stories, involving a surfacing and a sharing of that which constitutes us. This is difficult, but it provides the necessary means by which we can see one another in each other in a deep way—to get beyond pure difference to creative relation and the possibility of true care.

As a teacher it is impossible to reach and teach children effectively without knowing their stories, just as it is impossible to be available to another person's story unless one undertakes in an ongoing way the profoundly challenging, often fearsome task of deconstructing one's own. Not long ago in my *Introduction to Teaching* seminar, we were experimenting with this kind of exploration and I invited people to share family stories that might, say, be subjects of conversation around the dinner table. Stories concerned with school, business and work were ones most frequently shared—fruitful topics indeed by themselves. Then one person, whose parents were immigrants, said that in her house the story of how the family came to Canada from Latin America was often brought forward, usually as a way of relishing the family's good fortune here. I then asked the class, quite innocently, if others could relate why, say, their grandparents came to this land. Only ten of the fifteen students could do so. The rest, as it turned out, came from Germany after the war, and the subject of their journey to Canada was strictly taboo even within immediate family circles.[21] For one older student in particular this was an extremely difficult topic to discuss because she had very painful memories of the poverty, destitution and shunning she had, as a child, witnessed her parents suffering on arrival in Canada in the late 1940s. But her revelation broke open in an extremely positive way a new understanding on behalf of the group of the shortsightedness of making superficial judgements of other people, and an appreciation of how identity reproduces itself and stagnates in a bad way precisely to the degree that it refuses to be opened. The entire episode also made possible for the class a new appreciation of the contradictedness of human experience, and an acceptance of how that contradictedness is not to be taken as a problem-to-be-solved but somehow lived creatively within.

How can we overcome the fear of difference and learn to see ourselves in each other—how, in other words, can we become truly self-reflective persons, not just narcissistic "reflective practitioners"? Possibilities for this are well formulated by the metaphor of "Indra's Net" in the Hua-yen school of Mahayana Buddhism.[22] According to the story, in the heavenly abode there is hung a net that stretches out infinitely in all directions. In each eye of the net is a single glittering jewel, and since the net itself is infinite in all dimensions, the jewels are infinite in number. If one arbitrarily selects one of the jewels and inspects it closely, one discovers that in its polished surface there are reflected all the other jewels in the net. Not only that, but each of the jewels reflected in this one jewel is also reflecting all the other jewels so that there is an infinite reflecting process occurring. In the Mahayana school, the story of Indra's net is taken to symbolize a cosmos in which there is an infinitely repeated interrelationship among all the members of the cosmos. This relationship is said to be one of simultaneous mutual identity and mutual inter-causality.[23]

In teacher education terms, Indra's net suggests more than the obvious insights of mutual identity and mutual inter-causality taken in a vulgar way. Also, it seems to me there is a pointing to how a teacher must, in the most profound sense of the terms, take up his or her identity as a form of ethical responsible *self-work*, working to *be* that which can reflect the light of others. Without this, teaching takes the form of a projection *on* to others of everything that has not obtained resolution in oneself. In deep cultural terms this is what accounts, I suspect, for what Stanley Aaronowitz[24] has called the excessive "hyperbole" of educational discourse, reflecting a hyperextended desire to turn the world into an image of one's own limited shape and character, which in turn is also a way of trying to secure that identity even more intensely. Children, by virtue of both their malleability and the fact that they issue *from us,* are perfect targets for the multifarious machineries of self-reproduction available in a technological age. Unavailable or lacking in such a technological construction is a free availability *to* children and an acceptance of what they already are. There is a saying of Thich Nhat Hahn: "if you do not see the children you will not see the Buddha" because, insofar as they are already unselfconscious, "children are living Buddhas".[25] There are well-known parallels of this understanding in the Judeo-Christian tradition. The point is that education, including teacher education, is severely poverty-stricken if its momentum is only one-way, that is, projecting onto a self-defined externalized world of, say, children, or student teachers, a litany of plans and intentions, without an embracing of that agenda within a project of self-healing on our part as teachers. Teachers must understand the way in which their work, insofar as it operates unselfreflectively in the manner of which we have been speaking, is heavily implicated in the rationalist distortions of pure technique. Understanding "simultaneous mutual identity and mutual inter-causality" contains within itself a call to assuming full responsibility for oneself in the presence of others, a willingness to take up the hard work of attending to the tain of one's own mirror. The rhetoric one often hears in staff-rooms and faculty lounges about "What I do in private is of no public concern" belies a cultural heritage that is its own worst enemy.

9

The Problem for the South Is the North
(But the Problem for the North Is the North)

The Brazilian educator Paulo Freire used to say that his speaking and writing were always in the form of a "report from the workface" of his educational concerns and were never undertaken simply for academic and scholarly reasons. He wanted to emphasize the deeply human commitment which must be at the heart of anything we do and say as educators. The workface from which I wish to report concerns the question of how, as an educator, I can fulfill my responsibility to my own people—my own people whom I love yet who, as I do, live under an economic and epistemological dispensation which is a problem for most of the rest of the world.

Pedagogically speaking, understanding the link between First and Third Worlds is not simply a problem of information. Many First World students now have a good intellectual grasp of such economic issues as the operation of multinational corporations and the problem of the international monetary system crippling Third World economies, and so on. What we lack, typically, is something much deeper, call it a deeper sense of human communion or simple solidarity with the world. We lack a deep understanding of how we are all bound together on this planet. Maybe it could be said that what we lack is a simple love for life; perhaps that is *our* poverty. We are reluctant to understand how violence inheres in the deep substructures of our thinking and our everyday life practice, and here I speak of a violence that is subtle, often benign, but nonetheless real insofar as it breathes through most of our assumptions about what it means to live in the world. The work of George Lakoff and Mark Johnson,[1] for example, shows how even our everyday speech is permeated with the language of war:

Your claims are *indefensible*.
His criticisms were *right on target*.
I *demolished* his argument!
You disagree? Okay, *shoot*!

If you use that *strategy*, he'll *wipe you out*.
He *shot down* all of my arguments.

So in my own theoretical and academic work, I struggle to understand this particular poverty of ours in the West. I work to understand the historical, political and social reasons why, for example (and many empirical studies can document this) we increasingly cannot talk to one another meaningfully. Conversation, for example, becomes a war over concepts, definitions, and so on. Men and women learn to distrust one another under a banner of "gender differences" or gender wars; children and parents are increasingly alienated from each other under a rubric of "generation gap"; and, perhaps more disastrously, pedagogical handbooks are increasingly assuming a paramilitary language concerned with "discipline techniques", "classroom control", and "behaviour management".

Where does this come from, this inability to draw close, to be intimate, to simply be with others in a good way; and how can we act responsibly in response to it? There are many familiar points of analysis, such as the French Revolution and the elevation of the idea of the individual and individual human rights.

Another approach may be more significant in the long run. This is the tradition of inquiry that begins with the German philosopher Nietzsche in the nineteenth century and is followed through by Martin Heidegger, H-G. Gadamer, Michel Foucault, Jacques Derrida, Jean-Francois Lyotard and others. These thinkers might be named the "prophets of modernity" because they are the ones who mapped, in my view at least, the existential and living realities of modern western peoples most sensitively, even profoundly. I wish to briefly develop three themes from these thinkers and then give some examples of work with my own students where we try to work for a way through to new ways of speaking and acting.

Theme One

Western philosophy itself has moved humanity to a position of distancing, non-involvement and abstraction from meaningful life. It is the fundamental dilemma of a scientific and technocratic way of thinking about and organizing social life. J. Bouveresse, in his commentary on the work of the postmodern novelist Robert Musil, puts the matter this way:

Given the state of science in particular, a man is made only of what people say he is or of what is done with what he is.... The world is one in which lived events have become independent of man.... It is a world of happening, of what happens without it happening to anyone (in particular), and without anyone's being responsible.[2]

We don't have to look far to see how this form of thinking operates. A recent United Nations report argues that the world is in for a massive recession if

...cuts in the U.S. budget deficit are not combined with moves by Japan and West Germany to increase demand for goods in their economies. Domestic demand in the surplus market economies will need to be boosted if the slowdown is not to develop into a global recession.[3]

This is a strikingly good example of how theory (economic theory in this case) takes precedence over situated life, how human beings are asked to live in the service of theory at the expense of a trust in their own experience. Is the UN really suggesting that I, along with my friends, *must* go out and buy another television, refrigerator, washer and dryer, in order for the world to be saved? We are already living in deep suspense between our employers and our bank managers over credit ratings and financing schemes. We are already reduced to being anonymous actors in the unfolding inexorable drama of free market enterprise. How much more can we take? No, the point is that in the postmodern condition, human beings *in particular* (you and me) have been translated out of the discourse about humanity. We need to work to recover our Selves in the context of everything we do, and resist those pressures to perform in ways that rob us of our dignity.

Theme Two

High-technology societies become driven by the criteria of performance efficiency, testing, evaluation, accountability, and so on. This produces a rapid forward momentum in which individuals feel incredible pressure to perform but are never quite sure how. In the nineteenth century the philosopher Nietzsche described, prophetically, the condition of the modern university student:

He feels he can neither lead nor defend himself.... His condition is

undignified, even dreadful; he keeps between the two extremes of work at
high pressure and a state of melancholy enervation.... He seeks consolation
in hasty and incessant action so as to hide himself from himself.[4]

This sense of high-propulsion, out of control forward motion is experienced
at many levels, seeping deeply throughout our collective being. Jacques Derrida[5]
has noted that we refer to the nuclear arms race as a "race" precisely because we
are in the grip of a particular understanding of temporality, a movement from a
beginning to an end, an eschatological understanding of time which has
Judeo-Christian and biblical roots. It is as if nuclear war may result as
self-fulfilling prophecy, an end toward which we somehow feel inexorably
driven. Certainly much of the rhetoric from the Reagan-Bush era spoke from this
ground; and it is very dangerous, precisely because it is linked to our deepest
myths, our deepest beliefs about ourselves. Other examples are legion. I name a
few to let you fill in your own scenarios. Why is it now "in" to refer to "fast
tracking", "research tracking", and the importance of "being on the right track".
Tracks are a form of guidance that allow no deviation. In education, we need to
ask why the language of accountability, evaluation and supervision reigns
supreme. If it is driven simply by an interest in "improvement", it must be
asked in whose service is the improvement, in what direction is it moving? And
what is the effect on the quality of our life together? My sense is that it produces
paranoia, competitiveness and a generalized feeling of being ill. J-F. Lyotard
makes the same point.[6] He shows that a preoccupation with evaluation actually
destabilizes the social/education fabric and produces results exactly counter to
what was originally hoped for.

Theme Three

In Western consciousness, the fundamental split between subject and object
that began with Descartes produces a mode of acting which comes to be
understood as a performance *on* life and others, rather than *with* life and with each
other. Even our charity can take on a tone of condescension, because Cartesian
consciousness is not self-reflective, i.e., it does not, cannot, ask, what
difference does it make for me to know *you*? Yet experience tells us that any
"meaningful" relationship implies that my life must become different as a result
of knowing you; otherwise, we just go on living as two solitudes. As the
Trappist monk Thomas Merton, once said: "If I give you my truth but do not
receive your truth in return, there can be no truth between us."[7] Without true

reciprocity, human relations are reduced to a power struggle, but the recovery of reciprocity implies a new way of being together whereby we put emphasis on our collective journey rather than on, say, the accumulation of knowledge *per se*. Reciprocity means that ontology must take precedence over epistemology.

In education, this has implications for the way we think about children. Many are now suggesting that children are one of the most marginalized groups in contemporary Western society.[8] This is not to say that we do not express concern for children. We do, but the talk reflects a singular lack of self-reflexity on our part as adults. This is what undergirds the increasing alienation of children from meaningful participation in the life-stream of thought and action. David Kennedy[9] speaks of the way in which so much educational theory is "adultomorphic", taking some adult end-state as the norm towards which children should be driven. Thus, children grow up always feeling that they are missing something, or are fundamentally inadequate in some way.

Learning to Read Your Story in the Context of the Story

At the University of Lethbridge, in the graduate program, we have been working to design forms of pedagogical action which help us get in touch with our experiences of the world in ways not afforded through conventional or more prescriptive modes of inquiry. Many of these activities, which fall under the general rubric of "Learning to read your story in the context of the Story", have been inspired by the pedagogy of Paulo Freire and Ira Shor.[10]

"Pain-mapping" for example, involves learning to understand one's pains as a sign of the locale of insight into one's situation. We begin with an understanding that in a technocratic, instrumental culture, pain is always understood as pathology—something to be rooted out. We don't want to deny that; we simply want to take up the question of our difficulties as being not just reflective of personal problems but as somehow linked to the way we organize and live our lives collectively. Our diseases must be understood not just biologically but as dis-eases, signs of particular ruptural formations in the social fabric. Most diseases today in the West can be related to stress and isolation.

"Time Studies" involve learning to read how we spend our time. People are invited to stop-clock a typical day, itemizing what they are doing, specifically, every fifteen minutes. It is often a shock to realize how much of one's time is spent, for example, fulfilling bureaucratic expectations, or being involved in activities from which one feels somehow profoundly disengaged. We take this as a sign of modern "colonized" behaviour, i.e., behaviour which depends for its meaningful interpretation on referents outside of the insiders' experience of the action.

"Conversation Windows" is an activity whereby people will go out into the marketplace, stand on a street corner, sit in a bus station, or in a laundromat, and simply record/write down the conversations which are going on naturally around them. This is done in an attempt to bring the voice of the average person into formal deliberations about life together. We believe this voice is typically lost in conventional modes of research—even in so-called qualitative research, which, because it can still be interventionist in basic gesture, shuts down what is most naturally on people's minds. Conversation windows help to document what is on people's minds before a microphone is put in their face or an interview schedule predetermines the direction of a conversation.

"Sound Studies" involve learning to map all the subliminal sounds around us, such as the tempo of people walking the corridors, the sound of technical machinery such as air conditioners, cars honking, squealing. In identifying and naming these, we are then able to ask about their influence over, in and about us and to interpret the way in which they link up with the formal, generative, dominant themes of the culture. We want to gain a sense of how, when we talk of ideology, for instance, we are not talking just about some interesting intellectual idea but of how people's (our) deep consciousness of the world comes to be formed and structured in everyday commonplace events. Here I have been very much influenced by the work of Alfred Tomatis on hearing as the primary human sense. Also Stephen Feld at the University of Texas at Austin is doing fascinating studies on the relationship between sound structure and social structure.[11]

The pedagogical point of such exercises involves an identification of the deep structures of the world around us and then a re-interpretation of how to live with, for or against those structures in a more creative way. Our creative energy becomes more clearly focused. As an instructor, I have found it interesting to witness how, at the beginning, students seem dumbstruck when faced with the task of interpreting their commonplace world. It seems silly to pore over a transcript of conversation fragments searching for deep meaning. But this very incapacity to see the immediate world as a profoundly interpreted world is exactly a problem for our time in which powerful media machinery interprets the world for us as if the given interpretation was/is the real world. The ability to see that our world *is* an interpreted world, not just a given world, is the first step towards a more profound autonomy of persons. I might say that beginning this process of personal reclamation is very disturbing for some students. The sudden realization that so much of what one does in a highly materialistic, instrumental bureaucratic culture is simply ridiculous and "colonial" is like suddenly realizing you have got your pants on backwards or your shoes on the wrong feet, or that your father is a criminal. But there is an exhilaration and deep humour about it too and I think these are always signs of a breakthrough.

I am reluctant to end this paper with a typical "conclusion" because conclusions are dangerous. A key point to be made here is that the human conversation about what it is to live humanly is never over, and we have a deep responsibility to protect the conditions under which that conversation can continue. Suffice it to say for now that for us in North America, there are very severe oppressions, too. They are the oppressions of the "average person" in a massively mechanistic, technical culture, a culture with little capacity for surprise or spontaneity. Ours are different oppressions from those experienced by people in the Third/South World in the sense that Third World oppressions are so transparent, so easily identifiable. Ours are more hidden, more elusive, because everywhere, the impulse to allay a facing of ourselves is embroidered with a high gloss and a promise that if just one more thing is done, or purchased or rallied around, everything will be fine. The North survives on the basis of false promises: this is the hidden ghost of a consumerist mentality. Many of us, though, are suffering from exhaustion, but in the course of doing so, we are realizing that our pains are exactly what can form a foundation of solidarity with our brothers and sisters in the South. I think our suffering can be traced to common sources, common theoretical and philosophical roots in the sense that the essential theoretical and practical infrastructure of the world today is held together by loyalties to commonly recognizable figures such as Adam Smith and Karl Marx. The task for all of us is to deconstruct and reinterpret the Western Enlightenment project of absolutizing (dogmatizing) social theory as a form of truth, and then learn to trust our own experience of the world as our greatest gift. Let us unite in that trust and learn to live better, together.

10

On Being Critical About Language: The Critical Theory Tradition and Implications for Language Education

Since the end of the Cold War, not much is heard in educational circles about that tradition which reached its peak of influence in, say, the late 1970s, namely Critical Theory. Even in Germany where it all began shortly after World War II with the establishment of the Institute for Social Research at the University of Frankfurt—even there names like Jurgen Habermas and Max Horkheimer are virtually *passé*, or so a colleague from the University of Munich informed me recently. This is unfortunate because we owe that tradition much: it brought to our attention a basic lexicon of social criticism. Words like *ideology, dialectical, objectification* and *commodification* would not likely be as well known today without their popularization two decades ago during the cultural revolution in Europe, and especially in North America under the intellectual inspiration of the Frankfurt School.

The absence of an informed critical tradition in language education may be a sign of trouble, a sign not just of the reigning sovereignty of conservative forces today, but in a deep and subtle way a sign of the diminishment of language itself, which, since Wittgenstein, means also a diminishment of human life. The rise of religious fundamentalism, for instance, should be of critical interest to language educators because, in a certain way, biblical literalism, for example, is not so different from the kind of straitjacketing of language made necessary in the commands of the computer programmer. It has to do with the forcing of words to mean one thing and one thing only. It's what happens when one regards language primarily in instrumental terms, that is, as a tool of communication, a sign in turn of the technicization of our collective imagination.

Similarly the increasing literalism at work in the demands of our undergraduates ("Tell me exactly what it is you want in this assignment") reflects somehow a shaping of the imagination away from an ability to think analogically, metaphorically, poetically. Indeed as Robert Dana suggests, we are becoming "genuinely indifferent to poetry",[1] which means becoming indifferent to the full play of possibilities inherent in human discourse, a disposition which underwrites dogmatism. In this paper, then, I would like to resuscitate some of the central themes of the Critical Theory position in order to consider what it might mean to be critical about language and language education. In taking up this task I am very indebted to the historical work of Paul Connerton, Martin Jay and Susan Buck-Morss.[2]

Formally speaking, Critical Theory is associated with a group of scholars who fled the National Socialists of Weimar Germany in the 1930s. After the war, they established the Institute for Social Research at the University of Frankfurt, which became known internationally as "The Frankfurt School". The key figures were, or are, Max Horkheimer, Theodore Adorno, Herbert Marcuse, Erich Fromm, Walter Benjamin and later Jurgen Habermas. The group found its conceptual genesis in Marx's *Critique of Political Economy*, and the concept of totality in the Hegelian-Marxism of George Lukacs.

If one theme could be identified as being common to all Frankfurt thinking, it would be the belief that no specific detail of social life could be comprehended unless related to the historical whole, that is, to social structure in relation to superstructure. Horkheimer and Adorno, for example, argued that every word in a language can only be understood in its linkage to a semantic and material universe which carries its meaning.[3] Even simple words in children's books, like *ball, bat, dog,* carry an ideological trace of the structuration of social relations in any given society, connected as such words are to basic concerns about property, ownership and the organization and development of leisure activities.

The idea of *critique* central to Critical Theory is a product of the eighteenth century Enlightenment, and the project of *Aufklarung*, or the clarification of the conditions of enlightened reason. The interest of critique is to ensure that nothing, no prejudice or pre-judgement, should stand in the way of thinking itself. The basic gesture of such critique is "oppositional thinking", a reflex of "thinking against" in order that thinking itself does not become stuck in thinking only one way.

For the Frankfurt School, critique also denotes an interest in both the relationship between the *conditions* of possible knowledge and the *constraints* on the formation of it. The first aspect was the chief preoccupation of Kant's *Critique of Pure Reason*. Kant was concerned about how we come to perceive the world as an ordered place, and his answer was that ordering is the work of perception. The faculty of perception produces the mode in which reality appears to us; that is, we constitute reality by virtue of *a priori* ordering categories embedded between our ears.

Linguists who have taken Kant at face value dominate much language study today. Those who define their task as the identification and maintenance of linguistic rules are all basically Kantian in orientation. The most famous examples are the early Wittgenstein's analysis of *following a rule*, and Chomsky's concepts of *generative rules* and *linguistic competence*. For Critical Theory, however, far more important than the necessary conditions for possible knowledge are the systemic constraints which block and distort the formation of individuals and societies in their epistemic and social development.

Paradoxically, constraints contain within themselves the source of their own destruction. This idea came from Hegel, who, in his famous description of the master/slave relationship, showed how the constraints placed by the master on the slave open up for the latter the possibility of genuine growth through *negation*. Through his labour, the opportunity for which is provided by the master, the slave is able to produce works which in turn allow the slave insight into his own situation and thereby contribute to his power to change it.

Within this overall sense of critique, then, human rationality has a history grounded not just in reason *per se* or in perception or cognitive function, but also in the historic forms within which such activity arises. As has been shown by Basil Bernstein, for example, the implications of this are powerfully suggestive for understanding the language of the school and the dialectical origins of teacher and student talk.[4]

The assumed sense of criticism in Critical Theory can be transposed to a consideration of language in several ways. For one thing, the critical refusal to separate conditions from constraints in the development of language means we cannot speak of language simply as an abstraction. Attempts to cast a mode of speaking which is neutral or value-free (Esperanto, for instance, or the language of robots) miss an essential point, which is that to speak means to speak from a particular place and set of circumstances. Critical theory reminds us of our deep investment, our embodiment in everything we do or say. An attention to language means also an attention to the life conditions of those dwelling in the language. As a language teacher, one cannot urge a better way of speaking on children without at the same time addressing a better way of life for them. In relative and material terms, a poor speaker leads a poor life.

Furthermore, a language teacher who begins with an acknowledgement of the material, historical conditions under which any language comes to be what it is, also in that move provides an opening through which a language student can grasp his/her own future and sense of human agency. That is, when, as a language educator, I tell my students that we speak English here because nineteenth century political and military victories of the British brought English settlement and tongue to this land, I am also opening the possibility that things could in the future be different. Every non-Anglo student in the class should understand that inability to speak English is a political condition, not just a personal lack, and as a political condition it can be changed. The politicization of language also underscores the linguistic conditions of malleability and permeability, conditions which are a problem only for conservatives. The full possibilities inherent in language use always suffer from constraints (conventions, rules) which, by virtue of their link to historically constituted arrangements, can be criticized and changed.

We should note that if Critical Theory is essentially political and economic in nature, this is a sign of its own historical moment. European society in the 1930s was in political and economic chaos, and this was seen to indicate the inherent self-destructiveness of industrial capitalism and the inability of liberal democracy to address its own ills. While Marx in the *Critique of Political Economy* had produced a critique of social conditions via a critique of the categories used to justify those conditions (labor, commodity, exchange-value, etc.), the Frankfurt School recognized that the power of economic ideology went far beyond the basic propositions of discourse. For example, it was seen that fascism and organized capitalism had one thing in common. By breaking down the distinction between public and private spheres, both were able, through political propaganda and marketing psychology, to awaken artificial needs in support of a particular system. It became difficult to separate internal desire and external suggestion, such that the superstructure, the vast architectonics of the controlling social planners, became more firmly secured in individuals' own sub-structures, thereby ensuring people's obedience. For Critical Theory, therefore, "needs" were no longer to be interpreted as natural or fixed but rather the product of mechanisms of suggestion. The authoritarian personality, for example, is a product not only of a particular set of family relations, but of an authoritarian social structure, which becomes embedded within the psyche of each individual.

The point here for our purposes is that the pre-eminent means by which superstructure and individual sub-structure articulate in any collectivity is through language. Access, therefore, to an understanding of power relations must be achieved through the examination of both personal and public languages for the dominating metaphors, vocabularies, syntaxesand so on which legitimate and sustain the status quo.

A number of important studies have clarified this relationship between language and social structure. Jean Anyon,[5] for example, has done excellent work on comparing the language and syntax of pedagogy within different social classes. Working-class pedagogy takes place in the context of authoritarian language patterns (unilateral demands, servile academic labour involving drills, worksheetsand such) coupled with subversive, undercover language practices on the part of students (grafitti, plotting schemes against school authoritiesand so on). Middle-class pedagogy is imbued with the language of negotiation ("If you do this you will get that") while upper-class elite pedagogy is a form of training in the world of deals and making things happen, that is, learning the language of power management.

Some of Michael Apple's most interesting work examines the textbook industry as a chief broker of ideas in a culture.[6] When a publisher's principle aim is to turn a profit, only books guaranteed to sell target quantities will ever see the light of day. Apple sees such a condition as one which ensures a curriculum bleached of all fundamental controversy, of all possibilities for dealing with real issues today.

The women's movement also now well understands the connection between language and life. As Susan Aitkin has brilliantly shown, the exclusion of women from the basic canon of Western texts can only be taken as a sign of the exclusion of the voice of women from the heart of human affairs, and the predominance of male hegemony in the corridors of power. And changing that state of affairs must involve changing the face of the canon itself, a situation well addressed by Gilbert and Gubar in their compilation of *The Norton Anthology of Literature by Women*.[7]

A major contribution of both Horkheimer and Adorno was to clarify an antagonism in industrial culture between two concepts of reason: *practical* reason and *instrumental* reason. Practical reason is the older form and implies the modes of thinking and acting involved in the refined life when people are freed from externally imposed compulsions, such as the needs to produce food and build shelterand so on. Originating in classical Greek culture, it implies the presence of a slave or servant class to do the dirty work so that "purer", more aesthetic forms of human conduct can be practiced. Instrumental reason, on the other hand, is a source and function of technology, issuing from the need to control nature. According to Horkheimer and Adorno, in advanced industrial society instrumental reason has gained ascendance, but with the unfortunate consequence that the center of its focus is no longer simply the transformation of nature but now also of other people. This is especially true through the refined sciences of administration, which have borrowed rational models from the natural sciences and applied them to the study and management of human organizations such as schools. In *The Managed Heart*,[8] Arlie Hochschild has studied from a Critical Theory perspective several key service professions such as airline flight attendants and postal workers. She shows how, in such professions, basic emotional experiences such as joy, sadness, enthusiasm and anger themselves come to be controlled and "managed" in the service of "service". Emotions come to be used instrumentally rather than expressed authentically. Negative emotions are vetoed in the interest of "appearing to be happy" in order that customers and clients will in turn be happy with services rendered and hence in future be inclined to return. Such a condition has long-range effects in the lives of those concerned. It produces forms of deep repression with diverse corollary manifestations such as burn out, sexual impotence, and most drastically, an inability to take others at face value. That is, it produces a profound cynicism about human relations.

One wonders about the management of emotions in the teaching profession, and especially in the language of teaching itself. At a conference recently I heard a teacher enthusiastically extol the virtues of Whole Language instruction with the words, "It make kids feel good about language". There is something deeply disturbing about classrooms under the influence of a teacher who is compulsively driven to be "enthusiastic" and to provide a "good experience for the kids". It is not that such a predisposition is bad, only that it may be inadequate to articulate the full complexity at work, not only in children's lives, but also in the world at large. Critical Theorists would argue that the obsession to make classes "fun" is part and parcel of a consumerist approach to everything where the driving motive is to "sell" (Phonics yesterday, Whole Language today). Critical Theory would say, if we are to teach language wholly, then let us also attend to its dialectical oppositions, its negatives, such as the silences, the blockages and the unspeakables of life.

I also sensed in the teacher's remark a profound fear of this dialectical negative, an upholding of all those good ideas about positive reinforcement which teachers typically learn in college, a determination to be positive even at the expense of true feeling, a distinctive disallowing of all the hard conflict and struggle so necessary to the deep project of human authentication. Transposing such a prejudice to the teaching of language, does this mean that through such a teacher, Whole Language itself could only sponsor a half-truth about speaking and acting? Can Whole Language sponsor non-writing and non-speaking; that is, can it also sponsor restraint, modesty and all those other civil virtues which seem to have no place within that profligacy of self-annunciation which is a sure mark of any pedagogy putting language entirely and self-consciously at the service of the will? There, the soul has neither voice nor echo.

The search for not-ness, or the dialectical negative, was inspired by Herbert Marcuse, who in *One Dimensional Man*[9] argued that the greatest problem posed by the triumph of instrumental reason in modern culture is precisely that it brings with it a new ease of social functioning, a culture of efficiency and relative affluence. The result is that people come to feel quite happy in their oppression, like the prisoner who after ten years in jail decides it is not such a bad place, with its warm bed and three meals a day. Such an acquiescence, however, is a sign of political impotence, a giving up of one's sense of personal agency in favour of never having to be bothered again by life's basic difficulties. In an instrumentally guided and administered culture, the manipulation of public opinion and desire is an easy matter not just because the instruments of manipulation are so well refined, but because in fact people subliminally come to enjoy being manipulated. It makes them feel as if they are at the cutting edge of everything new.

Taking over the Freudian concepts of instincts and repression, Marcuse applied them to the question of how to awaken people to a renewed sense of personal and public responsibility. He argued that underneath the surface calm of efficient operations there lurked a veritable cauldron of primal drives and imagination. The key is to get people in touch with precisely those parts of their experience which lie beyond, behind, underneath and above the superficial pleasures of merely getting by.

It is in this sense that Brazilian educator Paulo Freire claimed he could teach any adult to read in forty minutes as long as every word was filled with political meaning.[10] Freire's critical dialogic pedagogy involved having people simply describe pictorially a situation in their everyday world and then collectively problematize and reflect on not just the power relations of the people, things and events in the picture, but also on one's own relationship to the people, things and events so described. In this way, students are able to see clearly that the world is an interpreted world, not just a received world in the brute sense of that term. And as an interpreted world, it can be interpreted differently, that is, the relationships within it can be different. I can find myself in the world in a different way than I presently do when I assume my ability to name and organize the world in a way that is truer to my experience of it. Such a task identifies the creative heart of a truly critical language pedagogy. It affirms an alliance between the critical spirit and the creative spirit, and in so doing points a way through the burden of dogmatic discourse.

There are many other things that could and perhaps should be clarified or amplified. For example, in spite of everything said so far, one of the difficulties Critical Theory has had to face is the true difficulty of going beyond simply naming problems. Critics of Critical Theory have pointed to the *theory* half of the term and thereby tried to dismiss the tradition as just another form of elitist arm-chair intellectualizing. But for me it is a matter more simply of maintaining an important truth: without a tradition which continually antagonizes the relationship between words and things, we run the even greater risk of falling in love with our own linguistic creations, taking those creations in such a way that our representations stand four-square in the way of that which cannot be named but without which we cannot go on. If Critical Theory has done nothing but clarify the relationship between words and things, and show that the way we use words is tied to much deeper issues about social structure, power relations, technology, capital interests and so on, well, if it has done only that, it has done a lot.

11

Modernism, Postmodernism and the Future of Pedagogy

I

That Education as a formal discipline is represented in the work of the Institute of East and West Studies at Yonsei University is a sign of the high priority given to education in Korea, a mark, perhaps, of its appreciated value in the long-range projects of modernization. In the West too, education commands widespread attention, but coupled with that is a generally low view of educators. Everybody believes in the value of education, but there seems to be a crisis regarding what character it should have, what can be expected from it, and its relationship to political interests. What I would like to do in this chapter is briefly discuss modern educational systems as precisely products of modernization, which therefore inevitably carry and reflect the underside difficulties of modernity.[1] Then I want to ask if the pedagogical mandate of standing alongside of the young does not in itself carry a special responsibility which needs to be articulated and which can help us understand certain essential human values which are in deep jeopardy in highly technical and industrial cultures. A recovery of these values has important implications for teaching and what we might understand about the meaning of the child in adult-child relations. In this endeavour I will draw on the insights of "postmodernism".

II

We know that public education as a feature of mass culture is a relatively recent phenomenon.[2] Its origins go back to the sixteenth century and the Protestant Reformation, when literacy programs became part of the agenda for getting people to read the Bible as the authority for their faith. The new sense of personal autonomy which the Reformation inspired also inaugurated the movement towards democratic process, and the rise of nationalism and the nation-state. Eventually the state took over from the churches responsibility for education, such that it could be said that nationalism as a form of secular

120

religion underwrites most modern educational practice, and that, in a way, teachers can be designated as the modern priest class or at least primary mediators of secular culture.

Another key element in the genesis of modern education was the rise of Cartesian science and the Enlightenment positivist projects of objective reason and methodological certitude. The methodological premises of the physical sciences directly catalysed all of the contemporary sciences of society such as economics and political science, as well as, in matters of pedagogy, the science of the child.[3] In the work of eighteenth-century philosophers like John Locke, for example, the child came to be viewed as an object fit for empirical investigation, separated off from any necessary connection to the adult world. Even the Romantics like Rousseau and Wordsworth, who reacted with horror against the new forms of social engineering, found their force precisely in positing a new kind of agenda for the child. And so, as David Kennedy suggests,[4] in the modern West the child has become a victim by virtue of his status as an isolable social phenomenon that can be studied and manipulated to serve predetermined definitions of the aims of society. Ashis Nandy, the Indian writer, has named "adultism" as one of the most pronounced features of modern industrial culture.[5]

Locating modern education and the question of the child in the context of the Enlightenment project of instrumental objective reason and the rise of science, in the same move opens the debate about certain poverties in that legacy. In the educational context, the poverty is most apparent in the inability of educational leadership to deal with what surfaces on a day to day basis as a questioning by the young of the auspices of the educational project. The increasing rebelliousness and diffidence shown by the young towards teachers and other school authorities can be read as an interrogation by the young as to whether time spent in school serves any other purpose than a rhetorical one, that is, fulfilling someone else's definition of destiny. For young people, the real reasons for their nine to twelve years of compulsory institutional confinement are not clear in any deep sense.

In North America, the school is also under increasing attack from parent groups and political lobbyists demanding not only greater accountability from the school in terms of quality of programs and such, but also expecting the school, as a receiver of public funds, to provide more and more services traditionally rendered by the family. From the perspective of teachers and administrators, however, things are already at a breaking point, with teacher burnout and dropout increasingly common features of the professional landscape.

Indeed, the point here is that the school, in the modern state, has become the crystallization point for most of the troubles of modernity. Teachers and administrators see at first hand the consequences of the loss of intimacy in family life, and the personal alienation and anomie which derive from the driven compulsive nature of dogmatic notions of enterprise and competition.

Unfortunately by virtue of their typical training in faculties of education or teachers' colleges, most teachers are scandalously ill-equipped to deal with the problems they face, except perhaps managerially. Undergraduate programs in education tend to be highly instrumental and technical in orientation, guided by rather vulgar notions of classroom management, curriculum strategies and discipline techniques. To say that teachers are singularly ill-prepared in the deep discourses about culture may again only be a sign of their double oppression as servants of the state. In a sense it is important that they not understand too well the foundations of their practices, otherwise their service function may be undermined. It is heartening to find more and more teachers searching for a language that can help them understand their personal and professional pains. In Canada, this is evident in the kinds of teacher autobiography studies of scholars like Richard Butt[6] and in school life-world studies such as those of Peter McLaren.[7]

III

The poverty of modernism, as the so-called postmodernists are helping us to understand,[8] is that it operates out of a unique and deep prejudice in the Western tradition which is the assumption that concepts, formulations and ideas refer eventually to something fixable, enclosable and nameable once and for all as reality. Highly imperial in basic gesture and nuance, this is the Western determination, with Platonic, Christian and Cartesian legitimation, to get things *right,* not just epistemologically (to have correct knowledge), but also to *be* right, to claim one's life as right. Philosophically it's a matter of getting one's concepts and ideas in proper order (one's theories of childhood, for example), then putting them into effect as being foundationally true. In educational terms, the modernist impulse accounts for the notorious theory/practice split, because modernism always begins with an intellectual cognitive act rather than an attention to life as it is lived. The objectification of others into formalized manipulable, theoretical categories means that any necessary connection between self and other is severed. Others become banished to the service of being examples of something you already know everything about; one is no longer related to others in any deeply human or ongoing sense. In formal terms, this way of proceeding has been called by the philosopher Richard Rorty as "representationalism".[9] The French writer Jacques Derrida names this deep Western predisposition "logocentrism" or "the metaphysics of presence".[10] Gregory Ulmer speaks of the "imperial dispensation" of the logocentric tradition.[11]

The difficulty presented by these foundations of modernism is that they are forgetful of what has been lost, deferred or suppressed in order for them to surface as such. Within every set of arrangements there are voices, desires and intentions which have been translated out of the present by virtue of the triumph of present interpretations. The most positive contribution of postmodernism, then, is the argument for the interpretive basis of human understanding rather than a stable declarative basis, so that while modernism gives full value to the surface of things, postmodern practices constantly destabilize the surface to show a fuller range of possible meanings. In pedagogical terms, postmodernism affirms what Derrida calls "not play *in* the world, but the play *of* the world".[12] Those who have paid careful attention to the way newly born children interact with the world sometimes describe the action as a form of play.[13] We might describe the postmodern commitment as being in the service of protecting the conditions under which play can go on, given that play is that through which human meaning itself is constituted.

The postmodern commitment to the motility of meaning is not a commitment to relativism or easy pluralism in which no one thing has any more value than anything else; rather it works in favour of a deep relationalism, towards an acceptance of the fact that the meaning of anything is never knowable purely in and of itself, but only in so far as it bears a relationship to something, or to others. The logocentric, modernist character we can describe as hierarchical, imperial, hard, argumentative and well defined. The postmodernist character is relational, ecological, modest, conversational and somewhat mysterious; it accepts the fact that the surface of things also contains a deep-structure which must be interrogated for the surface to be understood as such. The postmodern project is not analytical, declarative, war-like or punitive (wishing things were other than what they are) but rather it is intuitive, interpretive and always open to the play of possibilities inherent in the heart of life. It works from a sense that there is an integrity to life that always and everywhere exists prior to whatever we might say about it. Human thought and action are always second-order to the primacy of the world as it is always and already *there*. The pedagogical task involves learning how to live *with* the world instead of trying to force it into an identity we can recognize as conforming with our concepts of it.

Conventional orthodox pedagogy in the modern world can be characterized in two broad ways. Usually the guiding languages and practices are either *gericentric* or *pedocentric*. Gericentric pedagogy assumes the role of the teacher to be primarily that of transmitter of the cultural deposit and tradition, with the role of the student or child to be the passive docile recipient of the wisdom of the elders. As such, gericentric pedagogy is forgetful that texts and knowledges formalized in curriculum are not fixed and stable but rather are constitutive, i.e., arising as an answer to particular questions of a given time and place. Similarly, gericentric pedagogy undervalues the creative action of the young in constituting their own life and purpose, such that there is no genuine dialogue between old and young concerning the future that faces them together. Children and young people are inevitably seen as suffering a deficit which requires an adult remedy.

The neo-romantic pedocentric tradition begins with a sense of the child as one who must primarily be protected from the polluting and harsh realities of the contemporary world in order that his or her own true nature can have a chance to flourish. This rather sentimental view also, in a paradoxical way, leaves the child extremely vulnerable—abandoned, in a sense, to his or her own devices without benefit of the presence of lived experience embodied in significant adults. The child is without guide, isolated from the world in its full deep complexity. Pedocentric pedagogy can also produce a kind of generational warfare between adult and child as the child learns to see the adult simply as an impediment to his or her own plans and intentions.

Postmodern pedagogy, however, begins with a sense of the deep interconnectedness between adult and child. There is an ontological bond at work, the violation of which is at the heart of the generational wars of modernity, and which is the bad inspiration for the increasing marginalization of the young in late industrial cultures. The economist Leonard Silk has noted that, for example, the United States as a modern industrial state "has the highest child poverty rate of any industrialized country".14 The logocentric mind cannot abide the deep sense of play in the world, which the child understands so naturally, and so logocentrism forces a false wedge between play and work, even institutionalizing play as something only dutifully achievable, or commodifiable under state or capital interests. Postmodern pedagogy, on the other hand, openly enters into the play of the world, thereby enabling a kind of conversational dance with the young which ensures that they will not be abandoned, neither will teachers become sclerotic in their thought and action.

Again, logocentric pedagogy perpetuates a notion of curriculum as the cultural deposit of concepts, facts and figures which children must "master" in order to make their way in the world as it is already established. This conventional formulation of curriculum can be understood as the inevitable outcome of the instrumental metaphysics of presence, which underwrites the flourishing of technological values and apparatuses in the modern industrial world. Such a formulation, however, precisely prevents the kind of creative insight which is necessary to unveil the fixed strictures of modernity, such that students most successful at mastering the codes of the times are often the most shortsighted and undeveloped in terms of moral vision or social conscience. *That* kind of maturity requires an ability to see the claims of curriculum as simply possible interpretations given under certain situational constraints and historical moment. And an opening up of curriculum in *that* way, showing the motility of meaning in all texts and documents, showing their "desire", as Derrida would put it, as well as "the as-yet-unnameable-which-is-constantly-proclaiming- itself", [15] opens for students a sense of the possibility of their own creative involvement in the curricular task of creating meaning. Postmodern pedagogy gives students hope by showing the way of participation in the task of creating the future. Putting the matter in simplest terms, postmodern pedagogy is primarily the art of teaching students how to read, to understand not what texts mean in some fixed sense, but to learn to discern what is at work in the way in which meaning is achieved in them. In broadest terms, it is a matter of learning how to read one's own story in the context of the fuller cultural story. For teachers, this requires training in the arts of interpretation, a project we cannot elaborate on here, except to point to the ancient but now newly re-emergent tradition of hermeneutics.[16]

IV

As one who grew up in central Africa, and in later years has travelled in a number of non-Western countries, I have come to realize that the formulations and issues put forward in this paper have themselves a distinctly Western ring. In Africa, in the Philippines and even here in Korea it is quite striking how the young are precisely *not* marginalized in the way so observable in the West. In countries that have not had the long legacy of industrial and capital development, one still finds young and old interacting together with mutual respect and natural affection. I fear it is precisely these qualities that may be so easily lost in the blind race for economic and social development.

Not long ago in Seoul I struck up a conversation with a young graduate student, and, things going well, we went for lunch together. In the restaurant was a young family with a small child. After a while the child became restless and fretful. Out of the blue, my friend said, "You know, I hate kids. Now dogs I like, but kids, no." He said it with a smile so I know he meant it humourously. To be sure, young children's cries can sometimes be an irritant to adult ears. I have to admit, though, to being a bit saddened by my friend's almost reflex response. Because with his "Tom Cruise" sunglasses and surface cool, he was already voicing a problem which has reached tragic proportions in the West, namely, a cutting of the connective nerve with the young in favour of some sort of notion of smooth progress. The difficulties, dilemmas and ambiguities which children place in the path of adults are a reminder to us not to take ourselves too seriously. In postmodern terms, it could be said that children embody and keep alive a sense of the play of the world, giving voice to the powers of human regeneration. If modernization means putting children in jeopardy in the name of progress by institutionalizing them and separating them off from the living stream of things, then the times are truly dangerous.

I keep thinking of those icons of the Buddha which show him surrounded by children, or Zen scholar Toyoji Togo's words about the rustic saint Ryokan-osho, "Day after day he spends playing with children..."; or the words of Jesus, "Let the children come to me. Do not stop them. Unless you become like a child you cannot see the kingdom"[18] or Pierre Erny's wonderful study of the child in Africa and the child's special status as "one who brings a message from beyond". Modernity is not friendly to children because what is vulnerable, weak, or not fully understood is seen as a problem to be dealt with. Yet ancient wisdom points us back to the child as one who reminds us of our own deep adult vulnerability and our need for a more gentle way of being together on this earth. I hope education, as a human discipline, can eventually find the means by which to call a hardened world to its fuller senses.

Brighter Than a Thousand Suns: Facing Pedagogy in the Nuclear Shadow

The title of Robert Jungk's history of the first atomic scientists, *Brighter Than a Thousand Suns*,[1] is taken from the Bhagavad-Gita:

> If the radiance of a thousand suns
> were to burst into the sky,
> that would be
> the splendour of the Mighty One.

No one doubts the brilliance of an atomic explosion, but whether the kind of thinking that can produce it should also claim the status of the Mighty One is a question still facing us. Despite increasingly established critiques of Western science,[2] and especially the science within social science, it is still the monologic of Western empiricism as totalism[3] which underwrites virtually all the dominant political, economic, research and pedagogic discourses of the world today. The crisis of Western institutions is thus precisely a crisis about thinking, about what is embodied in a logic and structure of speaking and acting. It is a question of whether the form of thinking which has produced contemporary order[4] is itself adequate to deal with an increasingly insistent disorder. Disorder points to the political nature of all language, to how it is that speaking implies hearing, and that to be insistently not heard invites actions which are unspeakable. Disorder also reveals the limits of language, that is, the resistance of things to be fully named, yet also to the pull of freedom which lies beyond names but is itself the silent generosity out of which things find their voice.

If the ascendance of empirical science to epistemological guardianship has been at the cost of speech itself,[5] that is, of thinking,[6] as educators we are charged with a special question. That is, given that the language which dominates (us) allows us to speak but also prevents us from saying what cannot be said in it (any discourse is at the same time a violence against discourse), how should we conduct ourselves in a manner which, while acknowledging this contradiction, ensures we do not also give up on our own regeneration? It should be stressed that the contradiction is not a "problem to be solved" before another conceptual model can be produced and set beside all the others. To approach the matter this way would be to banish the question into a problem-solving subsumption which would ensure that things proceed as before. No, to raise the question of the limits of language is also to open its possibilities. But this requires a fidelity to that which calls out to us from within the heart of what we do not understand and for which we may not at present have words. Pedagogy then becomes a vocation to live and act within the difference between what we know and what we do not know, that is, to be drawn out to what calls us from both within and beyond ourselves.

Two temptations can divert us from this vocational task. One is to presume to speak and act as if one's (professional) discourse is already closed, that is, self-sufficient, self-contained. Indeed it might be said that Education, at present, is a field of clustered closed discourses. Not only are the formal subtexts of the discipline (educational psychology, curriculum and instruction, administration, foundationsand others) all bound within increasingly specialized languages of their own, and thus at greater and greater pains to know how to address each other, or even to know what the common text between them is—the worse result is a loss of the very thing hoped for. For the more tightly controlled a discourse, the more surely suffocated the very thing it is attempting to clarify or set free. This is a paradox which even the measurement sciences have taught us, namely, that any scale may be increasingly differentiated, but no matter how minutely, it will never completely close the distance between two points. Hence a pedagogy oriented to closure (fill in the blanks, complete this sentence) does violence to a basic phenomenological truth about our speaking together, namely, that it is never finished.

A second temptation is to speak and act as if all discourse is *nothing but* open. In education this is heard often in discussions about creativity, and the belief that, for example, every child is absolutely unique and that the structure of pedagogy should be principally to foster self-discovery. Again, such an orientation may deny an essential phenomenological insight not only about language (the means by which any pedagogic practice is mediated), but also about social relations. That is, no language is just an individually produced possession but is also a commonly held trust out of which one defines oneself to be who one is. Self-definition is contingent on an initial full (even though possibly rebellious) reception of the lexical and syntactic universe of the community of one's origins. There is no purely free language, that is, a language disengaged from historical, political, economic or familial antecedents. Indeed, it is just such rootedness which gives every language its character. In a sense, then, a view of possible discourse as nothing but free and open[7] is a kind of anti-language, a denial of that which makes its own discourse possible. Pedagogically speaking, abandoning language instruction to, say, a rubric of pure creativity would amount to nothing less than an abandonment of children through a declaration that the language they are learning has no sender. To live within the contradiction of (educational) discourse, then, means to be oriented to speech as being neither closed in on itself nor abandoned to a future which is out of our hands. It is to be held together in the search for, and articulation of, the text which holds us in common over, above, and under the surface of our talk. How is it possible to understand this, and what would it mean for us pedagogically speaking? I wish to explore three themes.

Theme One:
Ambiguity as Oracular

It is not the weakness but the strength of the oracle that it is ambiguous.[8]

In classical Greek thinking, an oracle was a person or thing regarded as serving as an infallible though mysterious guide through the precariousness of human life. The origin of the word in the term *to speak* (Latin *orare*) marked the way in which an oracle could offer a word—a word of advice, judgement, prophecy, to an otherwise incomprehensible situation.[9]

In *The Flight from Ambiguity*,[10] Donald Levine shows how the loss of a capacity to deal constructively with ambiguity is a recent (since the seventeenth century) and unique development in the West. An orientation to technology inspired by the rise of science creates a demand for precision and univocity in language, which in turn relies on a definitional approach to meaning rather than a discursive one. Words are defined to mean one thing and one thing only, a condition which predicates computer languages and the word processing/information science industries. Levine shows how such an orientation is completely foreign to the mode and function of natural language which is inexorably ambiguous, but which very ambiguity remains essential for the sustenance of discourse. Indeed, Levine shows how such key Western concepts as "rationality" and "freedom" are not, in practical use, fixed terms, but depend for their meaning on discursive exchange. That such a thesis could now be put forward by a mainstream North American sociologist is a positive sign: the interpretive/hermeneutic traditions of continental philosophy have been making such claims for over 100 years.

How is ambiguity oracular? Ambiguity brings forth a new speaking by pointing to the limits and finitude of our understanding at the same time as making us available to understanding. When everything is perfectly clear, speech grinds to a halt, or reduces to chatter, because there is nothing more to be said. This is when understanding becomes "narcotized", as Umberto Eco would say. [11] Narcotized understanding sleeps peacefully but unwittingly, unaware that the self-constructed boundaries of its comfort are permeable. Narcotized understanding, while happy on the surface, is inevitably paranoid and xenophobic because, though it can give account of the journey whereby it has arrived to where it is, it has forgotten that the journey is never over, or indeed that others are on a journey, too, and that their journey may depend on a new territoriality whereby established boundaries no longer make sense.

Ambiguity is oracular in that it calls forth a response, and one which, for sure, must be new because old knowledge/languages are inadequate to the task of naming what is now being confronted. This is why the language which emerges from meeting a stranger is always analogical—it speaks of resemblances, of how things are like one another even while quite different from each other. The analogical imagination,[12] as distinct from the literal, or the definitional, opens up speech because its interest is not power, or territorial claiming, but understanding: the capacity to search for how we are held in common on this earth. The analogical imagination, speaking from the heart of ambiguity, is the true friend of speech because it does not presume to wish to name everything exactly, as if by doing so all things could be subsumed under one code. The aim of analogical understanding is to let things speak for themselves in order that they may be understood on their own terms. An oracle will speak only if it is consulted by those whose eyes and ears are open, that is, attentive to what indeed is being said. Hence, it is the search for understanding which enables speech to go on, in the knowledge that understanding is never complete but is achieved as one lays oneself open to the conversation of life already in progress, instead of hiding within a set of fixed formulations marked, perhaps, as virtue.

Again, our task is to inquire into the meaning of these things for our conduct as educators. We know that the elevation of ambiguity to a positive status runs contrary to virtually all current practices, guided as they usually are by a frenetic search for rules, laws and protocols which can serve in the governing of what we do in schools, classrooms, day care centers and so forth.

And of course it would be silly to suggest that life with children can proceed without order. For us now, though, the question concerns what should be our fundamental pedagogic gesture. What should be embodied in our actions such that we are working on the side of true generativity even while in the midst of what we do not fully understand?

Theme Two:
No Longer Prescription but Interpretation and Understanding

What Clifford Geertz has said about social science in his important essay on "The Refiguration of Social Thought"[13] speaks equally to our thinking in education:

> The golden age (or perhaps it was only the brass) ... when, whatever the differences in theoretical positions and empirical claims, the basic goal of the enterprise was universally agreed upon—to find out the dynamics of collective life and alter them in desired directions—has clearly passed.

Geertz forsakes a gesture of planning, engineering, prescription and so forth, not to devalue it, but to acknowledge that the naive optimism or dogmatic methodologism which undergirds building in such a way cannot be supported in the face of the blurring that has occurred in our understanding of ourselves. We can no longer confidently proceed, for example, with the building of Utopias through shaping the lives of children in desired directions, because we now recognize the epistemological problematics inherent in most of our child-development knowledge, our social policy knowledge and so forth. Most important, we have come to recognize the inadequacy of the Cartesian underpinning of such knowledge, that is, the subject-object split which presumes we are not complicit in everything we say and do in our lives with others, including children. The shift, then, is away from interest in objective knowledge *per se* (which is always linked to a concern for utilization) toward the question of meaning, or what Geertz calls "sense and signification".[14] This he marks as the fundamental "interpretive turn" in social science, and it is a profound move noted contemporaneously by many others.[15]

In education a shift towards interpretation, meaning, sense, and signification means a turn away from the creation of knowledge, theories and so forth, which (we might hope) could exist in some underived form and thus used by anyone. A turn toward interpretation means a drawing close to what we already are, to the way in which we *are* together; to an attention to what is really going on in our lives with children, rather than having that attention deflected away by disembodied knowledge, media hype or the latest fad from some prominent educator with a loud voice. In pedagogical terms, a turn towards interpretation is interested in the way understanding is achieved between an adult and a child, with the deep question of what is required for them (us) to live together in a way that will ensure that life can go on.

Instead of being rendered insecure by harsh words about the decline of educational standards, the need for greater discipline in schools and so forth, interpretive pedagogy asks for the meaning of such judgements, deflecting attention away from schemes that show no concern for the quality of life as lived in schools and classrooms. Instead, interpretive pedagogy begins not with grand theory but with the way theory is already at work in day-to-day practices. Such a beginning point (right in the middle of things) orients pedagogy towards making action thoughtful, and thinking charged with political responsibility.

Interpretive pedagogy, concerned with sense and signification, is skilled in reading signs, both the signs of the times as well as signs of what is happening with children. Being able to read the signs of the times is not easy, but it is a discursive task which is informed by studies in political economy, international relations, critical sociology, semiotics and so forth. Such studies are important for loosening the grip of psychologism on educational theory and practice. Psychologism places an unfair burden on both teachers and students in making them feel that any difficulties they may be having in their life together is simply the result of the lack of personal commitment or personal weakness, not trying hard enough and so forth. Informed interpretive pedagogy is able to show that personal difficulties are also linked to political, economic and social arrangements designed to prevent genuine insight into problems by disallowing certain forms of questions or certain kinds of information from being generated and disseminated.[16] Interpretive pedagogy tries to show the way the specificities of our lives, while in a sense unique to each person, are also participant in the full texture of human life as a whole; that what we hold in common as human beings is at least of equal importance as what individually we maintain for ourselves; that individualism has an artefactual character.

While standing in the middle of things, interpretive pedagogy looks to the margins of collective life for the oracular word of signification, in the understanding that it is exactly at the boundary of experience, at the place of where we discover our limit, where we become available to that which addresses us. If we are at our wits' end with a child in school, that is where we begin to

133

interrogate most authentically our presuppositions about children and about our parental or pedagogic selves. If we feel threatened by new ideas, new political arrangements and so forth, this is a sign that we are being extended beyond our comfort, called forth to a new ability to respond.

Two examples of the radical limits of Western culture which promise to reinterpret our future include the emergent voice of the Third World, which calls into question the epistemic and axiological hegemony of the West,[17] and the question of nuclear war which, as Derrida says, places us "in the perspective of a remainderless destruction, without mourning and without symbolicity".[18] These two profound agitations on the boundaries of our comfort challenge us to re-evaluate the very foundation of our speaking and living together. They serve as reminders of the limits of our language, of our capacity to address the fullness of things. But an awareness of such limits also orients us phenomenologically to a fundamental reality about the relationship between the known and the unknown. This is the subject of our third theme.

Theme Three:
In the Presence Lives an Absence

The case of the (so-called) poststructuralist French philosophers,[19] especially Jacques Derrida, has been to propose that the orientation of Western metaphysics since Plato has been towards a "metaphysics of presence", or "logocentrism". By this is meant that the goal of Western thinking has always been to bring the meaning of things to the surface of awareness and then announce what has been surfaced as if it had some pure independent existence or essence. The consequence has been a tradition of announcements of truths taken to be of universal application, but spoken, as Derrida would say, without awareness of their own "hypocrisy" as "answer".[20] If, for example, answers lose connection with their questions, then they become hypocritical insofar as, in their self-confidence, they pretend to be something they are not. Derrida's projects of deconstruction emphasize the importance of *difference,* showing that what surfaces as known only does so on the basis of a suppression of something else. Deconstruction aims to bring that which is lost into the same domain of discourse as what has traditionally been accepted as found.[21] Michel Foucault's "archaeologies" of various Western discourses, such as those concerning sexuality, madness, the clinic and so forth, have much the same interest, namely, to show that they cannot be understood without their lost context, which still breathes as a living but lost presence within contemporary speech.

These insights are not necessarily unique or new, having their formal genesis in Plato, then later Kant, the phenomenologies of Husserl and Heidegger, as well as in the semiotics of Saussure.[22] What is distinctive is their radical insistence that it is the metaphysics of presence which is responsible for Western culture's assuming a self-appointed position of dominance in the world today, riding by necessity for its survival over an obliterated face and voice of an Other. It is when we consider our pedagogical practices in the light of this inevitability of an Other, on which/whom we ourselves depend for our Sameness, an Other which must be suppressed for the Sameness to be calm, but which very calmness knows itself to be agitated and anxious in spite of its best intentions—well, such considerations will indeed augur a new age for pedagogy. Because, instead of a pedagogy oriented towards mastery, closure, totalism, or towards nihilism, it will be oriented towards remembrance and the activation of voices rendered silent by contemporary narratives. It will know the fundamental ambiguity of all narrative, all story, an ambiguity which will be understood not as pathology but rather as essential to the very survival of speaking, thinking and acting.

What would be the face of pedagogy oriented by healthy remembrance? For one thing, it would not be nostalgic, with nostalgia as that selective recollection which only remembers what it can use to support, or tinker with, present practices.[23] Nostalgic pedagogy is guided by those who remember the good old days as being a time when everyone (so it is thought) knew his or her place. No, a true pedagogy of remembrance stands in the presence of young people remembering what it is like to be young, with all the idealism and chafing of youth, and all the insecurity which goes along with bold dreams. But such a pedagogy does not just encourage children to be bold and to dream more, but rather it gathers students and teachers together in a genuine conversation about life. For example, a teacher who lives well, with a healthy remembrance, is able to talk in such a way that students can learn to see that there is more to life than what appears on the surface—that there is indeed an Other side to everything, a silent archeology within every speech, a secret which inspires every saying,[24] indeed an absence which is always present. Furthermore, such a teacher also pays attention to that profound silence which often comes from children, and regards such silences not as voids to be filled with yet more facts, but as living spaces which are a sign that memory is in formation.

To remember that pedagogy is concerned with the formation of memory means to be fully responsive to the conditions by which a person learns to remember well. And remembering well does not mean just remembering happy times, that is, suppressing the fire by which we might be refined. More importantly, remembering well means remembering how each of us might struggle through life's bittersweetness with the kind of courage that enables life to go on. Good memory, then, is oriented towards the future, but realistically, not in a utopian fashion. A realistic future recognizes that whatever the future will be, it will contain what can endure today.[25]

A teacher who remembers well teaches curriculum as a story,[26] not just as a collection of trivia which seems to have no connection with anything but itself and which must be remembered in an unhealthy way, that is, crammed, to pass an exam. Teaching curriculum as a story means that teachers must be prepared in such a way as to be able to show that there are never facts without people for whom facts count as such and that all things read in books are somehow answers to questions that people pose or once posed. Take, for example, a simple statement often taught in primary grades: "The sun rises in the east and sets in the west". Such a statement is loaded with cultural memory. It reminds us that we once believed the earth was the center of things and that the sun actively circled the earth. But such a statement, residual in our common speech, could also remind us that we have a deep tenacity to forms of knowledge which will not be overcome by scientific knowledge, and that even though science may inform us that we live in a heliocentric universe, we know too that we are still at the center of our own knowing about it.

Teaching curriculum as a story means to have teachers response-able to children's questions, for we know that when children love a story they always want to know why things happened as they did. Teaching which can allow itself to be deeply interrogated by children and young people will be honest indeed, for it will show itself to be vulnerable, not having all the answers in advance. But in that very vulnerability it will provide a space for children, indeed for both adults and children together as they face a common world with a syntax and lexicon which cannot say everything. But exactly here there may be a true speaking, a form of dialogue which is beyond words, a creative silence which occurs when people are together in love, and out of which a new word may be spoken and shared for the first time. This is why such an orientation to curriculum is hopeful, because it draws young and old together in their common story in such a way that the story itself is generative, that is, not stuck in a worn-out stock of phrases and anecdotes.

"Education is suffering from narration-sickness", says Paulo Freire.[27] It speaks out of a story which was once full of enthusiasm, but now shows itself to be incapable of a surprise ending. The nausea of narration-sickness comes from having heard enough, from hearing many variations on a theme but no new theme. A narrative which is sick may claim to speak for all, yet has no *aporia*, no possibility of meeting a stranger because the text is complete already. Such narratives may be passed as excellent by those who certify clarity and for whom ambiguity is a disease to be excoriated. But the literalism of such narratives (speeches, lectures, stories) inevitably produces a pedagogy which, while passed as being "for the good of children",[28] does not recognize the violence against children inherent in its own claim. Because without an acknowledgement and positive appreciation of the full polysemic possibility which can explode from within any occasion when adult and child genuinely meet together (a possibility which resides precisely in the difference of every child, every person, a difference about which one can presume nothing despite the massive research literature available to us, and despite the fact that our children come from us, are our flesh and blood)[29]—without an appreciation of the radical mystery which confronts us in the face of every other person,[30] our theorizing must inexorably become stuck. For then we are no longer available for that which comes to meet us from beyond ourselves, having determined in advance the conditions under which any new thing will be acceptable, thereby foreclosing on the possibility of our own transformation. This radical difference of every child, every other person, renders our pedagogical narratives ambiguous but at the same time hopeful, because the imminent ambiguity held within them opens a space for genuine speaking, holding out the promise that something new can be said from out of the mists of the oracle of our own flesh.

13

Children and the Gods of War

"And what can the Joint Chiefs of Staff do for you today, little girl?"

A United Nations study examining the effects of the arms race on daily life should invite us to think about the relationship between increasing global militarism and children. In 1981, $1 million was spent on weapons every minute of every hour of every day,[1] and according to former UNICEF director James Grant, every year twelve to thirteen million children (the equivalent of one hundred and twenty Hiroshimas) die from hunger and malnutrition largely because funds for social and economic development are everywhere being diverted to the stockpiling of arms and the development of standing armies.[2]

So there's a certain irony in the *New Yorker* cartoon above, because what would the military mind accept as an answer to its own question about children? When the Joint Chiefs of Staff ask what they might do, today, for a child, educators should ask if this is merely a rhetorical questions or a real question, because there is much at stake in the answer. The irony may be that, in the face of a child, the military mind is powerless; i.e., the myths of "know-how" and "can do" which underwrite all vulgar interpretations of what is required today, pedagogically speaking, may be incapable of understanding that what is needed in our relations with young people is of a different order.

Several years ago, in New York, ambassadors from all the major world powers met to discuss questions of nuclear disarmament.[3] The meeting was both heated and fruitless as different parties argued fiercely for their own positions while making no progress at all towards the dismantling of nuclear stockpiles. At a cocktail party afterwards, however, a strange thing happened. One ambassador, who had just become a grandparent, enthusiastically pulled out a picture of his new grandchild to show the others. Before long all the members present were showing pictures of their children and grandchildren, nieces, nephews,and so on, swapping stories, jokes and comparing notes. Somehow the child had broken through the thick dumb husks of adult politics, generations of hostility and antagonism and arrogance of opinion, to bring people together, at least for a moment.

Without being sentimental, what is at issue here for educators? I think it has something to do with the nature of power, and the question of what it means to be mature or adult in our relations with children. We might begin by interpreting the question of the Joint Chiefs, "What can we do for you today...," as a question of genuine bewilderment, a bewilderment coming from a world, a way of thinking, so far removed from the radical simplicity, the closeness to life which the child represents, that, in the presence of a child, the most sophisticated planners of strategy, with all their information systems, their short, medium and long range geo-political agendas, genuinely do not know what to do. But also, we hear in the Joint Chiefs' query all the false confidence and braggadocio that imbues the speech of those who feel themselves to be in ultimate charge of the logics, rationales, conceptual schemes by which the world is to be understood. But it is precisely this confidence, this sure but foreclosed opinion which produces the unproblematized, unreflective desire to "help" children.

Education faculties are rife with this kind of powerful, confident assumption of knowing what to do with respect to children largely because they are foundationally deaf to the fuller question of what, in fact, children are for us. Contemporary educational paradigms are implicitly and increasingly militaristic with respect to children (witness the plethora of books on discipline, control, management and so on) because they are based on the will-to-power and a form of thinking (Cartesian) which cannot tolerate difference; i.e., which understands difference as a problem to be solved and subsumed under a condition of mastery and explanation.[4] This way of thinking cannot articulate the way in which the full meaning of a child, for us, resides in the paradox of being part of us but also apart from us. So as educators, we are in need of a new pedagogy which recognizes at its center the question of children as a question which calls for new self-reflection on our part. Hermeneutic studies of the meaning of children in the lives of adults[5] bring this theme home again and again, that living with children means living in the belly of a paradox wherein a genuine life together is made possible only in the context of an ongoing conversation which never ends yet which must be sustained for life together to go on at all. Homes, classrooms, schools wherein the people in charge cannot lay themselves open to the new life in their midst, always exist in a state of war from which children are driven either inward or outward but never forward. The openness that is required is not a vacuous licentiousness but a risky, deliberate engagement full of the conflict and ambiguity by which new horizons of mutual understanding are achieved. This is the fundamental requisite for giving children a sense of membership in the human community, for one learns to find one's voice only in an environment where speech itself is well understood as having a listening aspect.

John Martini's[6] study of the "moments" of pedagogy involved interviewing teachers about those occasions when they felt that something genuinely creative happened between themselves and their students. One common refrain spoke of a period of provocation, or "calling" (<L. *provocare*, call forth) from students followed by acts of anger, then conciliation on the part of the teacher. It is as if young people ask for, above all else, not only a genuine responsiveness from their elders but also a certain direct authenticity, a sense of that deep human resonance so easily suppressed under the smooth human-relations jargon teachers typically learn in college. Young people want to know if, under the cool and calm of efficient teaching and excellent time-on-task ratios, life itself has a chance, or whether the surface is all there is. And the best way to find out may be to provoke the teacher into showing himself or herself. How a teacher responds to that challenge determines whether a child will learn that growing up doesn't mean becoming forgetful about what it is like to grow, to be a child, but quite the opposite. For us as teachers, this means that we must become increasingly skilled in learning to read and understand our own childhoods, to understand our personal and collective pasts in a truly pedagogic way, that is, in a way that contributes positively and dialogically to a new understanding of and appreciation for the world.[7]

The most remarkable thing about contemporary North American teacher education may be that, in the name of inordinate concern for children, children themselves have been largely banished from any rightful place in the total human drama, banished under a dense cover of rationalistic, abstract discourses about "cognition", "development", "achievement" and so on. Once, at a conference on gifted girls, a keynote speaker introduced me (first words) to her two-year-old daughter as being in the "ninety-sixth percentile" on some important rating scale of ability. There is nothing wrong with this *per se*, but one must wonder if this is the most important, most valued, most attuned thing to be said about one's daughter. It doesn't really help me to understand the daughter personally, uniquely; i.e., in a way faithful to the child herself. Indeed one of the most frightening things about the new "science of teaching" studies geared to the "improvement of teaching"[8] is that they are so rational, so clear and without doubt. But as such they can tell us no more than a half-truth about the way life together is experienced at its fullest, most complex and meaningful. In fact, in terms of teacher education, such proposals often lead student teachers to believe that teaching is fundamentally an act of war. Many teachers have related to me that it took them several years of actual classroom practice to un-learn what they had learned in their teacher preparation programs.

The lack of credibility which teacher education programs typically face in university and public domains may be because we have yet to discover a language for our special task—the task of living and working with young people and all that that entails in our relations with the principalities and powers that be. Engaging in a discipline that is derivative primarily from psychology has prevented us from facing the political and economic challenges that inevitably arise when one stands on the side of those whose future is still open. The old unilateral options of *gericentrism* (appealing to the authority of age, convention, tradition, nostalgia) and *pedocentrism* (child-centered pedagogy) only produce monstrous states of siege which are irresponsible to the matters at hand, that is, to the question of how life is mediated through relations between old and young. The reported "rising tide of youngsters in trouble"[9] should be seen as a symptom of something horribly awry in the way we have thought about and organized our social, political and economic lives, because a child "in trouble" is a child without free, spontaneous and friendly access to adult thought and action, a condition brought about when adults are too busy, too self-preoccupied or too enamored of their own imperial projects to ask whether in fact they have any clothes on. As the old story says, it takes a child to tell the truth on that score, and that is why to separate the voice of the young from the center of our planning about the future is singularly perilous.

The Joint Chiefs' question of what to do must be understood as containing a genuine problematic, an invitation to those who consider themselves authorities on the subject of power to reconsider the nature of power in the light of what has just happened with the child's arrival in their midst. Of course, in terms of the military, such questioning is unlikely to occur, but I hope for us as educators the lesson isn't lost, not just because "children are our future" in some utopian, self-interested sense, but because our future is morally linked to the question of how we respond to new life in our midst here and now. We need to inquire critically and profoundly into all forms of thinking in our profession which take us away from our distinctly privileged mandate.

14

What Is Given in Giftedness?

Being gifted means something has been freely given—a special talent, a certain countenance, a capacity for laughter or song. It is this essential gratuity of giftedness which must be understood and protected if gifts themselves are not to be distorted, annexed or co-opted by vested interests dominant at any particular moment. Preserving the gratuity of giftedness also becomes important when we consider how to *live* with our gifts, because we see how difficult it is to live freely, that is, in a manner in which gifts may be freely lived and fully *realized*. I remember a little girl once telling me about her cat. She said she was sure her cat was a *real* cat, meaning that her cat had fully realized its cat-ness. Why? "Because I take care of it so well", she said. Obviously the cat enjoyed being a cat in her house, although I'm sure it was unaware of how much effort on the part of others went into making it possible for it to be itself.

In speaking of the gratuity of giftedness, of its free givenness, we not only rescue the possession of gifts from elitism or from questions about class and status, although such matters are all implicated in another way. Instead, we turn our attention to the givenness itself, to how the givenness shows itself as a gift. This is the phenomenological interest of trying to understand how something appears to be as it is. The phenomenological interest is the interest in how to stand with things in a way that the things can be seen for what they really are without the overlay of political agenda, dense theorizing or moralistic intent.

I offer the following considerations of what is at issue experientially, phenomenologically, in living with what is given.

1
Gifts Themselves Are Not Contingent

Any gift, insofar as it is a true gift, simply *is*: a gift given for a *reason* is not a true gift but is always in the service of something else. In the case of our own existential givens, the point is not so different. I have a friend whose youngest daughter is a child prodigy on the violin. At the age of ten she won a full scholarship to the Curtis Institute to study with the world's finest teachers, who are all amazed at her talent. Describing what it was like living with such a child, my friend said, "It's as if we're living in the presence of something that has nothing to do with us". No amount of extra work or practice could have forced this child's gift into being. But many children are sacrificed on the altar of their parents', or their own, ambition in a society where the deep myth is that "you can be whatever you want to be as long as you believe in yourself, put your mind to the task and are prepared to work hard". Pedagogically speaking, our response to such a belief must be both a yes and a no: some things are meant to be, other things are not.

I know a woman who, ever since she was an infant, wanted to be an opera singer. She started music lessons early, worked hard for fifteen years and eventually won the gold medal in voice from her local university. She won a scholarship to a prestigious music school in the East, and then after singing her first lesson with one of the world's finest voice teachers, she was told bluntly: "My dear, you don't have a good natural voice. You have an ordinary voice cultivated through sheer will, and already forced well beyond its limit. There's no point in your continuing your studies here...."

In 1984, at the auditions for the Metropolitan Opera, one of the judges, Eileen Farrell, was asked what she thought of today's young voices. She replied, "Voice today is in a state of crisis; they [the young singers] are simply promoting themselves. So that what is heard is not music rendered through voice, but a personality thrusting itself on the world". I take both these last examples as illustrations of something important, namely that it's easily possible to misinterpret as a gift that which in fact isn't a gift, often with terrible consequences, and that a bad orientation to a true gift produces results that are foreign to the gift itself. Gifts are not contingent; what is contingent is how we orient ourselves to what is given. What is given freely must be freely received without ulterior motive or agenda.

2
Finding One's Gift Means Being Found

Finding one's gift means finding what it is that makes one different, unique, i.e., what makes you you and me me. But this is not something I can simply discover for myself; it depends on the eyes and appreciation of others. In the case of my friend's child prodigy, so much depended on the discernment of others along the way. Without that recognition, the gift could never have come to fruition, and the child would never have "found herself". This fact underscores the necessity for a true pedagogy of giftedness, a pedagogy which is guided by careful discernment, discernment which is attentive to small signs of big things. For us as teachers, this requires tremendous maturity, which implies an authentic freedom on our part to watch over children in a way that is faithful to the full possibilities which are at work in children's lives.

Such an attentiveness involves an ability to become self-reflective, that is, to be able to discern and go beyond prejudices which could blind us to the full giftedness of the children in our midst. I know a teacher who used to be a fashion model. She's beautiful. Many of her female students think she's "great" and they emulate her, meaning they try to find themselves in her. But pedagogically speaking, we should be careful about this. In a culture where "looking good" has taken precedence over almost all other means by which it is possible to express oneself, a responsible teacher must be on guard against such deep cultural biases, rooted in ideological assumptions and socio-economic arrangements which occlude the expression of alternative ways of being in the world. The philosopher Nietzsche spoke of cultures being "inversely crippled", that is, highly developed in one way over and above all others. In nineteenth century Germany, said Nietzsche, everyone was "all ears", too dependent on the next new word from state authorities about this and that.[1] Every culture is inversely crippled in its own way, and children will go through life crippled to the degree that the significant adults in their lives have not understood their own crippledness, that is, their inevitable constraint within limits of knowledge and materiality. To find one's gift means to be found, but being found also depends upon another who is searching in the right way and in the right places.

Finding one's gift means being found in another sense as well. At Christmas time I always enjoy watching children "opening" their gifts. Usually they will head straight for the "special" gift, rip off the wrapping and forget about all the other things given to them. Sometimes they will say "This is what I've always wanted". The sense of being given what you've always wanted is very special because it's a sign that someone else understood you well enough, deeply enough, to know your heart's desire. It's a form of recognition, of being known by another in a way you've always known yourself, but which required the recognition of another for it to be personally understood. Sometimes it's possible to receive a "special" gift which is completely unexpected but precisely by virtue of its unexpectedness is the more appreciated. It is an even deeper sign of being understood, or known; a sign of being known in a way only dimly available to oneself. And that is how real advances are made in self understanding; how we find ourselves in what is given to us.

And then finally we find ourselves in our gifts, in the discovery of what is given to us, only to the degree we are prepared to lose ourselves in what we have found ourselves to be. This is not easy, but there is a deep dialectic between finding oneself and losing oneself which must be protected if what is given in giftedness is to go on showing itself as a gift. The fine tension at work here is evident in the ambiguity surrounding the term "self possession". A person who is "self-possessed" we understand as being well in charge of her faculties, her gifts, possessed of a certain poise, or "charisma", which means literally being in possession of something divinely given. But we also know self-possession to bear a negative meaning, and this is in the case of someone in whom we can discern many gifts, or a deep gift, but in whom somehow the gift is lost, hidden or suffocated because it is not realizing its true destiny as that which is found precisely in being given away, or shared with others.

Self-possession in this negative sense is sometimes associated with madness, that sign of a deep break in human bonding which is the result of profound distortions in the balance of relations between giving, receiving and giving away. Some people go through life feeling lost because their early primal desire to give (watch the way young children practice giving) was not received, acknowledged or appreciated. In terms of pedagogy we must learn to discern those moments when children in subtle, quiet ways are "opening" their gifts in front of us because how we receive them will determine whether or not the child will learn to find herself in the world creatively, that is, lose herself in a way that is also a gain. The early practices in giving which we see in young children are a form of inquiry as to whether there is a place in the world for what they have to offer, and many gifts are lost because there was a bad initial reception on the part of the significant receiver, be it parent, teacher or friend.

3
A True Gift Brings People Together

What is the silence that comes over an audience after a fine poetry reading, a well-played piece of music or a superb dramatization? If we describe the performances as "brilliant" we indicate our sense of something shining through the ordinary routine of things. But even more important is the effect of the performance on us—what it calls forth in our deep experience. The silence which reigns after the playing of a last note may be understood as a sign of our being "taken up" by that which has just been given into a new way of self-understanding, and a new way of being together. A well-developed gift which shines forth through the ordinary routine of things realizes something for us, something which we may well intuit subliminally yet which we cannot ourselves do or bring into effect. We might say, then, that when another person realizes her own gift in a special way, we too are drawn into our own fundamental potentiality. This accounts for the wonderful invigoration we often feel after witnessing a fine performance. We are inspired to go home and practice more regularly, or study harder or simply attend more deeply to the question of our own unique purpose. The point is that the mark of a true gift is its power to bring forth the question of others' gifts, that is, to bring others into the question of their gifts.

A gift realizes itself, then, not just in self-fulfillment but to the extent that others are drawn into a consideration of its broader, deeper and inner meaning. It is this capacity to engage others which signals the communalizing power of giftedness, and why, for example, gifted education may be an enterprise to be taken seriously. A true pedagogy of giftedness is oriented not simply to realizing the hidden potential of this or that particular student, but to bringing forth that which has the power to unite us as a human community through opening new possibilities for our own mutual regeneration. How we orient to what is freely given, how we care for it, will determine how well we can face what comes to meet us as new, which in turn holds (part of) the answer for our own authentication as persons.

Notes

Preface

1. Carl Gustav Jung, *Memories, Dreams, Reflections* (New York: Random House, 1989), p. 89.
2. Wilhelm Dilthey, *Gesammelte Schriften* (Gottingen: Vanderboeck und Ruprecht, 1, 1913/1967), p. 255.
3. David Loy, "Indra's Postmodern Net", *Philosophy East and West*. 43, no. 3 (Summer 1993), p. 503.
4. Harold Bloom, "The Pragmatics of Contemporary Jewish Culture". *Post-Analytic Philosophy*, edited by John Rachman and Cornel West (New York: Columbia University Press, 1985), p. 109.

Foreword: "It's All One Meditation"

1. Gary Snyder, "The Original Mind of Gary Snyder, June 1977." In *Meetings with Remarkable Men and Women*, from the editors of East West (Brookline MA: East West Health Books, 1989), p. 252.

1
Journeying: A Meditation on Leaving Home and Coming Home

1. *Revised Standard Version of the Bible*, Genesis 32:28.
2. Caesar E. Farah, *Islam* (New York: Barrons, 1987).
3. See for example, R. Amore, *Two Masters, One Message* (Nashville, TN: Abingdon, 1982).
4. Ashis Nandy, "Shamans, Savages and the Wilderness: On the Audibility of Dissent and the Future of Civilizations", *Alternatives* xiv, no. 3 (July, 1989), p. 68.
5. Tenzin Gyatso, *Kindness, Clarity and Insight*. J. Hopkins (trans. and ed.)

(New York: Snow Lion, 1985).

6. *Revised Standard Version of the Bible*, Psalm 46:10.

7. Chuang Tzu, *The Inner Chapters*, J. English (ed.) (Boston: Shambhala Press, 1993), p. 16.

8. See for example, R. Bultmann, *The Theology of the New Testament* (Oxford: Blackwells, 1969).

9. Thomas Merton, *The Asian Journal* (New York: New Directions, 1975), p. 34.

10. Chogyam Trungpa, Meditation and the Myth of Freedom (Boston MA: Shambhala, 1990), p. 68.

11. Quoted by H. Dumoulin (Ed.), *Buddhism in the Modern World* (London: Collier Macmillan, 1976), p. 31.

2
Teacher Education and Global Culture

1. Lao-Tzu, *Te-Tao Ching*, Robert Henricks (ed.), (New York: Ballantine Books, 1989), p. 32.

2. Wendel Berry, "The Futility of Global Thinking", *Harpers*, June 24, 1989.

3. Vaclav Havel, "After Communism", *New York Review of Books*, xxxiv, no. 3, 1991.

3
Identity, Self and Others in the Conduct of Pedagogical Action: An East/West Inquiry

1. See David Kennedy, *Young Children's Thinking: An interpretation from phenomenology* (unpublished Ph.D. Dissertation, University of Kentucky, 1984).

2. For the discussion on historical developments in the lineage of identity, I have been very much served by John Forrester, "A Brief History of the Subject," in *Identity: The Real Me*, ICA Document #6 (London: Free Association Books, 1987), 13–16.

3. For an extended discussion of Weber's argument, see David Loy, "Preparing for Something that Never Happens: The Means/Ends Problem in Modern

Culture," *International Studies in Philosophy* 26, no. 4 (1994), 49 f.f.

4. See, for example, Patrick Williams and Laura Christian, *Colonial Discourse and Postcolonial Theory: A Reader* (New York: Columbia University Press, 1995).

5. Terry Eagleton, "The Politics of Subjectivity," in *Identity: The Real Me*, *ICA Documents #6* (London: Free Association Books, 1987), 47.

6. In Forrester, "A Brief History of the Subject," p. 14.

7. Joanna Macy, *Mutual Causality in Buddhism and General Systems Theory* (Albany: State University of New York Press, 1991), p. 108.

8. Paul Ricoeur, *Self as Other* (Chicago: University of Chicago Press, 1992).

9. The concept of "Third Space" I borrow from Homi Bhabha but developed differently here. See Homi Bhabha, "The Third Space", in *Identity: Community, Culture, Difference*, edited by Jonathan Rutherford (London: Lawrence and Wishart, 1990).

10. Kazuaki Tanahashi, ed. *Moon in a Dewdrop: Writings of Zen Master Dogen* (San Francisco: North Point Press, 1985), p. 157.

11. D. T. Suzuki, *Living by Zen* (London: Rider, 1990).

12. Thich Naht Hanh, "Look Into Your Hand, My Child!" *The Acorn: A Gandhian Review* 3, no. 1 (March 1988), p. 10.

13. Vincente Fatone, *The Philosophy of Nagarjuna* (Delhi: Motilal Banarsidass, 1981).

14. Peter Hershock, "Person as Narration: the Dissolution of 'Self' and 'Other' in Ch'an Buddhism", *Philosophy East and West* 44, no. 4 (1994), p. 691.

15. In *The Diamond Sutra and the Sutra of Hui Neng*, translated by A. F. Price and Wong Mou-Lam. (Boston: Shambhala Press, 1969), p. 69.

16. David Loy, "Indra's postmodern net," *Philosophy East and West* 43, no. 3 (1993), p. 485.

17. For a discussion of this concept, see Achaan Chah, *A Still Forest Pool* (London: The Theosophical Publishing House, 1989).

18. This is discussed more fully in Donald S. Lopez, Jr., *Buddhist Hermeneutics* (Honolulu: University of Hawaii Press, 1988).

19. Thich Nhat Hanh, *The Sun My Heart* (Berkeley, CA: Parallax Press, 1988), p. 42

20. In Chinese, the one word *hsin* means mind-heart, in recognition that the work of mind and heart cannot be separated.

21. This story is recorded in Tchouang-Tseu, *Oeuvres Completes* (Paris: Gallimard, 1969), p. 47. Emphasis mine.

22. Psalm 46:10.
23. Ven. Song-chol, *Echoes from Mt. Kaya*, Ven. Won-tek ed. (Seoul, Korea: Lotus Lantern International Buddhist Centre, 1988), p. 81.
24. In Richard Palmer, *Hermeneutics* (Chicago: Northwestern University Press, 1969), 43.
25. Isaiah 30:20.
26. Ashis Nandy, "Modern Medicine and Its Nonmodern Critics: A Study in Discourse", in *The Savage Freud and Other Essays on Possible and Retrievable Selves* (Princeton, NJ: Princeton University Press, 1995); pp. 145–195.
27. In Koji Sato, *The Zen Life* (Kyoto: Tankosha, 1984), p. 177.
28. Mark 10:13.

4
The Hermeneutic Imagination and the Pedagogic Text

1. Information here concerning the character of Hermes has been drawn from M. Stapleton, "Hermes", *The Hamlyn Concise Dictionary of Greek and Roman Mythology* (London: Hamlyn, 1982), pp. 140–142.
2. S. B. Messer, L. A. Sass, and B. L. Woolfolk (eds.), *Hermeneutics and Psychological Theory*. New Brunswick, NJ: (Rutgers University Press, 1988).
3. *Market Process*, 6, no. 1(1988), entire issue.
4. The Canadian Society for Hermeneutics and Postmodern Thought, inaugurated in May 1985, made the following "Statement of Purpose" in its publication, *Bulletin* (1988), 3, no. 3 (1988), p. 15:

   [The society] was created to serve as a forum for interdisciplinary conversation. It is committed to the goal of opening up new and much needed channels of communication between the various human disciplines. For the success that these disciplines have enjoyed in defining their boundaries has been without attendant negative consequences. The more precisely each discipline has defined its own terrain, the more difficult the effort of communication between or across disciplines has become. The society does not propose to tear down fences. It would be more appropriate to think of conversations *over* fences, as one might converse with one's neighbours. What makes our particular conversations possible is an emphasis on methodological self-reflection, and the realization that the so-called facts that one discovers are already the product of many levels of interpretation. Interpretation is an activity common to all the human disciplines (in the humanities as well as in the social sciences, from the analysis of texts to the study of peoples and cultures), and hermeneutics is the study of this activity.

Those interested in membership in the society should write to CSH/SCH, Department of Philosophy, McMaster University, Hamilton, Ontario, Canada L8S 4K1.

5. K-O. Apel, "Scientistics, Hermeneutics, Critique of Ideology: An Outline of a Theory of Science from an Epistemological-Anthropological Point of View." In K. Mueller-Volmer (ed.), *The Hermeneutics Reader* (New York: Continuum, 1985), p. 333.

6. In English, the most comprehensive working out of the anti-foundationalist case is R. Rorty, *Philosophy and the Mirror of Nature* (Princeton, NJ: Princeton University Press, 1979).

7. H-G. Gadamer, "On the Origins of Philosophical Hermeneutics." In *Philosophical Apprenticeships* (Cambridge, MA: MIT Press), p. 100.

8. Whether or not there is such a thing as "postmodern hermeneutics" is a topic of debate. Here I simply prefer to say that all of the conversations about postmodernism are interpretive, hermeneutic endeavors. See the debate between the two primary players, Hans-Georg Gadamer and Jacques Derrida, *Dialogue and Deconstructionism: The Gadamer-Derrida Encounter* (Albany, NY: SUNY Press, 1989). John Caputo attempts to show the articulation between hermeneutics and postmodernism/deconstructionism in *Radical Hermeutics: Repetition, Deconstruction and the Hermeneutic Project* (Bloomington, IN: Indiana University Press, 1987).

9. United Nations, *Convention on the Rights of the Child* (New York: UNESCO, 1990). See also reports such as that of economist Leonard Silk: "The United States has the highest child poverty rate of any industrialized country". Reported in *The International Herald Tribune* (May 13–14, 1989), p. 9.

10. See David Kennedy's important study tracing the development of concepts of childhood in Western culture. He argues that under the Enlightenment rationality of the modern era the child has been reduced to child-as-object, a turn which undermines the ontological place of the child in the adult-child

relation. David Kennedy, "Young Children's Thinking: An Interpretation from Phenomenology". Ph.D. diss., University of Kentucky, 1986. Reviewed in *Phenomenology + Pedagogy* 6, no. 2 (1988), pp. 109–113.

11. Stapleton, p. 141.
12. The best general survey is still, in my view, R. Palmer, *Hermeneutics*. (Evanston, IL: Northwestern University Press, 1967). There is a good introduction in B. R. Wachterhauser, *Hermeneutics and Modern Philosophy* (Albany, NY: SUNY Press, 1986). For this paper I was greatly assisted by the historical survey of Kurt Mueller-Vollmer, note 5.
13. In English, the two most important documents for Schleiermacher's hermeneutics are H. Kimmerle (Ed.), *The Handwritten Manuscripts of Friedrich Schleiermacher* (Missoula, MT: Scholars Press, 1977), and F. D. E. Schleiermacher, "Outline of the 1819 lectures, *"New Literary History,* 10, no. 1 (1978), pp. 1–16. All of the quotations that follow are from the latter source.
14. F. deSaussure, *Course in General Linguistics*, C. Bally and A. Sechaheye (Eds.), (New York: Philosophical Library, 1959).
15. P. Sweet, *Wilhelm van Humboldt* (Columbus: Ohio State University Press, 1978).
16. J. Kristeva, *Desire in Language* (New York: Columbia University Press, 1980).
17. Paulo Freire discusses this theme in a film documenting experiments using his praxis model. See "Starting from Nina: The Politics of Learning". (Toronto: Development Education Centre, 1978).
18. See H. A. Hodges, *The Philosophy of Wilhelm Dilthey* (Boston: Routledge and Kegan Paul, 1952). R. Makreel, *Dilthey: Philosopher of the Human Sciences* (Princeton, NJ: Princeton University Press, 1975). H. P. Rickman, (Ed.) *Wilhelm Dilthey: Selected Writings*; New York: Cambridge University Press, 1976).
19. P. Ricoeur, "The Model of the Text: Meaningful Action Considered as a Text." In J. B. Thompson (Ed.), *Hermeneutics and the Human Sciences* (New York: Columbia University Press, 1985), pp. 197–221.
20. Students looking for an accessible introduction to Derrida would find helpful Richard Kearney's interview with him in R. Kearney, *Dialogues with Contemporary Continental Thinkers* (Manchester, England: University of Manchester Press, 1984), pp. 105–126.
21. A. Schutz, *On Phenomenology and Social Relations* (Chicago: The

University of Chicago Press, 1970).

22. H. Garfinkle, *Studies in Ethnomethodology* (Englewood Cliffs, NJ: Prentice Hall, 1967).

23. M. Heidegger, *Being and Time* (New York: Harper and Row, 1962), p. 43.

24. _____ , "The End of Philosophy and the Task of Thinking." In D. Krall (ed.) *Martin Heidegger: Basic Writings*. (New York: Harper and Row), p. 375.

25. H-G. Gadamer, *Truth and Method* (London: Sheed and Ward, 1979).

26. K. J. and M. M. Gergin, "Narratives of the Self". In T. R. Sarbin and K. E. Schiebe (Eds.), *Studies in Social Identity* (New York: Praeger, 1983), pp. 254-273. D. E. Polkinghorne, *Narrative Knowing and the Human Sciences*. (Albany, NY: SUNY Press, 1988). T. R. Sarbin (Ed.) *Narrative Psychology: the Storied Nature of Human Conduct* (New York: Praeger, 1986).

27. Play and desire are central themes throughout the work of both Derrida and Kristeva. See Derrida, note 20 above and Kristeva, note 16.

28. Z. Longxi, "The Tao and the Logos: Notes on Derrida's Critique of Logocentrism," *Critical Inquiry* 1, no. 3 (1985), pp. 385–398. Also "The Myth of the Other: China in the Eyes of the West. *Critical Inquiry* 15, no. 1 (1988), pp. 108–131.

29. O. M. Seng, *The Meaning of Moral Education: An Interpretive Study of Moral Education in Korea*. (Ph.D. dissertation, University of Alberta, 1986).

30. C. M. Chambers, *For Our Children's Children: An Educator's Interpretation of Dene Testimony to the Mackenzie Valley Pipeline Inquiry*. (Ph.D. dissertation, University of Victoria, British Columbia, 1989.)

31. I have in mind here a wide range of writing and inquiry that may be referred to generically as World Order Studies. Key figures include Ali Mazrui, Immanuel Wallerstein, Andre Gunder Frank, Ashis Nandy, Rajni Kothari, Richard Falk, R. B. J. Walker, Saul Mendelovitz and many others. The Centre for the Study of Developing Societies in Delhi, India, and the World Order Models Project, United Nations Plaza, New York, publish an important journal called *Alternatives*. A good introductory text is R. Walker (ed.), *Culture, Ideology and World Order*. (Boulder, CO: Westview Press, 1984). Major themes addressed in this field of discourse include North-South Relations, Peace and Disarmament, Colonialism and

Postcolonialism, and the future global habitat.

32. "Representationalism" as a basic gesture of Western thinking is well discussed by Rorty. See note 6 above. G. B. Madison discusses the critique of representationalism as a feature of postmodern philosophy in "Postmodern Philosophy?", *Critical Review* 2, no. 2/3 (1988), pp. 166–182.

33. See D. Jardine, "A Bell Ringing in an Empty Sky." Paper delivered at the eleventh annual conference of the *Journal of Curriculum Theorizing*, Bergamo Centre, Dayton, Ohio, October 18–21, 1989.

34. For a specific example, see L. Ellsworth, "Why Doesn't This Feel Empowering? Working Through the Repressive Myths of Critical Pedagogy," *Harvard Educational Review* 59, no. 3 (1989), pp. 299–324.

35. This position on a hermeneutic understanding of the tradition of ideology critique has been well worked out by Paul Ricoeur, "Ethics and Culture", *Philosophy Today* 17, no. 2/4 (1973), pp. 163–155.

36. P. Freire, *Pedagogy of the Oppressed* (New York: Herder and Herder, 1971), p. 121.

37. Gadamer elaborates on the conversational mode of inquiry in Part III of *Truth and Method*. Rorty deals with it explicitly in *Philosphy and the Mirror of Nature*. In a curriculum research context, see T. Carson, "Closing the Gap Between Research and Practice: Conversation as a Mode of Research", *Phenomenology +Pedagogy* 4, no. 2 (1986), pp. 73–85.

38. T. Merton, "A Letter to Pablo Antonio Concerning Giants". In *Emblems of a Season of Fury* (Norfolk, VA: New Directions, 1961) pp. 70–80.

39. Hence in the title Gadamer's key text, *Truth and Method*, "truth" and "method" are conjoined.

40. Schleiermacher, *Outline*, p. 28.

41. See the film series by Robert McNeil, "The Story of Language" (New York: Public Broadcasting System, 1987) for a good introduction to this topic.

42. The World Order Studies movement has crystallized in its work many of these themes (see note 13 above for the names of significant writers). Ashis Nandy has written eloquently and profoundly on all of these topics from a non-Western point of view. See A. Nandy, *The Intimate Enemy: Loss and Recovery of Self Under Colonialism* (Delhi: Oxford University Press, 1983), and *Tradition, Tyranny and Utopia* (Delhi: Oxford University Press, 1987). Nandy is also a frequent contributor to the journal *Alternatives*.

43. A useful introduction to semiotics is A. Berger, *Signs in Contemporary*

Culture (New York: Longmans, 1984). See also K. Silverman, *The Subject of Semiotics*. (New York: Oxford University Press, 1988).

44. See R. M. Schafer, *The Tuning of the World* (New York: Alfred Knopf, 1977), and Steven Feld, "Sound Structure as Social Structure", *Ethnomusicology* 28, no. 3 (1984), pp. 383–409.

45. See for example M. L. Dobbert, *Ethnographic Research: Theory and Application for Modern Schools and Society* (New York: Praeger, 1982). Also B. Glaser and A. Strauss, *The Discovery of Grounded Theory* (Chicago: Aldine, 1967).

46. A. Blum, *Self-Reflection in the Human Sciences*. (Atlantic Highlands, NJ: Humanities Press, 1984).

47. Foreword to the second German edition of *Truth and Method*. In *After Philosophy: End or transformation?*, Keith Baines and T. McCarthy (eds.), (Cambridge, MA: The MIT Press, 1987), p. 349.

48. I am thinking particularly here of Gregory Ulmer's description of the "imperial dispensation" of the logocentric tradition of the West, in "Textshop for Post(e) Pedagogy," in G. D. Atkins and M. Johnson (eds.), *Writing and Reading Differently* (Lawrence, KS: University of Kansas Press, 1985). Ashis Nandy has written of the culture of the West as one of "hyper-masculinity, adulthood, historicism, objectivism, and hypernormality". See *The Intimate Enemy*, p. 100.

5

Experimental Hermeneutics: Interpreting Educational Reality

1. M. Heidegger, *Being and Time*, J. Maquarrie and E. Robinson (eds.), (New York: Harper and Row, 1962), p. 32.

2. In L. Erwin and D. Maclennan (eds.), *Sociology of Education in Canada* (Toronto: Copp Clark, 1994), p. 27.

3. H-G. Gadamer, *Truth and Method* (London: Sheed and Ward, 1977), p. 420.

4. Cornel West, "The New Cultural Politics of Difference, *October* 53: no. 1, pp. 93–109.

5. J-F. Lyotard, *The Postmodern Condition* (Minneapolis: University of Minnesota Press, 1986).

6. See, for example, R. Fulford, "The Ideology of the Book", *Queen's Quarterly* 101: no. 4 (Winter 1994), pp. 800–812.

7. H. Bloom, "The Pragmatics of Contemporary Jewish Culture". In J. Rachman and C. West (eds.), *Post-Analytic Philosophy* (New York: Columbia University Press, 1985).

8. J. Mander, *In the Absence of the Sacred* (San Francisco: Sierra Club, 1991).

9. B. Hall, "Information Technology and Global Learning for Sustainable Development", *Alternatives: Social Transformation for Humane Governance* 19: no. 1 (Winter 1994), pp. 99–132.

10. For further development of this theme, see "On Discursivity and Neurosis: Conditions of Possibility for (West) Discourse with Others", in this volume.

11. J-F. Lyotard, *The Postmodern Condition: A Report on Knowledge* (Minneapolis, MN: University of Minnesota Press, 1986).

12. F. Jameson, *Postmodernism or the Cultural Logic of Late Capitalism*, (Durham, NC: Duke University Press, 1992).

13. A. Kroker, *Panic Encyclopedia* (Montreal: New World Perspectives, 1989).

14. M. Foucault, "Panopticism", in P. Rabinow (ed.), *The Foucault Reader* (New York: Pantheon Books, 1984).

15. T. Roszak, *The Cult of Information and the True Art of Thinking* (New York: Pantheon Books, 1986).

16. See, for example, W. Thompson, "The Cultural Implications of the New Biology," in *GAIA: A Way of Knowing* (Boulder, CO: Westview, 1988); and F. Varela, *Prospects for a Biology of Cognition* (Chicago: Pyrgammon Press, 1991).

17. T. Hahn, *The Sun My Heart* (Berkeley, CA: Parallax Press, 1989).

18. E. Husserl, *Cartesian Meditations* (London: Oxford University Press, 1952).

19. J. Hillman, *Blue Fire* (New York: Harper and Row, 1991), p. 37.

20. J. Gordon, "Why Students of Color Are Not Entering Teaching: Reflections from Minority Teachers", *Teacher Education* 45 no. 5 (1994), pp. 346–353.

21. M. Scheler, "Man in the Age of Compensation". In H. Doumelin, *Buddhism in the Modern World* (London: Collier, 1976), p. 48.

6
Modernism, Hyperliteracy and the Colonization of the Word

1. *Canada Yearbook 1992*, (Statistics Canada: Publications Division, 1991), p. 118.

2. See Alvin Kernan, *The Death of Literature* (New Haven: Yale University Press, 1990), pp. 1–10.

3. For a full discussion, see Jonathan Culler, *Structuralist Politics, Structuralism, Linguistics and the Study of Literature* (Ithaca, NY: Cornell University Press, 1975).

4. H-G. Gadamer, "Religious and Political Speaking", *Boston University Studies in Philosophy and Religion*, Vol. 1, Leroy S. Rouner, General Editor. (Notre Dame and London: University of Notre Dame Press 1980), p. 92.

5. See Paulo Freire and Don Macedo, *Literacy: Reading the Word and the World* (South Hadley, MA: Bergin and Garvey, 1987).

6. Discussed by James Burke in "Connections", a BBC documentary on the relation between science and culture. (London: The British Broadcasting Corporation, 1978).

7. Jacques Derrida, "No Apocalyse, Not Now (Full Speed Ahead, Seven Missiles Seven Missives", Catherine Porter and Philip Lewis. In *The Wallace Stevens Journal*, 14, No. 2 (Summer 1984), pp. 20–31.

8. Pierre Bourdieu, "Systems of Education and Systems of Thought." In Michael F. D. Young (ed.), *Knowledge and Control* (London: Collier-Macmillan, 1971), p. 191.

9. For example, L.W. Spitz, *The Protestant Reformation* (Englewood Cliffs, NJ: Prentice-Hall, 1966); and H. Brinton (1968), *The Context of the Reformation* (London: Hutchinson, 1968). For an interesting recent treatment of the relationship between protestantism, printing and Western pedagogical theory, see Carmen Luke, *Pedagogy, Printing and Protestantism: The Discourse on Childhood* (Albany, NY: SUNY Press, 1989).

10. George Steiner, "The Retreat from the Word", *Language and Silence: Essays on Language, Literature and the Inhuman* (New York: Atheneum Press, 1982), p. 25.

11. Paulo Freire, *Pedagogy of the Oppressed*, (Myra Ramos Trans.), (New

York: Continuum, 1970); *Education for Critical Consciousness*, Myra Ramos Trans.), (New York: Continuum Press, 1973); "Cultural Action for Freedom," *Harvard Educational Review*, Monograph Series, No. 1, 1970).

12. This point has been argued most strongly in recent days by Elspeth Stuckey in *The Violence of Literacy* (Portsmouth, NH: Boynton/Cook, 1991).

13. Plato, *Seventh Letter*, 341c, 344c and Phaedrus, 275. In *The Collected Dialogues of Plato Including the Letters*, Edith Hamilton and Huntington Cairns (eds.), (New York: Pantheon, 1961). For a full discussion of Plato's arguments about the relation of speech to writing, see H-G. Gadamer, *Truth and Method* (London: Sheed and Ward, 1978), part III.

14. Matt Groening, *School Is Hell* (New York: Pantheon Books, 1987).

15. Lao Tzu Tao Te Ching, 65. In Wee Chong Tan, *Lao Tzu and Gandhi (Friends of Jesus)* (Victoria, BC: Novissima Lectio, 1983), p. 19.

16. A good introduction to postmodernism is contained in the biographical essays of key figures, in John Sturrock (ed.), *Structuralism and Since* (London: Oxford University Press, 1978).

17. For a consideration of the "deep ethics" in deconstructionism, see Richard Kearney's interview with Derrida in R. Kearney, *Dialogues with Contemporary Continental Thinkers* (Manchester, UK: University of Manchester Press, 1984), pp. 105–126.

18. See E. D. Hirsch, *Cultural Literacy: What Every American Needs to Know* (Boston, MA: Houghton Mifflin, 1987); and H. Bloom, *The Closing of the American Mind* (New York: Simon and Schuster, 1987).

19. David G. Smith, "Pedagogy as an International Narrative Practice". A paper delivered at the Invitational Banff International Pedagogy Conference, Banff, Alberta, May 26–29, 1990.

20. William Thompson, "The Cultural Implications of the New Biology", *GAIA: A Way of Knowing* (Great Barrington, MA: Lindisfarne Press, 1987), p. 33.

21. In B. Commoner, *The Closing Circle: Nature, Man and Technology* (New York: Knopf, 1971).

22. See J. Heimlich and S. Pittleman, *Semantic Mapping.* (Newark, DE: International Reading Asociation, 1986); and Umberto Eco, *Semiotics and the Philosophy of Language* (Bloomington, IN: Indiana University Press, 1984), p. 53.

23. In J. Batz, "The Many Faces of Walter Ong", *Universitas* (Fall 1988), p. 40.

24. Jacques Derrida, *Of Grammatology*, G. Spivak Trans. (Baltimore, MD: Johns Hopkins University Press, 1976), p. 66.

25. For a discussion of the "new literacy", see John Willinsky, *The New Literacy: Redefining Reading and Writing* (New York: Routledge, 1990).

26. R. Murray Schafer, *The Tuning of the World* (Toronto: McClelland and Stewart, 1977).

27. T. Berry, "Ecology and Society". A public address at the Ontario Institute for Studies in Education (April 19, 1990).

28. See David Jardine, "Awakening from Descartes' Nightmare: On the Love of Ambiguity in Phenomenological Approaches to Education", *Studies in Philosophy and Education* 10, no. 12, (1990), pp. 211–232.

29. In Zhang Longxi, "The Tao and the Logos: Notes on Derrida's Critique of Logocentrism", *Critical Inquiry* 11, no. 4 (March 1985), p. 394.

7

On Discursivity and Neurosis: Conditions of Possibility for (West) Discourse with Others

1. For an excellent discussion of the historical background of the new politics of identity, see Cornel West, "The New Cultural Politics of Difference", *October,* 53:1, 93–109.

2. See especially M. Foucault, *Power/Knowledge: Selected Interviews and Other Writings,* Colin Gordon (ed.), (New York, NY: Pantheon Books, 1980).

3. A good introduction to Derrida is Jonathon Culler's "Derrida" in John Sturrock (ed.), *Structuralism and Since* (London: Oxford University Press, 1979).

4. The strongest claim about the end of grand narratives comes from J-F. Lyotard, *The Postmodern Condition* (Boston: MIT Press, 1986).

5. See particularly *Cutting Through Spiritual Materialism* (Boston: Shambhala Press, 1986) and *Meditation and the Myth of Freedom* (Boston: Shambhala Press, 1988).

6. Ibid., p. 10.

7. For a discussion of how the rise of the ideal of public literacy was linked to a concern for public discipline, see Carmen Luke, *Printing, Protestantism and Pedagogy* (New York: SUNY Press 1988). The point made here I

162

discuss more fully in "Modernism, Hyperliteracy and the Colonization of the Word", *Alternatives* 17 (1992) 247–260.

8. I am indebted to William I. Thompson's discussion of this in "The Cultural Implications of the New Biology". See William I. Thompson (ed.), *GAIA: A Way of Knowing* (New York: Lindisfarne Press, 1988) pp. 27–29.

9. Vaclav Havel, "Words on Words", *The New York Review of Books*, January 18, 1990.

10. For a discussion of the child-as-monster in the cultural struggle between *puer* and *senex*, see David Jardine, "Student-Teacher, Interpretation, and the Monstrous Child". *Journal of Philosophy of Education* (in press).

11. See Ashis Nandy, "The Uncolonized Mind: A Post Colonial View of India and the West", in *The Intimate Enemy: Loss and Recovery of Self Under Colonialism* (Delhi: Oxford University Press, 1983), pp. 70–93.

12. Pierre Bourdieu, "Systems of Education and Systems of Thought." In M. F. D. Young (ed.), *Knowledge and Control* (London: Collier and Macmillan, 1967), p. 191.

13. H-G. Gadamer "Foreword to the Second German Edition of *Truth and Method.*" In Kenneth Baynes, James Bohman and Thomas McCarthy (eds.), *After Philosophy: End or Transformation* (London: MIT Press, 1987), p. 349.

14. For a discussion of Luther's excesses, see Hartmann Grisar, *Martin Luther: His Life and Work* (New York: AMS Press, 1930). So far as I know, no research to date has investigated the relationship between the increasing violence in Luther's later life and his prodigious fondness for beer, but, in the light of so much recent work in the field of addictions on the link between long-term alcohol consumption and the development of "rages", such a line of inquiry could be useful. Certainly, the violence of his verbal and written tirades became a source of great concern to his friends: see John M. Todd, *Martin Luther: A Biographical Study* (New York, NY: Paulist Press, 1964), p. 275. It is interesting to compare, for example, the evolution of Luther's attitude towards Jews. His youthful sermon of 1523, "That Jesus Christ Was Born a Jew" is open and generous; his sermon of 1543, "Concerning the Jews and Their Lies," is virulently anti-semitic. See *Disputation and Dialogue: Readings in the Jewish-Christian Encounter*, edited by F. E. Talmage (New York, NY: Ktav Publishing House Inc. 1975), pp. 33–36.

15. Again in the context of Luther, Gerhard Ebeling suggests that the clue to

understanding Luther "seems to lie in the observation that Luther's thought always contains an (unresolved) antithesis, tension between strongly opposed but related polarities...the letter and the Spirit, the law and the gospel...faith and love", etc. See *Luther: An Introduction to His Thought* (Philadelphia, PA: Fortress Press, 1983), p. 25. In another context, Rudy Weibe's novel *Peace Shall Destroy Many* (Toronto, ONT: MacLellan and Stewart, 1974) is a telling example of how a community committed to absolute pacifism has its own forms of violence, which arise precisely from attempts to suppress it.

16. Edward Said's *Orientalism* (New York: Vintage Press, 1978) is the work that more than any other illuminated the condition of interdependence between oriental and occidental worlds. For other contexts, such as the experience of Latin America and India, see respectively, Andre Gunder Frank, *Capitalism and Underdevelopment in Latin America* (New York, NY: Basic Books, 1977), and Ashis Nandy, *Tradition, Tyranny and Utopia: Essays in the Politics of Awareness* (New Delhi: Oxford University Press, 1988).

17. In a book with a generally very anti-Western tone, Kiang Kang-Hu grudgingly acknowledges the contribution of Western missionaries to the emancipation of women in China. See "Women and Education in China", in *On Chinese Studies* (Shanghai: The Commercial Press, 1934), pp. 191–204.

18. Reported by Henry Louis Gates in "Blood and Irony: How Race and Religion Will Shape the Future." *Economist*, 11 September, 1993, p. 37.

19. D. T. Suzuki, *Living by Zen* (London: Century Hutchinson Limited, 1990), p. 150.

20. For a discussion concerning the relation of the Biblical creation myth to the rise of science, see D. Homans, *Science and the Modern World View* (New York: Colliers, 1967).

21. Peter Berger and Thomas Luckmann, *The Social Construction of Reality* (New York: Anchor Books, 1967).

22. For a further discussion of the origins of the cognitive self-enclosure of Western consciousness, see David Jardine, *Speaking With a Boneless Tongue* (Bragg Creek, Alberta: Makyo Press, 1992). Also, William Barrett, *The Illusion of Technique* (New York: Anchor Doubleday, 1972).

23. See various papers of Berry's on this theme in *The Dream of the Earth* (San Francisco, CA: Sierra Club Books, 1988).

24. *Revised Standard Version of the Bible*, Luke 12: 27; Matthew 6: 26.

25. R. Murray Schafer, *Ear Cleaning* (Don Mills, ONT: BMI Press, 1967). On the relationship of sound structure to social structure, see Steven Feld, "Sound Structure as Social Structure", *Ethnomusicology* 28: 3 (1984), pp. 383–409.

26. The relation of geography to modes or styles of cognition is being fruitfully researched by Derek Gregory, *Geographical Imaginations* (Oxford: Blackwells, 1993).

27. This is a term I coined after reading William Thomson, *Imaginary Landscapes: Making Worlds of Myth and Science* (New York: Lindisfarne Press, 1990).

28. David Campbell, *Writing Security: United States Foreign Policy and the Politics of Identity* (Minneapolis: University of Minnesota Press, 1992). For the point which follows, I am indebted to the brilliant exposition of Campbell by Sankaran Krishna in "The Importance of Being Ironic: A Postcolonial View on Critical International Relations Theory", *Alternatives* 18 (1993), pp. 385–417.

29. Thomas Merton, *The Asian Journal of Thomas Merton*, Naomi Burton, Patrick Hart and James Laughlin (eds.), (New York: New Directions, 1975) p. 117.

30. Vaclav Havel, "How Europe Could Fail", *The New York Review of Books*, vol. XI, no. 19, 18 November, 1993, p. 3.

31. Ira Shor, *Culture Wars: School and Society in the Conservative Restoration* (Boston, MA: Routledge and Kegan Paul, 1986).

32. Gayatri C. Spivak, "Postmarked Calcutta, India", in *The Postcolonial Critic*, ed. Sarah Harasym (New York: Routledge, 1990), p. 93: "(America has) the most opulent university system in the world, where clearly the humanities have as an ideology know-nothingism, so that they cannot be critical in this society".

33. *Meditation and the Myth of Freedom, p. 73 .*

34. David Loy, "Indra's Postmodern Net", *Philosophy East and West* 43, no. 3, July 1993, p. 485.

35. For those wishing to further investigate the meditative tradition, see especially Chogyam Trungpa, *Meditation and the Myth of Freedom,* and Thich Naht Hahn's *The Miracle of Mindfulness: A Manual on Meditation,* Mobi Ho (trans.) (Boston, MA: Beacon Press, 1987). Hahn's *The Sun My Heart: From Mindfulness to Insight Contemplation* (Berkeley,

CA: Parallax Press, 1988) contains a very sophisticated, brilliant analysis of the resonances between the insights of contemplative practice and the findings of the new physics regarding, for example, the unity of time and space. There are notable similarities between the meditative practice of stopping and the Western phenomenological strategy of "bracketting" to reveal the essences of experience. The major difference is that in Buddhism, essence is an illusion.

36. For an accessible discussion of this, see Wilfred Cantwell Smith, *The Faith of Other Men* (New York: Vintage, 1967).

37. Loy, p. 497.

38. Martin Buber, *The Eclipse of God*, Maurice S. Friedman (trans.), (New York: Harper Torchbook, 1975), p. 35. The above quote is a paraphrase of Buber by Loy, p. 497.

39. Personal communication from N. Radhakrishnan, Director of the Gandhi Centre, New Delhi, October 12, 1993.

40. Thomas Berry, "Technology and the Healing of the Earth", in *Dream of the Earth*, p. 142.

41. Max Scheler, "Man in the Age of Compensation" (1929). Quoted by Ernst Benz in *Buddhism in the Western World*, Heinrich Dumoulin (ed.), (London: Collier, 1976), p. 321.

42. Loy, p. 503.

43. Jacques Derrida, *Writing and Difference*, Alan Bass (Trans.), (Chicago: University of Chicago Press, 1984), p. 184.

44. Karl Marx, *The Eighteenth Brumaire or Louis Bonaparte* (New York: International Publishers, 1981) p. 15.

45. Wendell Berry, "The Futility of Global Thinking", *Harper's Magazine*, September, 1989, pp. 16–22.

46. *Cutting Through Spiritual Materialism*, pp. 74 and 97 respectively.

47. See Ashis Nandy, "Reconstructing Childhood", in *Traditions, Tyranny and Utopia* (Delhi: Oxford University Press, 1987), pp. 56–76.

48. For a journalistic account of the seriousness of this issue, see the special theme issue of *Mother Jones Journal*, May/June 1991: "America's Dirty Little Secret: We Hate Kids".

49. *Revised Standard Version of the Bible*, Mark 10: 13–16.

8
Teacher Education as a Form of Discourse: On the Relation of the Public to the Private in Conversations About Teaching

1. Pierre Bourdieu, "Systems of Education and Systems of Thought." In M. F. D. Young (ed.), *Knowledge and Control* (London: Collier Macmillan, 1967).
2. J. Karabel and A. H. Halsey, (eds.) *Power and Ideology in Education* (New York: Oxford University Press, 1977)
3. A good readable introduction to the key postmodernism figures and issues is J. Sturrock, (ed.), *Structuralism and Since* (London: Oxford University Press, 1979). See also G. Madison, "Postmodern Philosophy", *Critical Review*, 2, no. 3 (Spring/Summer 1988), pp. 31–40.
4. For a moving treatment of this issue, see D. Jardine, "Wild Hearts, Silent Traces and the Journeys of Lament", *The Journal of Educational Thought*, 27, no. 1 (1993), pp. 18–27.
5. The manner in which television itself encourages people to think and act *one* way, with all of the political and cultural implications embedded in the influence of centralized television *production*, is a topic too broad to be addressed here. See Todd Gitlin, *Watching Television* (New York: Pantheon, 1987).
6. J-F. Lyotard, *The Postmodern Condition: A Report on Knowledge* (Boston: MIT Press, 1983).
7. On the relation of Piaget to Darwin, see William Kessen, *The Child* (New York: Wiley, 1967). For a discussion of the politics of domination and exclusion in Darwin, and by implication, Piaget, see William I. Thompson "The Cultural Implications of the New Biology," in W. Thompson (ed.), *GAIA: A Way of Knowing* (Great Barrington, MA: Lindisfarne, 1987).
8. In C. Norris, *Deconstruction: Theory and Practice* (London: Methuen, 1982), p. 41.
9. Paul Ricoeur, "The Model of the Text: Meaningful Action Considered as a Text". In J. B. Thompson (ed. and trans.), *Hermeneutics and the Human Siences* (Cambridge, UK: Cambridge University Press, 1985).
10. For a full discussion of this point, see D. Jardine, "Awakening from Descartes' Nightmare: On the Love of Ambiguity in Phenomenological Approaches to Education", *Studies in Philosophy and Education* 10, 12 (1990), pp. 15–25.

11. John of the Cross, "The Ascent of Mount Carmel (1587)", in *John of the Cross, Selected Writings*, K. Kavanaugh (ed.), (New York: Paulist Press, 1987), p. 1.

12. Jacques Derrida, *Of Grammatology*, G. Spivak (trans.), (Baltimore, MD: Johns Hopkins University Press, 1976), p. 66.

13. Gregory Ulmer, "Textshop for Post(E)Pedagogy". In G. D. Atkins and M. L. Johnson (eds.), *Writing and Reading Differently* (Lawrence, KS: University of Kansas Press, 1985).

14. Howard Coward, *Derrida and Indian Philosophy* (Toronto: Macmillan, 1993), p. 41.

15. Derrida, *Of Gammatology*, p. 66.

16. Ibid, p. 80.

17. David Loy, "A Buddhist Response" (1990). A paper presented to the Invitational Conference on Derrida and Negative Theology, the Institute for the Humanities, University of Calgary, Alberta, p. 14.

18. C. Trungpa, *Cutting Through Spiritual Materialism* (Boston: Shambala Press, 1987), p. 31.

19. This is discussed by Derrida in "Deconstruction and the Other," in R. Kearney, *Dialogues With Contemporary Continental Thinkers,* (Manchester, UK: Manchester University Press, 1984).

20. For a working through of the main themes of the interpretive/hermeneutic material see David G. Smith, "The Hermeneutic Imagination and the Pedagogic Text", in this book.

21. This phenomenon of historical suppression has been brilliantly and disturbingly portrayed in the recent German film *The Nasty Girl*, a story of a young girl who, in researching an essay on the topic "What people in my town did during the Third Reich", finds herself confronted with thick walls of community resistance.

22. F. Cook, *Hua-yen Buddhism: The Jewel Net of Indra* (University Park, PA: The Pennsylvannia State University Press, 1977), p. 2.

23. Ibid.

24. In H. A. Giroux, *Ideology, Culture and the Process of Shooling* (London: Falmer Press, 1981), p. 2.

25. C. Ingram, "In the Footsteps of Gandhi", in *Conversations with Spiritual Social Activists*. (Berkeley, CA: Parallax Press, 1990).

9
The Problem for the South Is the North
(But the Problem for the North Is the North)

1. George Lakoff and Mark Johnson, *Metaphors We Live By* (Chicago: University of Chicago Press, 1980), p. 4.
2. Quoted by Jean-Francois Lyotard in *The Postmodern Condition: A Report on Knowledge* (Minneapolis: University of Minnesota Press, 1986), p. 90.
3. Report on the United Nations Economic Commission for Europe, 1987. Cited in "UN Body Warns of World Recession", *The International Herald Tribune,* 32, no. 578 (Hong Kong: Saturday-Sunday, November 21–22, 1987), p. 1.
4. Friedrich Nietzsche, *On the Future of Our Educational Institutions*. (New York: Russell and Russell, 1964), pp. 132, 133.
5. Jacques Derrida, "No Apocalypse, Not Now," *Diacritics*, 3, 4 (1982).
6. Lyotard, J-F. *Post Modern Condition.*
7. Thomas Merton. "A Letter to Pablo Antonio Cuadra Concerning Giants", in *Emblems of a Season of Fury* (New York: New Directions, 1965), p. 38.
8. For an example of research that documents this isolation of children, see Valerie Saranski, *The Erosion of Childhood* (Chicago: University of Chicago Press, 1982).
9. David Kennedy, "Young Children's Thinking: An Interpretation from Phenomenology." Unpublished Ph.D. dissertation, University of Kentucky, Lexington, KY, 1986.
10. P. Freire, *Education for Critical Consciousness*. (New York: Seabury, 1978). Ira Shor, *Critical Teaching and Everyday Lfie* (New York: Black Rose Books, 1983).
11. "A l'écoute de l'univers: An Interview with Dr. Alfred Tomatis". CBC Radio, *Celebration Series*, May 1978. Steven Feld, "Sound Structure as Social Structure", *Ethnomusicology* 13, 5 (1988), pp. 25–40.

10
On Being Critical About Language: The Critical Theory Tradition and Implications for Language Education

1. R. Dana, "Poetic Injustice", New York Times Magazine, May 29 (1988), p. 22.
2. P. Connerton (ed.), *Critical Sociology* (Harmondsworth, England: Penguin Books 1978). M. Jay, *The Dialectical Imagination* (Boston: Little, Brown, 1979). S. Buck-Morss, *The Origin of Negative Dialectics* (New York: The Free Press, 1979).
3. M. Horkheimer and T. Adorno, *The Dialectic of Enlightenment* (New York: Continuum Press, 1975).
4. B. Bernstein, *Class, Codes and Control* (London, England: Routledge and Kegan Paul, 1971).
5. J. Anyon, "Social Class and the Hidden Curriculum of Work", in H. Giroux, A. Penna and W. Pinar (eds.), *Curriculum and Instruction: Alternatives in Education* (Berkeley, CA: McCutcheon, 1981).
6. M. Apple, "The Text and Cultural Politics", *The Journal of Educational Thought* 24, no. 3A(1990), pp.17–33.
7. S. Gilbert and S. Gubar (eds.), *The Norton Anthology of Literature by Women: The Tradition in English* (New York: Norton, 1985).
8. A. Hochschild, *The Managed Heart* (Berkeley, CA: The University of California Press, 1985).
9. H. Marcuse, *One Dimensional Man: Studies in the Ideology of Advanced Industrial Society* (Boston: Basic Books, 1964).
10. P. Freire, *Education for Critical Consciousness* (New York: Seabury, 1978).

11
Modernism, Postmodernism and the Future of Pedagogy

1. The concept of modernization I am assuming here is David Apter's paradigm of "modernization I" (compared to "modernization II", characterizing neo-marxist dependency theory). Modernization theory is an attempt to describe modern capital industrialism as a symbol of developmental evolutionary progress. Modernization relies on

"strategic norms of work, values of social discipline, and beliefs about equity and motivations representing the internalization of these norms, values and beliefs in a manner ensuring role performance through appropriate behaviour.... Political development adds ideology to the mix to secure a 'fit' between structural, innovative and behavioural components, enabling them to become mutually reinforcing and so achieve... 'steady state'".

According to Apter, other general theoretical questions built into "modernization I" include:

"how best to convert growing complexity into social integration, how to create the nation by means of the state and how to incorporate within the state social networks that generate development". In this view, "state legitimation depends on the expansion of choice, with the state mediating the negative effects of developmental processes".

Apter argues that this conventional view of modernization is in a state of exhaustion. It cannot account adequately for the most pronounced negative effects of modernization, which include the downward spiral of the middle classes, increased polarization of society and the creation of "superfluous man". See David E. Apter, *Rethinking Development: Modernization, Dependency, and Post-Modern Politics* (New York: Sage, 1987), esp. Chs.1 & 10.

2. I am indebted here to Ralph Pound's excellent historical survey, *The Development of Education in Western Culture* (New York: Appleton-Century-Crofts, 1968).

3. On the question of the child as an object of psychology, see W. Kessen, *The Child* (New York: Wiley, 1965).

4. David Kennedy, *Young Children's Thinking: An Interpretation from Phenomenology*. Unpublished Ph.D. Dissertation, University of Kentucky, 1986.

5. Ashis Nandy, *The Intimate Enemy: Loss and Recovery of Self under Colonialism* (Delhi: Oxford University Press, 1983), p. 100.

6. Richard Butt and Danielle Raymond, "Arguments for Using Qualitative Approaches in Understanding Teacher Thinking: The Case for Biography", *Journal of Curriculum Theorizing* 7, no.1 (1987), p. 62–93.

7. Peter McLaren, *Life in School* (New York: Longmans, 1989).

8. Two good introductions to the discussion about postmodernism are: G. B.

Madison, "Postmodern Philosophy?" *Critical Review* 2, nos. 2, 3 (Spring/Summer, 1988); and Steven Best, "After the Catastrophe: Postmodernism and Hermeneutics", *The Canadian Journal of Political and Social Theory* 12, no. 3, (1988), pp.71–86.

9. See Richard Rorty, *Philosophy and the Mirror of Nature* (Chicago: University of Chicago Press, 1980).

10. Jacques Derrida, *Writing and Difference* (Chicago: University of Chicago Press, 1978).

11. Gregory Ulmer, "Textshop for Post(e) Pedagogy", G. D. Atkins and M. L. Johnson (eds.) *Writing and Reading Differently* (Lawrence, KS: University of Kansas Press, 1985).

12. In John Caputo, *Radical Hermeneutics* (Chicago: University of Chicago Press, 1988).

13. See Dorothy Day's description of interacting with her four-day-old daughter in *By Little and Little: The Selected Writings of Dorothy Day* (New York: Knopf, 1988), p.32.

> She is only four days old but already she has the bad habit of feeling bright and desirous of play at four o'clock in the morning. Pretending that I am a bone and she is a puppy dog, she worries me fussily, tossing her head and grunting. Of course, some mothers will tell you this is because she has air in her stomach and that I should hold her upright until a loud gulp indicates that she is ready to begin feeding again. But though I hold her up as required, I still think the child's play instinct is highly developed.

14. Leonard Silk noted the following recently in *The International Herald Tribune*. May 13–14, 1989, p. 9:

> The United States has the highest child poverty rate of any industrialized country. In the last decade, the well-being of American children has deteriorated as divorce rose and as unemployment insurance and means-tested benefits shrank in both coverage and level of benefits.

15. For Derrida's discussion of desire in texts, see the interview with him in Richard Kearney, *Dialogues with Contemporary Continental Thinkers* (Chicago: Chicago University Press, 1985). The quotation is from *Writing and Difference*, p. 12.

16. The literature on hermeneutics is burgeoning. The best introduction is still Richard Palmer, *Hermeneutics* (Evanston, IL: Northwestern University Press, 1969); and H-G. Gadamer, *Truth and Method* (London: Stheed and Ward, 1976) is still the classic foundational text. For the relation of hermeneutics to Education, see chapter "The Hermeneutic Imagination and the Pedagogic Text" in this volume.
17. In Koji Sato, *The Life of Zen* (Tokyo: Tankosha, 1984).
18. *Revised Standard Version of the Bible*, Mark 10: 13–16.
19. Pierre Erny, *Childhood and Cosmos* (New York: New Perspectives Press, 1974).

12

Brighter Than a Thousand Suns: Facing Pedagogy in the Nuclear Shadow

1. R. Jungk, *Brighter Than a Thousand Suns* (New York: Harcourt Brace, 1958).
2. See especially the work of J. Habermas and the Frankfurt School. Also H-G. Gadamer, *Reason in the Age of Science* (Cambridge: MIT Press, 1982); and K. Winkler, "Questioning the Science in Social Science, Scholars Signal a Turn to Interpretation", *The Chronicle of Higher Education*, June 26, 1985.
3. The concept of *totalism* is explored most fully by Emmanuel Levinas in *Totality and Infinity,* translated by Alphonso Lingis (Pittsburgh: Duquesne University Press, 1979). Totalisms speak out of finitude yet claim to speak for all, whereas understanding which acknowledges the "infinite totality of the Other" is modest, recognizing that an acceptance of the fullness of the Other calls for a relationship to a mystery which both confronts us and hides from us. See also Michel Foucault's discussion of "the tyranny of globalizing discourses"; "the inhibiting effect of global, totalitarian theories"; and how "the attempt to think in terms of totality has in fact proved a hindrance to research". In Michel Foucault, *Power/Knowledge: Selected Interviews and Other Writings,* Colin Gordon (ed.), (New York: Pantheon Books, 1980), pp. 80–83.

Empiricism in the sense used here refers not to the Greek sense of *empeira*, that is, the full sense of experience, but to the legacy of the 18th century. Modern empirical science grounds knowledge on observation and experiment. Its key words are hypothesis, test, measurement, validity, reliability, explanation. It forsakes metaphysics, philosophy-as-thinking or questions about the meaning of being human. In regarding empiricism as the modern totalism, I interpret it (empiricism) not simply as a set of credal statements or propositions (Berkeley, Hume) which guide research procedures, but as a deep, fundamental sedimented attitude in Western culture. It is an attitude which sponsors a particular relationship to life, one based onspectatorship (research-as-pornography), disengagement, rationalism, the objectification and reification of human beings and their relationships. As such, empiricism shuts out all those traditions against which it has defined itself: the religious, the aesthetic, the poetic and so forth.

4. I mean order in the sense that Foucault connotes the term, that is, as taxonomizing, categorizing and so forth, which is never arbitrary but subject to the organizing power of prevailing discourses. See Michel Foucault, *The Order of Things* (New York: Vintage Books, 1973).

5. Hannah Arendt:

> If we would follow the advice, so frequently urged upon us to adjust our cultural attitudes to the present status of scientific achievement, we would in all earnest adopt a way of life in which speech is no longer meaningful. For the sciences today have been forced to adopt a "language" of mathematical symbols which, though it was originally meant only as an abbreviation for spoken statements, now contains statements that in no way can be translated back into speech. The reason why it may be wise to distrust the political judgment of scientists qua scientists is not primarily their lack of "character"—that they did not refuse to develop atomic weapons—or their naivete—that they did not understand that once these weapons were developed they would be the last to be consulted about their use—*but precisely the fact they move in a world where speech has lost its power.* And whatever men [sic] do or know or experience can make sense only to the extent that it can be spoken about.

The Human Condition (Chicago: University of Chicago Press, 1958), pp. 4–5 (Emphasis mine).

6. Jacques Derrida:

> Empiricism always has been determined by philosophy, from Plato to Husserl, as *nonphilosophy:* as the philosophical pretension to nonphilosophy, the inability to justify oneself, to come to one's own aid as speech. "cf." It was a Greek who said, 'If one has to philosophize one has to philosophize; if one does not have to philosophize, one still has to philosophize (to say it and think it). One always has to philosophize.

"Violence and Metaphysics", in *Writing and Difference* Alan Bass(tr.), (Chicago: University of Chicago Press, 1978), p. 152.

7. Habermas's projection of a community of discourse free from distortion seems to suggest something of this. J. Habermas, *Communication and the Evolution of Society* (New York: Beacon Press, 1979).

8. H-G. Gadamer, *Truth and Method* (London: Sheed and Ward, 1979), p. 444.

9. "Oracle" in *The Shorter Oxford English Dictionary* (Oxford: The University Press, 1980).

10. Donald N. Levine, *The Flight From Ambiguity* (Chicago: University of Chicago Press, 1985).

11. Umberto Eco, *Semiotics and the Philosophy of Language* (Bloomington: Indiana University Press, 1984), pp. 79–80.

12. See David Tracy, *The Analogical Imagination* (New York: Crossroads Press, 1981).

13. Clifford Geertz, "Blurred Genres: The Refiguration of Social Thought," *The American Scholar,* 49 (Spring 1980), pp. 165–179.

14. Ibid.

15. See Winkler, note 2 above. Also Paul Rabinow and W. Sullivan (eds.), *Interpretive Social Science: A Reader* (Berkeley: University of California Press, 1979).

16. I am thinking here particularly of the work of the Frankfurt School and especially Herbert Marcuse, *One Dimensional Man* (New York: Basic Books, 1969); also the educational theorizing of M. Apple and H. Giroux.

17. In the June 1986 edition of *The New York Review of Books* (volume XXXIII, number 11, 29) there appears this announcement of an international conference under the title "The Challenge of Third World Culture":

> Do the forces of the rich new literary and cultural production outside the West force us to modify traditional critical categories essentially derived from First World texts? Is there anything in common between

the various spaces of this nonwestern cultural production (Latin America, Africa, and Far East, India)? What are the publics of Third World Cultural producers, and are their works ever directly or indirectly meant to address a First World Public? *Is it possible that the so-called "crisis in the humanities" in the United States may be related to our parochialism and our systematic exclusion of Third World culture?* These are some of the fundamental issues to be raised in an exchange between a group of North American critics and some of the most important Third World writers and film makers. (Emphasis mine).

18. Derrida says nuclear war would be

a war without a name, a nameless war, for it would no longer share even the name of war with other events of the same type, of the same family. Beyond all genealogy, a nameless war in the name of the name. That would be the End and the Revelation of the name itself, the Apocalypse of the Name.

"No Apocalypse, Not Now (Full Speed Ahead, Seven Missiles, Seven Missives," *Diacritics* 14 , no. 2(1984), p. 31.

19. An excellent introduction to the French poststructuralists is John Sturrock (ed.), *Structuralism and Since* (London: Oxford University Press, 1979).

20. Derrida calls for

A community of the question, (living) within that fragile moment when the question is not yet determined enough for the hypocrisy of an answer to have already initiated itself beneath the mask of the question, and not yet determined enough for its voice to have been already and fraudulently articulated within the very syntax of the question.

Jacques Derrida, *Writing and Difference* (Chicago: University of Chicago Press, 1978), p. 80.

21. This is not quite Derrida's meaning, if taken that what is lost must be simply reabsorbed into a fuller subsumption. Derrida's experimental writings, which include crossings out, erasures, realignments of linear text, and so forth, all are attempts, on the one hand, to acknowledge that which is suppressed for a text to surface as such (difference as deferral) as well as, on the other hand, an attempt to provide a space for genuine difference (difference as difference). See Jacques Derrida, *Margins of Philosophy,* Alan

Bass (tr.), (Chicago: University of Chicago Press, 1982).

22. Such dialectics/antinomies (the absence in the presence; the unsaid in the said; the invisible in the visible, etc.) are seminal also in mystical traditions, for example, in the writings of Nicolas de Cusa, Meister Eckhart and more recently, Thomas Merton.

23. For an excellent description of the character of nostalgic memory, see H-G. Gadamer, *Truth and Method*, Part III (London: Sheed and Ward, 1979).

24. In *After Babel: Aspects of Language and Translation* (London: Oxford University Press, 1976), George Steiner suggests that every language is inspired by a secret known only to the native speakers.

25. Paul Ricoeur discusses the operation of "schizophrenic utopian discourse which projects a static future without ever producing the conditions of its realization", in *Dialogues*. See note 30 below.

26. Kieren Egan, *Teaching Curriculum as a Story* (London: Althouse Press, 1986).

27. Paulo Freire, *Pedagogy of the Oppressed* (New York: Continuum, 1984).

28. See Alice Miller, *For Your Own Good: Hidden Cruelty in Child-Rearing and the Roots of Violence* (New York: Farrar, Strauss, Giroux, 1983). Miller is a proponent of what may be called "anti-pedagogy".

29. This theme of the "difference" of our children is one I explore in *The Meaning of Children in the Lives of Adults: A Hermeneutic Study*. Unpublished doctoral dissertation, University of Alberta, 1983.

30. The question of what faces us in the face of another is interrogated by Emmanuel Levinas in "Ethics of the Infinite," *Dialogues with Contemporary Continental Thinkers*, Richard Kearney (ed.), (Manchester: University of Manchester Press, 1984), pp. 49–63.

13
Children and the Gods of War

1. United Nations, *Economic and Social Consequences of the Arms Race and of Military Expenditures* (New York:UNESCO, 1983), p. 7.

2. Swee Hin Toh, "Survival and Solidarity: Australia and Third World/South Peace", *Social Alternatives*, 6, 2 (1986), p. 59.

3. This story was related by the Canadian Ambassador for Disarmament, Douglas Roche, at the International Institute for Peace Education,

University of Alberta, Edmonton, Alberta, July 18, 1987.

4. I do not wish, here, to rehearse the history of the critique of Cartesian thinking. Interested readers should consult the works of J. Habermas, M. Heidegger, H-G. Gadamer, R. Rorty and others. A good exposition of these issues is contained in William Barrett, *The Illusion of Technique* (New York: Anchor Books, 1979). Barrett describes the consequences of Cartesian epistemology this way: "Behind the faltering steps of the doubter marches the conquistador", p. 126.

5. David Smith, "The Meaning of Children in the Lives of Adults: A Hermeneutic Study". Unpublished Ph.D. dissertation, University of Alberta, Edmonton, 1983.

6. John Martini, "Teaching Moments". Unpublished paper, University of Lethbridge, Lethbridge, Alberta, 1987.

7. See, for example, Deborah P. Britzman, "Cultural Myths in the Making of a Teacher: Biography and Social Structure in Teacher Education," *Harvard Educational Review* 56, no. 4 (1986). Also Richard Butt and Danielle Raymond, "Arguments for Using Qualitative Approaches in Understanding Teacher Thinking: The Case for Autobiography", *Journal of Curriculum Theorizing* 7, no. 1 (1987).

8. I am thinking here of the work of Madeleine Hunter, Gere Brophy, Barak Rosenshine, etc.

9. Lisa Church, "City's Probation Service Stretched to Crisis Point", *Calgary Herald*, August 2, 1987, p. 1, Calgary, Alberta.

14
What Is Given in Giftedness?

1. Jacques Derrida deconstructs Nietzsche's concept of "inverse cripples" in "All Ears: Nietzsche's Otobiography", *Yale French Studies,* no. 63 (1982), pp. 245–250.

References

Aiken, S. (1986). "Women and the Question of Canonicity". *College English,* 48(3), pp. 288-301.

Amore, R. (1982). *Two Masters, One Message.* Nashville TN: Abingdon Press.

Anyon, J. (1981). "Social Class and the Hidden Curriculum of Work". In H. Giroux, A. Penna & W. Pinar (Eds.), *Curriculum and instruction: Alternatives in Education* (pp. 317–341). Berkeley, CA: McCutchan Corporation.

Apel, K. (1985). "Scientistics, Hermeneutics, Critique of Ideology: An Outline of a Theory of Science from an Epistemological-Anthropological Point of View". In K. Mueller-Vollmer (Ed.), *The Hermeneutics Reader* (pp. 321–345). New York: Continuum.

Apple, M. (1986). *Teachers and Texts: A Political Economy of Class and Gender Relations in Education.* New York: Routledge and Kegan Paul.

Apter, D. (1987). *Rethinking Development: Modernization, Dependency, and Postmodern Politics.* New York: Sage.

Arendt, H. (1958). *The Human Condition.* Chicago: University of Chicago Press.

Atkins, G. D., and Johnson, M. (Eds.). (1985). *Writing and Reading Differently.* Lawrence, KS: University of Kansas.

Barrett, Wm. (1979). *The Illusion of Technique.* New York: Anchor Books.

Batz, J. (1988). "The Many Faces of Walter Ong". *Universitas,* Fall, pp. 22–27.

Berger, A. A. (1984). *Signs in Contemporary Culture.* New York: Longmans.

Bernstein, B. (1971). *Class, Codes and Control.* London: Routledge and Kegan Paul.

Berry, T. (1990). "Ecology and Society". A public address at the Ontario Institute for Studies in Education, April 19.

Berry, W. (1988). *Home Economics.* Boulder, CO: Westview Press.

Berry, W. (1989). "The Futility of Global Thinking". *Harpers* (June) .

Best, S. (1988). "After the Catastrophe: Postmodernism and Hermeneutics". *The Canadian Journal of Political and Social Theory,* 12(3).

Bloom, H. (1985). "The Pragmatics of Contemporary Jewish Culture". In J. Rachman and C. West (eds.), Post-Analytic Philosophy. New York: Columbia University Press.

Bloom, H. (1987). *The Closing of the American Mind.* New York: Simon and Schuster.

Blum, A. (1984). *Self-Reflection in the Arts and Sciences*. Atlantic Highlands, NJ: Humanities Press.

Bourdieu, P. (1971). "Systems of Education and Systems of Thought." In M. F. D. Young (Ed.), *Knowledge and Control*. London Collier: Macmillan.

Brinton, H. (1968). *The Context of the Reformation*. London: Hutchinson.

Britzman, D.P. (1986). "Cultural Myths in the Making of a Teacher: Biography and Social Structure in Teacher Education". *Harvard Educational Review*, *56*(4).

Buck-Morss, S. (1979). *The Origin of Negative Dialectics*. New York: The Free Press.

Bultmann, R. (1955). *The Theology of the New Testament*. New York: Scribner's.

Burke, J. (1978). Discussed in *Connections*. {A BBC documentary on the relation between science and culture.} London: The British Broadcasting Corporation.

Butt, R., and Raymond, D. (1987). "Arguments for Using Qualitative Approaches in Understanding Teacher Thinking: The Case for Autobiography". *Journal of Curriculum Theorizing*, *7*(1).

Canada Yearbook 1992. Statistics Canada: Publications Division, 1991.

Caputo, J. (1987). *Radical Hermeneutics: Repetition, Deconstruction, and the Hermeneutic Project*. Bloomington, IN: Indiana University Press.

Carson, T. R. (1986). "Closing the Gap Between Research and Practice: Conversation as a Mode of Research". *Phenomenology + Pedagogy*, *4*(2), pp. 73–85.

Chambers, C. M. (1989). *For Our Children's Children: An Educator's Interpretation of Dene Testimony to the Mackenzie Valley Pipeline Inquiry*. Ph.D. dissertation, University of Victoria, British Columbia.

Chuang, T. (1993). *The Inner Chapters*. J. English (ed.), Boston: Shambhala Press.

Church, Lisa. (1987). "City's Probation Service Stretched to Crisis Point". *Calgary Herald*, August 2, Calgary, AB.

Commoner, B. (1984). *The Closing Circle: Nature, Man and Technology*. New York: Knopf.

Connerton, P. (ed.), (1987). *Critical Sociology*. Harmondsworth, England: Penguin.

Cook, F. (1977). *Hua-yen Buddhism: The Jewel Net of Indra*. University Park, PA: The Pennsylvania State University Press.

Culler, J. (1975). *Structuralist Politics: Structuralism, Linguistics and the Study of Literature*. Ithaca, NY: Cornell University Press.

Dana, R. (1988). "Poetic Injustice". *New York Times Magazine*, May 29.

Day, D. (1988). *By Little and By Little: The Selected Writings of Dorothy Day*.

New York: Alfred Knopf.

de Saussure, F. (1959). *Course in General Linguistics* C. Bally and A. Sechehaye (eds.); W. Baskin (trans.). New York: Philosophical Library.

Derrida J. (1984) "No Apocalypse, Not Now (Full Speed Ahead, Seven Missiles, Seven Missives". C. Porter and P. Lewis (trans.). *The Wallace Stevens Journal* 14 (2), pp. 22–31.

Derrida, J. (1976). *Of Grammatology*, G. Spivak, (trans.). Baltimore, MD: Johns Hopkins University Press.

Derrida, J. (1978). "Violence and metaphysics." In A. Bass (trans.), *Writings and Difference.* Chicago: University of Chicago Press.

Derrida, J. (1981). "Diaglogue." In R. Kearney (ed.), *Dialogues with Contemporary Continental Thinkers* Manchester, UK: Manchester University Press.

Derrida, J. (1982). *Margins of Philosophy,* A. Bass (trans.), Chicago: University of Chicago Press.

Derrida, J. (1982). "All Ears: Nietzsche's Otobiography". *Yale French Studies* 63, pp. 254–250.

Dobert, M. L. (1982). *Ethnographic Research: Theory and Application for Modern Schools and Society.* New York: Praeger.

Doumelin, H. (1976). *Buddhism in the Modern World.* London: Collier.

Eco, U. (1984). *Semiotics and the Philosophy of Language.* Bloomington, IN: Indiana University Press.

Ellsworth, E. (1989). "Why Doesn't This Feel Empowering? Working Through the Repressive Myths of Critical Pedagogy". *Harvard Educational Review, 59*(3), pp. 299–324.

Erny, P. (1974). *Childhood and Cosmos.* New York: New Perspectives Press.

Farah, C. (1987). *Islam.* (New York: Barrons).

Feld, Steven. (1984) "Sound Structure as Social Structure". *Ethnomusicology*, 5 (3), pp. 59–70.

Foucault, M. (1973). *The Order of Things.* New York: Vintage Books.

Foucault, M. (1980). *Power/ Knowledge: Selected Interviews and Other Writings.* C. Gordon (ed.), New York: Pantheon Books.

Freire, P. (1970). "Cultural Action for Freedom." *Harvard Educational Review*, Monograph Series, No. 1.

Freire, P. (1971). *Pedagogy of the Oppressed,* D. E. Linge (trans.) Berkeley: University of California Press.

Freire, P. (1973). *Education for Critical Consciousness.* M. Ramos (trans.) New York: Continuum Press.

Freire, P. and Macedo, D. (1987). *Literacy: Reading the Word and the World*. South Hadley, MA: Bergin and Garvey.

Fulford, R. (1994). "The Ideology of the Book". *Queen's Quarterly* 101 (4), pp. 801–812.

Gadamer, H-G. (1979). *Truth and Method* (W. Glen-Doepel, trans.). London: Sheed and Ward.

Gadamer, H-G. (1983). "Hermeneutics as Practical Philosophy." In F. G. Lawrence (trans.), *Reason in the Age of Science* (pp. 18–138). Cambridge, MA: The MIT Press.

Gadamer, H-G. (1985). "On the Origins of Philosophical Hermeneutics." In *Philosophical Apprenticeships*. Cambridge: MIT Press.

Gadamer, H-G. (1987). Foreword to the second edition of *Truth and Method*. In K. Baynes, J. Bohman and T. McCarthy (eds.), *After Philosophy: End or Transformation*. Cambridge MA: MIT Press.

Garfinkle, H. (1967). *Studies in Ethnomethodology*. Englewood Cliffs, NJ: Prentice-Hall.

Geertz, C. (1980). "Blurred Genres: The Refiguration of Social Thought." *The American Scholar,* 49 (Spring).

Gergin, K. J., and Gergin, M. M. (1983). "Narratives of the Self". In T. R. Sarbin and K. E. Schiebe (eds.), *Studies in Social Identity* (pp. 254–273).

Gilbert, S., and Gubar, S. (eds.), (1985). *The Norton Anthology of Literature by Women: The Tradition in English*. New York: Norton.

Giroux, H. A. (1981). *Ideology, Culture and the Process of Schooling*. London: Falmer Press.

Gitlin, T. (1987). *Watching Television*. New York: Pantheon.

Glaser, B. C., and Strauss, A. (1967). *The Discovery of Grounded Theory: Strategies for Qualitative Research*. Chicago: Aldine.

Gordon, J. (1994). "Why Students of Color Are Not Entering Teaching: Reflections from Minority Teachers". *Teacher Education* 45 (5), pp. 346–353.

Groening, M. (1987). *School Is Hell*. New York: Pantheon Books.

Gyatso, T. (1985). *Kindness, Clarity and Insight*. J. Hopkins (trans. and ed.) New York: Snow Lion.

Habermas, J. (1979). *Communication and the Evolution of Society*. New York: Beacon Press.

Hall, B. (1994). "Information Technology and Global Learning for Sustainable Devleopment: Promise and Problems". *Alternatives: Social Transformation and Humane Governance* 19 (1), pp. 99–132.

Hamilton, E., and H. Cairns (eds.) (1961). *The Collected Dialogues of Plato*. New York: Pantheon.

Hahn, T. (1989). *The Sun My Heart*. Berkeley, CA: Parallax Press.

Havel, V. (1991). "After Communism". *New York Review of Books*, June 23, pp. 10–15.

Havel, V. (1990). "Words on Words". *The New York Review of Books*, January 18, pp. 36–39.

Heidegger, M. (1962). *Being and Time*, J. Maquarrie and E. Robinson (trans.). New York: Harper and Row.

Heidegger, M. (1977). "The End of Philosophy and the Task of Thinking". In D. Krall (Ed.), *Martin Heidegger: Basic Writings* (pp. 369–392). New York: Harper and Row.

Heimlich, J., and Pittleman, S. (1986). *Semantic Mapping*. Newark, DE: International Reading Association.

Hillman, J. (1991). *Blue Fire*. New York: Harper and Row.

Hirsch, E. D. (1987). *Cultural Literacy: What Every American Needs to Know*. Boston: Houghton Mifflin.

Hochschild, A.R. (1983). *The Managed Heart*. Berkeley: University of California Press.

Hodges, H.A. (1952). *The Philosophy of Wilhelm Dilthey*. London: Macmillan.

Horkheimer, M., and Adorno, T. (1975). *The Dialectic of Enlightenment*. New York: Continuum Press.

Husserl, E. (1952). *Cartesian Meditations*. London: Oxford University Press.

Ingram, C. (1990). *In the Footsteps of Gandhi: Conversations with Spiritual Social Activists*. Berkeley, CA: Parallax Press.

Jameson, F. (1992). *Postmodernism, Or The Logic of Late Capitalism*. Durham, NC: Duke University.

Jardine, D. (1989). "A Bell Ringing in an Empty Sky". Paper delivered at the Eleventh Annual Conference of the *Journal of Curriculum Theorizing*, Bergamo Center, Dayton, Ohio, October 18–21.

Jardine, D. (1990). "Awakening from Descartes' Nightmare: On the Love of Ambiguity in Phenomenological Approaches to Education". *Studies in Philosophy and Education*, *10*(12).

Jardine, D. (1994). "Student-Teacher, Interpretation and the Monstrous Child". *Journal of the Philosophy of Education*, 4 (3), pp. 36–45.

Jay, M. (1979). *The Dialectical Imagination*. Boston, MA: Little, Brown.

John of the Cross. (1968). *The Ascent of Mount Carmel*. New York: Orbis Press.

Jung, C. G. (1969). "The Phenomenology of the Child Archetype". In C. G. Jung and C. Kereny (eds.), *Essays on a Science of Mythology*. Princeton, NJ: Princeton University Press.

Jungk, R. (1958). *Brighter Than a Thousand Suns*. New York: Harcourt Brace.

Karabel, J., and Halsey, A. H. (Eds.). (1977). *Power and Ideology in Education*. New York: Oxford University Press.

Kearney, R. (Ed.). (1984). *Dialogues with Contemporary Continental Thinkers*. Manchester: Manchester University Press.

Kennedy, D. (1986). "Young Children's Thinking: An Interpretation from Phenomenology". Unpublished Ph.D. dissertation. University of Kentucky, Lexington, KY.

Kernan, A. (1990). *The Death of Literature*. New Haven: Yale University Press.

Kessen, W. (1965). *The Child*. New York: Wiley.

Kimmerle, H. (ed.). (1977). *Hermeneutics: The Handwritten Manuscripts of Friedrich Schleiermacher*, J. Duke and J. Frostman (trans.) Missoula, MT: Scholars Press.

Kristeva, J. (1980). *Desire in Language*. New York: Columbia University Press.

Kristeva, J. (1983). "Psychoanalysis and the Polis." In W. J. T. Mitchell (Ed.), *The Politics of Interpretation* (pp. 75–98). Chicago: The University of Chicago Press.

Kroker, A. (1989). *Panic Encyclopedia*. Montreal: New World Perspectives.

Lakoff, G., and Johnson, M. (1980). *Metaphors We Live By*. Chicago: University of Chicago Press.

Lao-Tzu. (1983). "Tao Te Ching". In Wee Chong Tan, *Lao Tzu and Gandhi (Friends of Jesus)*. Victoria, BC: Novissima Lectio.

Lao-Tzu. (1989). *Te-Tao Ching*. R. Henricks (ed.). New York: Ballantine Books).

Levinas, E. (1979). *Totality and Infinity,* A. Lingis (trans.). Pittsburgh: Duquesne University Press.

Levinas, E. (1984). "Ethics of the Infinite". In R. Kearney (ed.), *Dialogues with Contemporary Continental Thinkers*. Manchester: University of Manchester Press.

Levine, D. N. (1985). *The Flight from Ambiguity*. Chicago: University of Chicago Press.

Longxi, Z. (1985). "The Tao and the Logos: Notes on Derrida's Critique of Logocentrism". *Critical Inquiry, 11*(3).

Longxi, Z. (1988). "The Myth of the Other: China in the Eyes of the West".

Critical Inquiry, *15*(1), pp. 108–131.

Loy, D. (1990). "A Buddhist Response". A paper presented to the Invitational Conference on Derrida and Negative Theology, at the Institute for the Humanities, University of Calgary, AB.

Luke, C. (1989). *Pedagogy, Printing and Protestantism: The Discourse of Childhood*. New York: SUNY Press.

Lyotard, J.-F. (1986). *The Postmodern Condition: A Report on Knowledge*. Minneapolis: University of Minnesota Press.

Madison, G. B. (1988, Spring/Summer). "Postmodern Philosophy?" *Critical Review*, *2* (2,3).

Makreel, R. (1975). *Dilthey: Philosopher of the Human Sciences*. Princeton: Princeton University Press.

Mander, J. (1991). *In the Absence of the Sacred: The Failure of Technology and the Survival of the Indian Nations*. San Francisco: Sierra Club.

Marcuse, H. (1964). *One Dimensional Man: Studies in the Ideology of Advanced Industrial Society*. Boston: Basic Books.

Market Process. (1988), *6*(1).

Martini, J. (1987). "Teaching Moments". Unpublished paper. University of Lethbridge, Alberta.

McLaren, P. (1989). *Life in School*. New York: Routledge and Kegan Paul.

Merton, T. (1975) *Asian Journal*. New York: New Directions.

Merton, T. (1961). "A Letter to Pablo Antonio Caudra Concerning Giants". In *Emblems of a Season of Fury*. Norfolk, VA: New Directions.

Messer, S. B.; Sass, L. A.; and Woolfolk, B. L. (eds.). (1988). *Hermeneutics and Psychological Theory*. New Brunswick, NJ: Rutgers University Press.

Miller, A. (1983). *For Your Own Good: Hidden Cruelty in Child-rearing and the Roots of Violence*. New York: Farrar, Strauss, Giroux.

Mueller-Vollmer, K. (1985). "Language, Mind, and Artifact: An Outline of Hermeneutic Theory Since the Enlightenment". In K. Mueller-Vollmer (ed.), *The Hermeneutics Reader* (pp. 1–53). New York: Continuum.

Nandy, A. (1983). *The Intimate Enemy: Loss and Recovery of Self under Colonialism*. Delhi: Oxford University Press.

Nandy, A. (1987). *Traditions, Tyranny, and Utopia: Essays in the Politics of Awareness*. Delhi: Oxford University Press.

Nandy, A. (1987). "Shamans, Savages and Wilderness: On the Audibility of Dissent and the Future of Civilizations." *Alternatives* 14 (3) (Spring), pp. 65–76.

186

Nietzsche, F. (1964). *On The Future of Our Educational Institutions*. New York: Russell and Russell.

Norris, C. (1982). *Deconstruction: Theory and Practice*. London: Methuen.

Palmer, R. (1969). *Hermeneutics*. Evanston, IL: Northwestern University Press.

Polkinghorne, D.E. (1988). *Narrative Knowing and the Human Sciences*. Albany NY: SUNY Press.

Pound R. (1968). *The Development of Education in Western Culture*. New York: Appleton, Century, Crofts.

Rabinow P., and Sullivan, W. (eds.) (1979). *Interpretive Social Science: A Reader*. Berkeley: University of California Press.

Rickman, H. P. (ed.) (1976). *Wilhelm Dilthy: Selected Writings*. New York: Cambridge University Press.

Ricoeur, P. (1973). "Ethics and Culture." *Philosophy Today, 17*(2/4), pp. 153–165.

Ricoeur, P. (1985). "The Model of the Text: Meaningful Action Considered as a Text." In J. B. Thompson (ed. and trans.), *Hermeneutics and the Human Sciences*. Cambridge: Cambridge University Press.

Rorty, R. (1979). *Philosophy and the Mirror of Nature*. Princeton: Princeton University Press.

Roszak, T. (1986). *The Cult of Information: The Folklore of Computers and the True Art of Thinking*. New York: Pantheon Books.

Rouner, L. S. (Ed.) (1980). "Religious and Poetical Speaking." *Boston University Studies in Philosophy and Religion, Vol. 1*. Notre Dame, IN and London: University of Notre Dame Press.

Seng, O. M. (1986). *The Meaning of Moral Education: An Interpretive Study of Moral Education Curriculum in Korea*. Ph.D. dissertation, University of Alberta.

Sarbin, T. R. (ed.). (1986). *Narrative Psychology: The Storied Nature of Human Conduct*. New York: Praeger.

Sato, K. (1984). *The Zen Life*. Tokyo: Tankosha.

Schafer, R. M. (1977). *The Tuning of the World*. Toronto: McClelland and Stewart.

Schleiermacher, F. D. E. (1978). "Outline of the 1819 Lectures". *New Literacy History, 10*(1), 1–16.

Schutz, A. (1970). *On Phenomenology and Social Relations*. Chicago: The University of Chicago Press.

Shor, I. (1983). *Critical Teaching and Everyday Life*. New York: Black Rose Press.

Silk, L. (1989). "Child Poverty in the U.S." *The International Herald Tribune*, p.

9, May 13–14, 1989.

Silverman, K. (1983). *The Subject of Semiotics*. New York: Oxford University press.

Smith, D. (1983). *The Meaning of Children in the Lives of Adults: A Hermeneutic Study*. Unpublished doctoral dissertation, University of Alberta.

Smith, D. (1990). "Pedagogy as an International Narrative Practice". A paper delivered at the Invitational Banff International Pedagogy Conference, Banff, Alberta, May 26–29.

Smith, D. (1988). "Brighter Than a Thousand Suns: Facing Pedagogy in the Nuclear Shadow." In T. R. Carson (ed.), *Toward a Renaissance of Humanity* (pp. 275–285). Edmonton: Faculty of Education, University of Alberta.

Smith, D. (1991). "The Hermeneutic Imagination and the Pedagogic Text". In Edmund Short (ed.), *Forms of Curriculum Inquiry*. Albany, NY: SUNY Press.

Spitz, L.W. (1966). *The Protestant Reformation*. Englewood Cliffs, NJ: Prentice-Hall.

Stapleton, M. (1982). "Hermes". In *The Hamlyn Concise Dictionary of Greek and Roman Mythology* (pp. 140–142). London: Hamlyn.

Steiner, G. (1976). *After Babel: Aspects of Language and Translation* . London: Oxford University Press.

Steiner, G. (1982). "The Retreat from the Word". In *Language and Silence: Essays on Language, Literature and the Inhuman*. New York: Atheneum Press.

Stuckey, E. (1991). *The Violence of Literacy*. Portsmouth, NH: Boynton/Cook.

Sturrock J. (ed.). (1979) *Structuralism and Since*. London: Oxford University Press.

Suranski, V. (1982). *The Erosion of Childhood*. Chicago: University of Chicago Press.

Sweet, P. (1978–80). *Wilhelm von Humboldt: A Biography* (2 volumes). Columbus: Ohio State University Press.

The New York Review of Books (1986, June). *The Challenge of Third World Culture, 23*(11).

Thompson, W. (1987). "The Cultural Implications of the New Biology". In W. Thompson (ed.), *GAIA: A Way of Knowwng*. Great Barrington, MA: Lindisfarne Press.

Toh, Swee Hin (1986). "Survival and Solidarity: Australia and Third World (South) Peace", *Social Alternatives, 6*(2).

Tomatis, A. (1978). "A l'écoute de l'univers: An Interview with Dr. Alfred Tomatis". CBC Radio, *Celebration Series,* May.

Tracy, D. (1981). *The Analogical Imagination*. New York: Crossroads Press.

Trungpa, C. (1990). *Meditation and the Myth of Freedom*. Boston: Shambhala Press.

Trungpa, C. (1987). *Cutting Through Spiritual Materialism*. Boston: Shambhala Press.

Ulmer, G. (1985). "Textshop for Post(e) Pedagogy". In G. D. Atkins and M. L. Johnson (eds.), *Writing and Reading Differently*. Lawrence, KS: University of Kansas Press.

United Nations Economic Commission for Europe. (1987). "UN Body Warns of World Recession". In *The International Herald Tribune, No. 32*. Hong Kong: November 21–22.

United Nations. (1983). *Economic and Social Consequences of the Arms Race and of Military Expenditures*. New York: United Nations.

Van den Berg, J. H. (1961). *The Changing Nature of Man*. New York: Norton.

Varela, F. (1991). *Prospects for a New Biology of Cognition*. Chicago: Pyrgammon Press.

Wachterhauser, B. R. (ed.). (1986). *Hermeneutics and Modern Philosophy*. Albany, NY: SUNY Press.

Walker, R. B. J. (ed.). (1984). *Culture, Ideology, and World Order*. Boulder, CO: Westview Press.

West, C. (1992). "The New Cultural Politics of Difference". October 53 (1), pp. 93–109.

Willinsky, J. (1990). *The New Literacy: Redefining Reading and Writing*. New York: Routledge.

Winkler, K. (1985, June 26). "Questioning the Science in Social Science, Scholars Signal a Turn to Interpretation". *The Chronicle of Higher Education*.

Studies in the Postmodern Theory of Education

General Editors
Joe L. Kincheloe & Shirley R. Steinberg

Counterpoints publishes the most compelling and imaginative books being written in education today. Grounded on the theoretical advances in criticalism, feminism and postmodernism in the last two decades of the twentieth century, Counterpoints engages the meaning of these innovations in various forms of educational expression. Committed to the proposition that theoretical literature should be accessible to a variety of audiences, the series insists that its authors avoid esoteric and jargonistic languages that transform educational scholarship into an elite discourse for the initiated. Scholarly work matters only to the degree it affects consciousness and practice at multiple sites. Counterpoints' editorial policy is based on these principles and the ability of scholars to break new ground, to open new conversations, to go where educators have never gone before.

For additional information about this series or for the submission of manuscripts, please contact:

Joe L. Kincheloe & Shirley R. Steinberg
637 West Foster Avenue
State College, PA 16801